CONSUMER SURVIVAL KIT

CONSUMER SURVIVAL KIT

adapted by John Dorfman
from the television series
by Maryland Center for Public Broadcasting

PRAEGER PUBLISHERS
A DIVISION OF HOLT, RINEHART AND WINSTON
NEW YORK

First published in the United States of America in 1975
by Praeger Publishers, Inc.

© 1975 by Maryland Center for Public Broadcasting

Third printing, 1977
by Praeger Publishers
A Division of Holt, Rinehart and Winston
New York

Library of Congress Cataloging in Publication Data
Dorfman, John.
    Consumer survival kit.
    1. Consumer education.   I.   Marylan ' Center for
Public Broadcasting.   II.   Title.
TX335.D67   640.73   74-29312
ISBN 0-275-22010-9
ISBN 0-275-63830-8 pbk.

Printed in the United States of America

Contents

Foreword

This foreword should include the names of hundreds of people who gave time, energy, and creative unselfishness to the success of the television series upon which this book is based. Those whose efforts were so valuable included scores of volunteers, upon whom public television relies so continuously for so many forms of help. They often came to us at times when the where-withal to complete the project seemed doubtful; they stayed long enough to see us through crisis, then moved on—in many cases not to be heard from again. To those who were unpaid and stood to gain nothing material from our success, we extend the first of our thanks. To what exactly did they contribute, and why? We believe they recognized a meritorious idea, a potential for doing some good.

The idea was initiated in December 1969 in a proposal submitted at the Maryland Center for Public Broadcasting. The suggestion was to produce a series on consumerism that would present information the consumer could apply directly to his or her pocketbook. It would not bemoan the system or scatter blame for the problems of the market place. The series would deal with solutions to consumer problems.

It would be designed to attract viewers, something so many information series on commercial and public television had not been able to do. The series would serve little purpose if no one watched. Because we believe that television is basically an entertainment medium and we are not going to change that fact, the format included some sketches, song and dance routines, quizzes, and other variety show devices. But it was stressed that no routine was to be developed that did not use information as the basis for its dialogue or lyrics. Between entertaining pieces we would present straight information. The end of each program was to include a segment telling viewers what recourse agencies were available to them, whom to call or write at those agencies, and how to reach them. Finally, to get some idea of how many people were watching, we decided to offer a packet of topical information, which we would compile from government and private sources.

The very difficult task of taking all these ideas and formulating them into a pilot script fell to a talented but relatively inexperienced writer, twenty-four-year-old Dick George. An equally inexperienced twenty-four-year-old director, Earl Neal, and an inexperienced producer took Dick's script and turned out an $1,800 pilot program that proved they all had been in "show business" only a short time. But if the pilot was clumsy and rough, it was fresh in concept and approach. Warren Park, the program director at the Center, saw beyond the pilot's flaws and agreed to try twenty-six half-hour shows. We were off . . . with one change.

The consumer information packet was too good an idea to be a "throw-away" segment. It became a significant part of each program. One selfless volunteer, Fran Johannson, offered to handle the packet project. She would compile stuff, and mail the 150 packets we guessed we'd need for our first program. On March 6, 1971, the initial program, "Auto Repairanoia," was aired. Within five days, we had received more than 1,000 requests for packets. Much of the information in those packets is included in this book.

Since that first program the staff has grown. Many creative, hard-working individuals have contributed talent and energy to the series. The chapters in this book were originally shooting scripts by Cherrill Anson, Christina Pogoloff, Carter Clews, and Dick George, who is now our script supervisor. For these scripts, the research burden was shared by the writers and occasional volunteer and staff researchers—among them Ruth Silverstone, Mack Lee, Marilyn Bereson, Sara May Gold, Narda Clews, and Sandee Harden, who now supervises our researchers.

During the past two years, some very special people have turned the scripts into television shows. Donna Faw worked as a project assistant beginning in January 1973; she is now associate producer. Her energies have been untiring, and she deserves a special commendation. Our first director, Earl Neal, has moved on, and Tom Barnett now makes the television magic happen. Both gentlemen have been instrumental in making our programs watchable. Throughout the series, the music has been original, not only in the literal but in the creative sense. Don Swartz and Don Barto have composed it.

There are, of course, others whose efforts are not listed here. We hope they understand that their work is no less appreciated. Time and space are so restrictive.

Michael Magzis and Praeger Publishers saw in the program the potential for a book. John Dorfman has truly caught and reflected the flavor of the series. The CSK staff considers him one of us.

Finally, to you the reader—and we hope viewer—our thanks for your support. We truly believe that changes in consumer concerns will come only through an enlightened public. While it is certainly the responsibility of the government and business to keep our interest and safety in mind, too often we cannot afford to wait for the crises that are their only cue to act. If the buying citizenry is purchase-wise, the time will come when business will have to produce quality products, and the regulators will regulate out of the knowledge that we will not permit them to be lax.

In 1972, Virginia H. Knauer commented on the "buyer's bill of rights." She said that too often the public is lost at the second right, the right to information. We on the staff of Consumer Survival Kit are trying to help remedy that situation. Our success will be measured by the dollars you save.

VINCE CLEWS
Producer,
Consumer Survival Kit,
Maryland Center for Public Broadcasting

FOOD

1

Supermarket Strategy

Supermarket Rag!
Supermarket Rag!
Ultra-convenient—
Boil it in a bag.
Hydrogenated, butylated . . .
Pocketbook is mutilated
As we go on singing
That supermarket rag.
Woke up this morning
Took myself to town
Went to the market
And put my money down.
I got instant coffee
And some instant tea,
And I got some sugar-coated
Instant poverty.

Is the supermarket running you ragged? Are you spending more for food and enjoying it less? The chances are you are. The cost of feeding a roast beef dinner to a family of four, for example, has gone from about $5.85 in 1970 to about $8.25 in 1974. During that same period, the cost of a chicken dinner (including an appetizer, vegetables, salad, bread and butter, beverages and dessert) has gone from $4.18 to $5.56.

To these jarring statistics, some would reply that things are always darkest just before the dawn. But there's some truth, too, in what a cynic said: "Things are always darkest just before they go completely black." The fact is that food prices are likely to keep rising. The whole world is clamoring for food. The United States, which traditionally has had a surplus, is not likely to refuse to export food, because we need the raw materials we get in exchange, as well as the goodwill. So food prices in your supermarket will be influenced for years to come by booming worldwide demand.

Besides that, weather has been freakish and unstable in the mid-1970s. The drought of summer 1974 is an example. It destroyed a large part of the Midwest corn crop. That doesn't only raise the price of corn. With less corn to feed their animals, farmers bid up the prices of other feed grains. That makes cereal and bread more expensive. Meat becomes higher-priced, too, since farmers must make up for their swelling feed costs. Since it costs more to feed beef cattle, for example, farmers tend to send the animals to market early, trimming the size of the herds. And that only makes meat prices rise more.

Faced with vicious circles of this kind, the consumer still wants to set a decent table in spite of inflation. To fight back, you need some knowledge—some skill in the art of how not to be ripped off in a supermarket. Do you know the basics about protein? How to read a label? How to use the dates that appear on containers? If not, you soon will. But first, you might want to try this *Consumer Survival Kit* quiz as an introduction to the question of supermarket strategy.

CSK Quiz

1. True or false: A typical American family (mother, father, and two school-age children) spends $2,000 a year on food.
2. True or false: That same family spends $800 a year at the supermarket on things that aren't food—paper products, pet food, cleaning supplies, and the like.

3. True or false: One third of the typical family's food budget is spent on meat.

Now let's look at the answers. Number 1 is false. The typical American family spends more than $2,000 a year on food. In the fall of 1974, it took $2,440 to feed an urban family of four on what the U.S. Labor Department calls a "low-budget" basis. On an "intermediate budget" basis, it took $3,183. And figures like these assume that the family always eats at home. Real families like to eat out once in a while.

Number 2 is also false. Our typical family spends more than $800 a year on nonfood items. In fact, it spends a little bit over $1,000 (at 1974 price levels). That means that if our typical family had an income of $12,000, it would be spending about 35 per cent of it at the supermarket!

Number 3 is true. About one third of the typical family's food budget does go to pay for meat. Back in 1972 people were so concerned about soaring meat prices they organized boycotts. Then things sort of simmered down. But many of us started reassessing the subject of protein in our diets. While we were at it, we should have kept going and re-examined the whole menu. Somewhere along the line, many of us got the idea that the good life means eating more sugar, fat, and protein than we need.

Your great-great-great-great-great grandfather managed to get along on about 10 pounds of sugar a year. You, if you're average, socked away 20 pounds of candy, 450 servings of soft drinks, and 135 sticks of chewing gum last year. And that was just a start. If your eating habits are typical, you ate about 100 pounds of sugar altogether. Sugar has its uses—it supplies energy. After all, that's what calories are: units of energy used by the body as fuel. The trouble is, if you get too many of your calories from sugar, it dulls the appetite for more needed foods. Unless your body burns up calories very fast, gobbling sugar is flirting with overweight. And dentists have a few choice words to say about sugar's effect on the teeth that won't be repeated here. So, if either you or your food bill is overweight, sweets are one of the first things you can consider cutting out.

A second area for trimming is fat. Like sugar, it isn't a total villain. Some fats are needed as carriers of vitamins A, D, E, and K. The body should have some fat as a temperature-regulating mechanism and as just plain padding. And foods with fat in them —let's face it—tend to taste better. Fat adds some of the tang to spare ribs, some of the succulence to roast beef. Nonetheless, many doctors have been having (pardon the expression) heart-to-heart talks with their patients about fat consumption. The typical American gets about 40 per cent of his or her calories from fat. Medical authorities think a 20 per cent ratio would be healthier. In countries like Japan, where fat intake is about 20 per cent, there seem to be fewer heart and circulatory problems than in the United States. The case isn't conclusive. But if you're trying to pare down a food bill, it makes sense to start with items that perhaps should be consumed in smaller quantities anyway.

That brings us to protein. There's simply no more important part of the diet than this. Without protein—in fact, without protein every day—our bodies would deteriorate. Without enough protein our organs don't function properly, our blood doesn't carry enough oxygen, our fluid balance goes haywire, and we can't fight off infections. Hair, skin, and nails all require protein. Adults need it to replace tissues that are always breaking down in a normal body. Children need it in order to grow.

In many people's minds, the epitome of protein has always been a succulent steak. But now that a good steak is priced as if it should be kept under glass, it's time that we retouched our mental picture. Beefsteak and roast beef, delicious as they are, are not the only source of protein, the most economical source of protein, or even necessarily the best source of protein. Protein doesn't have to be beef or anything else that comes from an animal. In fact, all protein is vegetable to begin with. For 21 pounds of vegetable protein you feed to a cow, you end up with only one pound of beef. That's not going to win any efficiency awards. Besides, it uses huge amounts of protein at a time when there's a serious worldwide shortage.

If you're on a tight budget, you want protein that's good and cheap. Beans and peanut butter—vegetable proteins—are among the cheapest. A lot of doctors believe that more vegetable protein and less animal protein would be a healthy thing for American diets. A normal body isn't that picky about protein—as long as it's getting enough complete protein. "Complete" means that the protein has all eight of the amino acids the body needs. These acids, like tryptophan and argenine, are the "active ingredients" in protein. Dairy products, sea food, meat, and poultry get an A+ for completeness. A lot of vegetable proteins are incomplete. But if you put them together right, at the same meal, they combine and complement each other to form complete proteins.

Here are some incomplete proteins that combine to form complete ones:

- rice and beans
- Boston brown bread and baked beans
- "Hopping John," which is rice and black-eyed peas
- tabouili, which is a Middle Eastern salad of chick peas and cracked wheat

If those dishes sound to you like peasant food, you're right. But they certainly deserve a trial. If you try such combinations and don't like them, there's another way you can boost the nutrition content of your meals. A small amount of a complete protein will give a big boost to an incomplete protein. For instance, try a turkey sandwich on whole wheat bread. It doesn't take very much turkey to activate the nutritive potential of the bread.

All kinds of casseroles accomplish the protein-activation trick. In tuna fish casserole, the tuna activates the nutritive potential of the noodles. (Noodles, like macaroni and spaghetti, have protein because they're made from wheat. It's incomplete protein, of course, but a touch of meat, poultry, or dairy food will take care of that. The same goes for potatoes and for rice. Thus, rice pudding can make a fine meal. (The milk completes the protein value of the rice.) A large potato dish can supplement a relatively small meat portion. And lasagna with meat sauce is a very healthy meal.

Unfortunately, all too many people either don't have basic nutritional knowledge or are unable to act on it. One nutritional economist estimates that poor nutrition—both hunger and food abuse—costs American society $30 billion a year. That toll, however, is expressed not in dollars but in undernourished mothers, sickly children, dental decay, absenteeism, and nutritional diseases.

Even before the superinflation of the mid-1970s, a lot of us were striking out nutritionally. In 1955, 60 per cent of us had an adequate diet, according to the U.S. Department of Agriculture. In the same Department's survey in 1965, only 50 per cent of us were getting the right amounts of the substances necessary for good nutrition. The most serious diet deficiencies were in calcium, vitamins A and C, and iron. The preliminary report of a U.S. Public Health Service study in 1974 showed that about 95 per cent of all preschool children and women of childbearing age may not have enough iron in their diet.

These deficiencies needn't occur. Vitamin A is abundant in liver, egg yolks, butter, carrots, yellow corn, sweet potatoes, apricots, and peaches. Vitamin C is found in citrus fruits, tomatoes, cabbage, strawberries, melons, and potatoes. (Potatoes don't have much of it, but people who eat a lot of them end up getting considerable quantities of vitamin C.) As for iron, it's found in liver (and other organ meats), whole-grain breads and cereals, raisins, molasses, green leafy vegetables, and egg yolks.

Why, then, are so many people inadequately nourished? Some blame poverty, others ignorance, our high-pressure lifestyle, or even the disintegration of the family. Dr. Jean Mayer, Professor of Nutrition at Harvard University, puts part of the blame on food commercials. Says Dr. Mayer: "It's obvious to any even casual television viewer that national advertising expenditures are in reverse order to the usefulness of the foods."

One excellent device for combating nutritional ignorance and inspiring enthusiasm for eating the right foods is the Scoreboard for Better Eating developed by Dr. Michael Jacobson. Dr. Jacobson holds a doctorate in microbiology from MIT. He has served as a research associate at the Salk Institute and as a consultant to Ralph Nader's Center for the Study of Responsive Law. In 1970 he helped found the Center for Science in the Public Interest, of which he is now codirector. Dr. Jacobson has assigned plus and minus number values to dozens of common foods, including many brand-name products. Foods gain points for important nutrients. They lose points for saturated fat, for having more than 20 per cent fat, or for containing added sugar and corn syrup. A glass of orange jucie comes out plus 62; a can of soda pop, minus 92. Certainly, the scoreboard isn't the whole answer to poor nutrition in this country. But children and adults who were never interested in nutrition may be hooked by its competitive, "batting average" approach. Excerpts from the scoreboard appear below.

Excerpts From Nutrition Scoreboard
by Dr. Michael Jacobson

(*Nutrition Scoreboard: Your Guide to Better Eating* was originally published by the Center for Science in the Public Interest, Washington, D.C. It is to be republished in 1974 by Avon Books, New York. The scoreboard is reproduced with the permission of the Center.)

Protein Foods

		Nutritional Score
beef liver	2 oz.	172
chicken liver	2 oz.	158
liver sausage*	2 oz.	104
chicken breast	2.7 oz.†	62
tuna fish	3 oz.	55
round steak, very lean	3 oz.	53
turkey meat	3 oz.	52
pork chop, lean	1.7 oz.†	47
hamburger, lean	3 oz.	46
veal cutlet	3 oz.	45
round steak, lean and fat	3 oz.	43
lamb chop, lean	2.6 oz.†	43
leg of lamb, lean, roasted	2½ oz.	43
soybeans, cooked	½ cup	41
cod, broiled	3 oz.	40
salmon, pink, canned	3 oz.	39

		Nutritional Score
flounder, baked	3 oz.	38
eggs	2	36
roast ham, lean and fat*	3 oz.	35
hamburger, regular	3 oz.	34
pot roast, lean and fat	3 oz.	33
navy beans	½ cup	32
Alpo dog food	3 oz.	30
pork chop, lean and fat	1.7 oz.†	29
salami*	2 oz. (2 slices)	27
pork sausage	2 oz. (2 links)	27
drumstick, chicken, fried	1.3 oz.†	26
shrimp	1½ oz.	24
ham, boiled and sliced*	2 oz.	22
sirloin steak, lean and fat	3 oz.	19
McDonald's small hamburger	1 oz.	18
peanut butter	1 Tbsp.	17
hot dog, pure beef*	1	6
Spam*	3 oz.	4
bacon*	3 slices	4
bologna*	2 oz. (2 slices)	2

*These foods contain sodium nitrite, an additive that should be avoided.

†weight does not include the bone.

Desserts

cantaloupe with ice cream	¼ melon, 1½ oz. ice cream	90
watermelon	2 lbs.*	74
peach	1	29
pineapple, canned in juice	½ cup	27
canned peaches, water pack	½ cup	16
apple	1	12
applesauce, unsweetened	½ cup	9
pineapple, canned in heavy syrup	½ cup	4
blueberry muffin	1	0

		Nutritional Score
canned peaches, light syrup	½ cup	-6
angel food cake	1/12 cake	-15
Cool 'n Creamy	½ cup	-18
ice cream	3 oz.	-18
Hunt Snack Pack fruit cup	1	-19
Hunt Snack Pack vanilla pudding	1	-20
canned peaches, heavy syrup	½ cup	-24
coconut	1½ oz.	-30
brownie	1	-30
applesauce, sweetened	½ cup	-35
apple pie	6 oz.	-40
Del Monte vanilla pudding	1	-43
Jell-O	½ cup	-45
popsicle	one (3 oz.)	-45
chocolate cake	3 oz.	-52
Morton coconut cream pie	¼ pie	-62
Hunt Snack Pack gel	1	-63
ice cream soda	8 oz. soda, 3 oz. ice cream	-79

*The weight includes the rind; however, any nutrients in the rind were not included in the score.

With aids like the Jacobson scoreboard, or with your own knowledge of nutrition, it's easy to choose a menu for yourself and your family. But then you face the problem of turning that menu from a theory into a reality without tearing your pocketbook to shreds. Here's where supermarket strategy comes in. We're going to look at a number of techniques. Among the key ones:

- Use store brands.
- Buy in large quantities.
- Pretend you're Ulysses (don't worry, we'll explain).
- Read the labels.
- Check unit prices.

Let's start with store brands. They aren't *always* cheaper than "name" brands of canned or frozen goods. But they usually are. And many times they were packaged at the very same factory. Even when that's not the case, they may still taste just as good as better-known brands. The only way to know is to try. The savings can be considerable. *Money* magazine recently priced a market basket of thirty-one common grocery items. Using name brands, the tab was $21.18. Substituting store brands, the register rang up $18.26—a saving of 14 per cent.

Next, consider increasing the quantities in which you purchase your food. A lot of items are cheaper if purchased by the dozen, keg, sack, barrel, or box instead of one portion at a time. Buy large cans, if you can possibly use them. If you're thinking that won't work for you, consider this: Sidney Margolius, a well-known consumer writer, calculates that small households or people who live alone could actually waste almost one third of a large or medium container of some items and still come out ahead. We're not suggesting that you waste food—but do give some thought to these larger sizes.

Pretending you're Ulysses is another way to struggle for lower food bills. The analogy we have in mind here refers to the time the Greek hero sailed by the land of the sirens. Those beautiful creatures crooned an alluring melody that could tempt the sternest of men to their destruction. Ulysses had his crew stop their ears with wax, while he, bound to the mast, listened to the seductive song. Well, we don't suggest you enter the supermarket with handcuffs, or even ear wax. Instead, we suggest the psychological equivalent: that you go after true bargains and resist the siren lures of the store's display and packaging practices. Do shop the ads and pay attention to sales. Chicken on sale for 39 cents a pound may actually have cost the chain 41 cents. It's a perfect chance to stock up, and the store is content because the offer has brought in customers. Once you're there, though, you have to start binding yourself to the mast, mentally. Supermarkets have an almost hypnotic effect on a lot of shoppers. Merchandisers are paid to help bring on the trance, or make the most of it while it lasts. Thus: colorful mass displays . . . items displayed in a special island where you almost trip over them . . . impulse items placed at adult—or child—eye level, or near the checkout counter . . . shortcake tucked temptingly next to the strawberries . . . and so on, and on. The store may take a loss on an advertised item to bring you in. But the items displayed most alluringly once you're there are probably those on which they have the fattest mark-up. For bargains, reach up or down, or look in the corners.

The next hint: Read the labels. This may seem like an obvious or even an insulting injunction. But the fact is, too many shoppers don't. And even people who do read labels don't always know how to take full advantage of what's printed there. Take a can or package of "mushroom soup." A lot of people assume that the law requires one of its main ingredients to be mushrooms. That's not so, although the laws are moving in that direction and maybe we'll get there some day. For the time being, it's possible to pick up a package of mushroom soup like one we encountered recently. It sold for $2.99 a pound, a little arithmetic told us. And on the side of the box, the ingredients were listed. Spray-dried vegetable fat came first. That's made up of quite a batch of things —vegetable fat, corn syrup solids, sodium caseinate, mono- and diglycerides, di-potassium phosphate, sodium silico aluminate, and artificial flavor and color. After that came ten more ingredients, including salt and vegetable gum. Then, way down at the bottom, were dehydrated mushrooms and caramel color.

What some people don't realize is that manufacturers are required to list ingredients in descending order, according to the weights of each ingredient contained in the product. What you see first is what you get most of. So a more accurate name for the mixture described above would have been not mushroom soup but spray-dried vegetable fat soup.

Another example: We recently looked at a can of fruit drink, which called itself a citrus cooler. That might suggest to most of us that the main ingredient is citrus juice. But when we looked at the label and read the ingredients, we found that water was first in line, followed by sugar, followed by corn syrup. The label also said the product contained "not less than two percent orange juice." You can make discoveries like this for yourself at the supermarket every day.

As it happens, most 46-ounce cans of fruit drink are about 90 per cent water, and the second-largest ingredient is usually sugar or corn syrup. For exactly the same price per quart as the product we examined, you could buy 100 per cent orange juice in the form of frozen concentrate. It takes about three minutes to prepare, as against no time at all for the fruit drink. But it contains about 70 per cent more vitamin C, plus assorted other vitamins— and tastes better.

Reading labels not only tells you the ingredients in order of weight; it also gives you nutritional information. Under rules promulgated by the Food and Drug Administration, any food processor or packager that makes nutritional claims or that adds nutrients to a product must provide nutritional information on the product's label. This information follows a standard format. First comes the size of one serving or portion. Then, the number of portions in the container. After that come the number of calories per portion; then the amount of protein, carbohydrate, and fat in each portion—expressed in grams. (It doesn't really matter if you're unfamiliar with metric measurements. One gram happens to equal about .035 ounce, but the point of the information is really to let you compare the proportions of the nutrients in the product and to let you compare one brand's nutritional merits against another's.)

Following that basic information, the label will give the product's percentage of the U.S. recommended daily allowance (RDA) of various vitamins and minerals. The RDA—set by the National Academy of Sciences—is the daily intake of each nutrient that is believed to be desirable for from 95 to 99 per cent of the population. The label must tell you what percentage of this recommended level the product in question will provide for each of eight nutrients: protein, vitamin A, vitamin C, thiamin, riboflavin, niacin, calcium, and iron. If, for example, the label says "riboflavin . . . . . 10," that means one serving of the product provides 10 per cent of the riboflavin you need for the day. If a company wants to show information for other vitamins and minerals besides the eight mentioned here, that's okay. But it must show the figures for the eight.

There's no question: Reading the labels takes time. But the benefits are considerable. With careful label-reading, you can direct your food dollar toward foods that will do you the most good and away from products that consist primarily of water, sweeteners, chemicals, and the like.

A final element in successful supermarket strategy is using unit pricing. The way unit pricing works varies from place to place. Some states require it; others only encourage it. Where it's required, the regulations often apply only to stores that do a certain volume of business. Regardless of the situation in your state, you certainly have the prerogative of making your own requirement—shopping only at stores that do offer this service.

Unit pricing is an answer to the dilemma shoppers have faced for years: the jumble of odd package sizes, weights, and prices. Which is better, 165 square feet of "Super Soak" paper towels for 38 cents, or 180 square feet of "Wonder Wipe" towels for 45 cents? Questions like that can give you a headache, and by the time you've answered them, the ice cream has melted or your child has to go to the bathroom. The problem is compounded by the fact that this sort of annoying arithmetic must be repeated time and again. There are some fifty-nine different sizes of cookies, sixteen sizes of cereal, nine sizes of laundry soap.

Enter unit pricing. On the shelf, underneath those paper towels, you'll find a unit price label. It tells you the price per 100 square feet. For this standard quantity, Super Soaks are 23 cents, Wonder Wipes 25 cents. Now you know that Super Soaks are cheaper, so you buy them, unless there's a difference in quality that outweighs the price difference. The same technique applies to other products, from toothpaste (where you check the price per ounce) to meat (price per pound). With unit pricing, the information's right there, on either the product label or the shelf label.

The five techniques we've examined—store brands, large-quantity buying, the Ulysses trick, label reading, and unit pricing—can help almost anyone chop a food budget down to a better size. There are some additional techniques that can help certain people. For example, consider food stamps. Some people think food stamps are the same as welfare. That's wrong. Food stamps are part of a federal program to help all kinds of people, including working people, afford more and better food. About one in five Americans is eligible for food stamps. You can find out if you're eligible by contacting your county welfare or public aid office. They'll tell you what documents you need and where to obtain them.

The way it works is this: You pay for some food stamps, and when you do you get additional bonus food stamps free. A family of four in 1974, for example, could get from $24 to $150 extra to spend on food each month just by joining the food stamp program. The amount a household gets depends on the size of its income. You still buy your usual foods in your usual stores, and you pay with food stamps instead of cash. In 1974, families of four could join the food stamp program if they had incomes of up to $500 a month—after taxes and a number of deductions. Families could earn quite a bit over $500 a month and still qualify.

Another idea: How about growing your own food? If you'd like to but don't own any land, there may still be a way. Some cities have "adopt a lot" programs. With those, you lease a vacant lot from the city, either for free or for a slight fee. The city supplies the land. You supply the seeds—and the sweat.

Then there are free or 10-cent school lunches and breakfasts. There's federal money available for these. If your school isn't taking advantage of them, it might be worth rounding up a few parents and talking with the principal. Under the school programs, if your income falls within certain limits, your children can get two nutritious meals a day for either nothing or 20 cents.

You may be able to save a little bit extra by learning about open dating standards in your area. Like unit pricing, open dating is a hodgepodge. It's required in some areas, voluntary in others, and nonexistent in some. Open dating doesn't mean you can run in Friday night and pick up that lovely redhead at register seven, or that handsome butcher's assistant. It has to do with food freshness. For a long time, perishable items were marked with a code only the store manager could understand. With open dating, they're marked in plain English, with a month and a date. As a rule, the date shown for dairy products is the "pull date," the date by which a product should be sold. (In some places it's illegal to sell dairy goods after the pull date, in others it's not.) How long a product will still be good after the pull date depends on how well it was refrigerated in the store and on how fast you get it home to your refrigerator. As a rule, a product should stay fresh for about a week. With meat products, the date stamped on the package is normally not a pull date but the date on which the meat was packed. How long it will stay fresh is something you'll have to develop a feel for. Again, it depends partly on the store's storage practices. Besides pull dates and packing dates, there's a third kind of date stamped on some foods in some states. That's a spoilage date—a date after which the food shouldn't be eaten. What you need to do is check the regulations in your city and state (and even in your individual supermarket, in some cases) so you'll know what the rules of the dating game are in your own area.

As you shop, you'll develop some of your own techniques for saving money and spotting good values, or perhaps you already have. Talking with some sophisticated shoppers, *Consumer Survival Kit* has run into a number of helpful miscellaneous hints about food shopping. We'd like to close our session on supermarket strategy by passing some of them along.

• Potato chips cost almost four times as much per pound as raw potatoes.
• Soft drinks are among the worst nutritional buys in the supermarket; ditto for fruit drinks that are mostly water and sugar and for sugary, fruit-flavored drink powders in little packets.
• Watch out for baked goods that contain synthetic fruit.
• Sugar-coated cereals that are highly refined and contain artificial colorings and flavorings are a bad value. They may contain as much as 40 per cent sugar, and you may be paying an exorbitant amount for that sugar.
• Special baby juices may cost twice as much as what you drink. Baby can drink the same juice as the rest of the family if you don't start him or her too early.

• Processed meats like bacon, hot dogs, and bologna are costly sources of protein. Besides, they contain nitrates and nitrites—additives that some scientists suspect may increase your chances of getting cancer if eaten in fairly sizable quantities over a period of years.

• With convenience foods, you pay for the convenience. For example, take beef stroganoff in a box. You usually get about three ounces of beef, plus seasonings, and wind up paying about $2.50 a pound for the noodles. Regular egg noodles were about 44 cents a pound in 1974.

• Prepared rice mixes are expensive. Again, you could buy the ingredients separately for much less.

• Frozen dinners usually cost twice or two and a half times as much as the equivalent home-cooked meal. You usually end up with only a couple of ounces of meat and a lot of expensive gravy.

• A tremendous money-saver is nonfat dry milk. It contains large amounts of protein at a very low price. If your kids don't like the taste, you can mix it with whole milk or use it in desserts, soups, and meat loaves.

• Plain oatmeal is cheaper than instant.

• Small eggs are cheaper than large ones. If you like the big ones for breakfast, you can still use small ones for cooking and baking.

• Buy condensed soup, not prewatered. You can pay up to $1.20 a gallon for the water.

• A good buy in cheese is natural cheddar in blocks or wedges, not individually sliced and wrapped. To be labeled simply "cheese," a product can't have more than 41 per cent water. "Cheese food" can have up to 43 per cent; "cheese spread" up to 59 per cent. And "imitation cheese spread" can have even more water.

• Vegetables should be cooked with the smallest possible amount of water. When you drain water off vegetables, you drain off vitamins. When you can, buy vegetables in one-and-a-half- or two-pound bags, rather than the small packages.

• Products that come in boiling pouches cost more.

• Watch out for packages of frozen goods stacked above the freeze line marked on the inside of a store's freezer compartment. Ice crystals on the outside of a package or frost inside a package are signs that a product has been thawed and refrozen.

• Request checkout personnel to put your frozen goods in insulated bags, if they don't do it on their own.

• Fruit with discoloration on the skin and nothing else wrong with it is perfectly good and sometimes cheaper.

• Buy bread by weight, not size. Some bread is puffed up with air like a balloon.

Using all the supermarket strategy you can will certainly hack away at those towering food bills that hang over all of us. It makes shopping less of a routine and more of a challenge, a contest of wits in which you try to wrest the most nutrition possible from the supermarket with the least possible damage to your pocketbook.

CLOTHING

2

Keeping the Shirt on Your Back

The average American spends nearly $300 a year on clothing. Is the money well spent? Not always. In the never ending war between restraint and impulse, the frequent victor is impulse. Too often, consumers pay for merchandise of poor quality. And sometimes money spent on clothing simply disappears down the drain—of the washing machine.

There *are* ways to get more from your clothing dollar, and we'll be looking at several of them in this chapter. The techniques involved include tricks for spotting quality construction in a garment, rules for taking care of clothes once you've bought them, and methods for getting your money back if a garment is defective. Right now, let's get a glimpse of how much you already know about the clothes you buy.

CSK Quiz

1. True or false: In the long run, it pays to buy the best-quality garment you can afford.
2. True or false: You can always save money by making your own clothes.
3. True or false: The law now requires that all clothing must have cleaning instructions on the label.

Now let's see the answers. Number 1 is false. It may actually be more economical to buy a garment of lower quality—if you are planning to wear it only a few times, for instance, or if it is an item that will go out of style quickly. It also makes sense not to buy the highest quality in garments for a child going through a growth spurt who will outgrow, say, a pair of jeans before they've even been properly scuffed up. For garments you expect to wear often, however, the best quality you can afford is usually the best buy. The garment will wear longer than a cheaper alternative and will be less likely to develop split seams, wrinkles, loose buttons and all the other ills that cheap clothes are heir to.

Number 2 is also false. You can't always save by making your garments rather than buying them. One woman we know, a very inexperienced seamstress, decided to economize by purchasing a secondhand sewing machine and making some of her own clothes. She bought several yards of some rather costly material and a moderately complicated pattern. Full of enthusiasm, she set to work. That was more than a year ago. After several frustrated attempts, the dress was abandoned in the preliminary stages of its construction. The moral of the story: Don't expect to save money by sewing unless you know what you're doing, have plenty of time, and enjoy spending it at a sewing machine. If you think you'd like to sew, it would be a good idea to take a course in the basics before you go out and buy a machine, accessories, and material. For an experienced seamstress (or seamster), of course, sewing can be both rewarding and economical.

Number 3 is true. All items of clothing purchased after July 1973 should bear permanent labels with cleaning instructions such as "hand wash in warm water" or "dry clean only." Products covered by the clothing-care labeling law include practically all articles of textile wearing apparel, even hosiery. Yardgoods must also be sold with care labels that can be attached to the finished garment. Exempted from the law are shoes, hats, gloves and articles whose utility or appearance would be impaired by a permanent label. Completely washable items costing less than three dollars are also exempt. If you're thinking about buying an item that doesn't bear a permanent care label, ask the salesperson about it. If he makes unwritten claims about the performance or the care of the garment, ask to have these promises written on the sales receipt. Not all sales people will do this for you, of course. But a store where they will do it is more likely to merit your continued patronage than one where they won't.

If you check permanent care labels before you buy clothing, you can save yourself hours of ironing and quite a few dollars on dry-cleaning bills. And if you remember to keep reading the labels after the garments are at home, you can prevent the early demise of many a garment that would otherwise emerge from your dryer tattered, discolored, or wrinkled. And that will save you money on the cost of replacement garments.

When you're shopping for clothes, it helps to have a basic knowledge of the materials clothes are made of—textiles. It's impossible for most consumers to be familiar with all the different materials on the market. There are more than 700 man-made fibers, from Acele to Zefran. When it comes to these, you have to try them and see if you like them. Anyone, however, can start out with a knowledge of some of the basic components used in complex fabrics.

First, there's cotton. The one-time king of the South still reigns supreme in a lot of garments. And there are good reasons why. Cotton is strong, colorfast, and powerfully resistant to moths and heat. Most important, it's highly resistant to perspiration, and it's very absorbent, so you don't get all clammy when you're wearing it. Cotton is also versatile—you'll find it in a large variety of garments. But you usually won't find it by itself. That's because, for all its virtues, cotton is only fair-to-poor at retaining a crease. As a result, it's often blended with other fibers or given special treatment to make it wrinkle-resistant. Another reason why you may have a hard time finding garments of 100 per cent cotton is that cotton has become increasingly expensive in the mid-1970s.

The same thing has happened to the cost of another of the world's great natural fibers—wool. Like cotton, wool is a very versatile fiber. It's warm, absorbent, colorfast, and resilient. It isn't the easiest thing in the world to care for, however. It doesn't have much resistance to bleaches, moths, perspiration, or strong soaps.

It certainly can't be called wash-and-wear, either, as anyone who has washed a heavy wool sweater can tell you. (The sweater stays damp for a while, during which time the environment may smell slightly like a sheep meadow.) To care for your wool garments, let them rest twenty-four hours between wearings, so the fibers can relax back into their natural shape. Wool absorbs odors, so hang your sweater or whatever where the air can circulate around it. Or better still, if you don't live in a sooty area, lay it out flat in front of an open window. Don't forget to mothproof your wool items before you store them over the summer.

Now let's move on to a couple of the synthetic, or man-made fibers. The granddaddy of them all is nylon. Nylon is probably the strongest of all man-made fibers in common use. It's strong enough to be used in tire cords. Yet so versatile is it that it can also be used in sheer hosiery (which many women call "nylons" as a matter of course). Despite its strength, nylon is light—as witness its use in parachute cloth, backpackers' tents, and panty hose. When you buy a nylon garment, you can be pretty sure it will wash easily, dry quickly, and need little pressing. Nylon holds its shape quite well, since it hardly shrinks or stretches. It's not very absorbent, though: You probably wouldn't want to wear a nylon shirt or dress in warm weather. Another weakness of nylon is sunlight resistance. You wouldn't, for example, want 100 per cent nylon drapes in a sunny room. They'd fade. To overcome these weaknesses, nylon is often blended with other fibers.

A second man-made fabric is polyester. This is the material that made the dream of wash-and-wear garments come true. It has outstanding wrinkle resistance and shape retention. It also happens to have good colorfastness and resistance to sunlight, abrasion, mildew, moths, and perspiration. Polyster, though, has its own Achilles' heel: When used by itself it lacks absorbency, and it's susceptible to oily stains. Some fabrics are given soil-release treatments to reduce this last problem. But, because of the absorbency factor, polyester is almost always used in blends —often with cotton, rayon, or wool.

Rayon was the first man-made fiber to be manufactured. It was exhibited in 1889 at an exposition in France. It's soft and comfortable to wear because of its high moisture absorbency. Its texture is rather like that of linen. Unfortunately, most rayon garments don't wash well. For this reason, garments made primarily of rayon usually have to be dry-cleaned—which can be expensive.

One more common synthetic is acrylic. Acrylic might be described pretty accurately as imitation wool. If you're wearing a sweater and it's not wool, it's probably acrylic. Fake furs are often made from acrylic fiber, too. It feels like wool and has pressed-crease retention, good wrinkle resistance, and some wash-and-wear qualities. The main thing to remember about acrylic is that it doesn't like to get too hot. To avoid ruining an acrylic garment, wash it and press it at moderate temperatures.

The basic man-made fibers, like nylon, polyester, rayon, and acrylic, are easier to spot if you know some of the common trade names under which they're sold. Below is a chart to help you do that.

Common Trade Names of Man-Made Fibers

Nylon is sold as:
  Antron (by DuPont)
  Blue "C" (by Monsanto)
  Caprolan (by Allied Chemical)
  Celanese nylon (by Celanese)
  Qiana (by DuPont)
Polyester is sold as:
  Dacron (by DuPont)
  Fortrel (by Celanese)
  Kodel (by Eastman)
  Trevira (by Hystron)
Rayon is sold as:
  Avril (by American Viscose)
  Bemberg (by Beaunit)
  Cupioni (by Beaunit)
  Fibro (by Courtaulds)
  Nupron (by IRC)
Acrylic is sold as:
  Acrilan (by Monsanto)
  Creslan (by American Cyanamid)

Orlon (by DuPont)
Zefran II (by Dow Badische)
(Source: "Facts About Man-Made Fibers," by Celanese Corp.)

One thing you've probably noticed from reading labels in stores (or from the discussion so far in this chapter) is that very few garments are made of 100 per cent *anything* these days. That doesn't mean a basic knowledge of fibers isn't helpful. But it does explain why consumers were somewhat at a loss as to how to use garments wisely, in the absence of specific care instructions. Now, thanks to permanent care labels, those instructions are available. So, unless you have a taste for throwing money away, read the care labels and follow their suggestions!

Some further suggestions for garment care come from the International Fabricare Institution, a trade association, which is the successor to the National Institute of Drycleaning and the American Institute of Laundering. You can get the Institute's guide to home spot removal (a four-page brochure) by writing to International Fabricare Institute, P.O. Box 940, Joliet, Ill. 60434. Enclose a self-addressed, stamped envelope. As you might expect, the Institute recommends that you take a stained garment to a dry-cleaner if the stains are extensive, if the garment is very expensive, or if you think the fabric may be fragile.

There are three basic methods of removing a stain: dry-cleaning, wet-cleaning, and bleaching. If you know what caused a particular stain, the chart on pages 29-30 may help you choose the appropriate method. Otherwise, you should try them in the order listed, using bleaching only as a last resort. The word "dry" in cleaning, by the way, is a bit deceptive. It's most often done with cleaning fluid. The procedure is dry only in that the fluid used contains no water. (At times, the cleaning agent used will be a powder rather than a fluid, in which case the procedure is literally dry.)

As the Institute points out, "Some stains will dissolve in water but not in cleaning fluid, others in cleaning fluid but not in water. For instance, sugar dissolves in water but is totally unaffected by cleaning fluid. Tar dissolves in cleaning fluid but is unaffected by water." Some stains, like lipstick, are complex and need both water and cleaning fluid to dissolve them. Remember that, men, before engaging in any illicit adventures.

With both the wet and the dry procedures, you should spread a spare towel (preferably white) underneath the stained garment. You then apply the agent (that is, cleaning fluid or water—never both) to the stain, and rub gently with your fingertips. The idea is to make the stain soak through the fabric onto the towel. It takes a good deal of patience. With wet-cleaning, if water alone doesn't do the job you may add some liquid detergent. If you do this, be sure all the detergent is flushed out afterwards; it can leave a ring. After the stain seems to be gone, you should wet a piece of cheesecloth with the cleaning agent you've been using (that is, water or fluid, not detergent) and wipe from the edges of the area toward the center. This will help prevent a ring.

When you're coming to the rescue of a stained garment in distress, time is of the essence. A stain that goes untreated can become permanent—especially if it gets exposed to heat (as in a dryer). Watch out for soft-drink stains! These can sometimes be invisible once they dry. But let the garment be exposed to heat, and—wham! You have a brown stain that won't come out. Some fruit juices and fruit drinks also leave stains that start out invisible but show up later. So if you spill something on yourself, take care of the stain as quickly as possible.

The chart below will give you some ideas on what kind of stains should be dry-cleaned and what kind should be wet-cleaned (as well as what kind you shouldn't try to clean yourself).

Stain Removal Table

Use the "dry" method on:
    Ballpoint ink
    Printing ink
    Rouge, mascara, foundation and leg makeup
    Carbon paper
    Typewriter ribbon

Road oil or tar
Cooking oil or grease
Candle wax
Lipstick*
Shoe polish*
Gravy*
Salad dressing*
      (*Items marked with an asterisk should be cleaned first
with the dry method, then the wet method.)
   Use the wet method on:
   Milk, cream, ice cream
   Soft drinks
   Wine and berry stains
   Solid food stains
   Catsup
   Urine
   Washable inks (not ballpoint)
   Library paste, LePage's glue, Elmer's glue (but most glue
      and adhesive stains require professional care)
   Take these stains to a professional:
   Glues and adhesives (except as noted above)
   Coffee
   Tea
   Medicines
   Paint
   Fingernail polish
   Mustard
   Grass
   (Source: International Fabricare Institute.)

Following the advice in the chart may save you money, even if it
means taking a garment to a dry-cleaner's. It's rare that the cost
of cleaning a garment professionally once or twice will exceed the
cost of replacing the garment itself. If it should happen that a
professional cleaner ruins a garment of yours, though, don't
simply shrug it off. Ask him to reimburse you. If he declines, take
the matter up with the Better Business Bureau in your area.
When the bureau gets a complaint, it sends a copy of the letter to

the cleaner. Sometimes this is enough to resolve the dispute. If no agreement is reached, the bureau will often send the garment itself to the International Fabricare Institute for analysis. If the Institute determines the cleaner is at fault, the BBB urges him to reimburse you. If the analysis reveals that the fault lies with the manufacturer (in other words, that the garment was defective in the first place and therefore was easily damaged in the cleaning process), you'll be given a copy of the Institute's letter to that effect.

Take the letter with you when you go to see the retailer who sold the garment to you. Unless you've moved far away from the store where you bought the item, the retailer should be your first recourse. It will help, of course, if you still have the sales slip. If the retailer demurs, you can enclose a copy of the letter when you complain to the manufacturer. If none of these procedures brings you satisfaction, you can try going to a small claims court in your area and suing the party you think is responsible for the damage. Of course, the amount of time you are willing to spend getting your money back will depend on how costly the garment was and on how fired-up you are about the damage.

Taking good care of your clothes is one important way to keep the shirt on your back, and we hope we've given you some useful hints for doing it. Another way of saving on clothes that deserves some discussion is making a careful selection, so you won't be stuck with a garment that you really don't want to wear very often. If the size isn't quite right, or if the garment looked great on the rack but lousy on you, you'll have wasted your money. The same is true if the garment looks fine but matches hardly anything else in your wardrobe. The best way to judge whether you're prone to these mistakes is to ask yourself if you have made them in the past. If you have, try to keep a tighter rein on your impulses—or have a friend or spouse join you in shopping for clothes. A second opinion may help you avert a mistake. Pick out two or three colors in which you look good and feel at home. Then try to coordinate your wardrobe around those colors. You can, of course, have different color schemes for summer and for winter. "Mixing and matching" tops and bottoms in compatible colors is a good way to stretch your clothing dollar.

If you follow certain basic principles of fashion, you'll be less likely to end up with a garment sitting in your closet gathering dust. *Always* try on clothes before buying them. Sizes are not really uniform, and tailoring varies from one manufacturer to another. You might have a 30-inch waist when you're buying one brand of pants, for example, and need a 32-inch waist for another. Even if you've bought the brand before, it pays to try the garment on. If you're short, you'll probably look good in garments with vertical lines or stripes. If you're tall, vertical lines will accentuate your height, which is probably something you don't want. Horizontal lines usually draw attention to the part of the body where they appear. So keep that in mind of there's a part of your body you want to keep hidden (or show off). Fashion details, like patches, buttons, pockets, lace, or unusual material tend to draw people's eyes. So use them to attract eyes to your good features, away from your bad ones. Not that *you* have any bad ones. . . .

Some special considerations enter into buying clothes for young children. It must be a mystery to every baby and toddler why grownups design clothes with such teeny-weeny head holes. Getting dressed, as every parent knows, is not a young child's favorite activity. Garments that are tight around the neck and sleeves only make it harder.

Even before they can walk, kids do a lot of bending, stretching, stooping, sitting, and reaching. And once they're on their feet children are mobile to an astonishing degree: Their garments should be able to withstand cartwheels, races, fights, games, and miscellaneous exploring. That means they should be reasonably tough and adequately roomy. Shirts should be long enough to stay tucked in during play. On the other hand, pants legs and dresses should be short, or kids will trip over them. Coats, jackets, and snowsuits for winter should be carefully fitted while the child is wearing clothes similar to those that will normally be worn under these outer garments. It's no fun to be jammed into a snowsuit that hardly fits over your other clothes.

Whether you're buying for a child, man, or woman, certain signs will help you recognize good workmanship in clothes. Where the fabric is decorated with a pattern, that pattern should be continuous even where the garment isn't. With a sport jacket, for example, buttoning the center button should be analogous to completing a jigsaw puzzle—the pattern should fit together perfectly. Pockets on men's clothes should be full and sturdy. Hems on dresses should be neatly stitched, with enough material provided for lengthening as required. Seams on sleeves should be single, not double, and should run along the inside of the arm. Sleeves look better and last longer this way, according to Aileen Knapp, a fashion consultant to whom Consumer Survival Kit is indebted for several of the hints given here. Perhaps the most important indicator of workmanship is the appearance of the seams. They should be completely and evenly sewn, not loose or ragged. But there should be an adequate amount of material inside the garment at most seams so that the garment can be let out if the buyer needs a little bit of extra room (or puts on some weight later).

Recognizing quality workmanship, buying clothes you'll actually use, caring properly for your garments—all of these will help stretch your clothing dollar. But none of what we've said so far is of much help when it comes to shoes. And shoes are a vital part of everyone's wardrobe, both financially and in terms of health. Most people put a lot of mileage on their feet. Every inch of it can be torture if shoes don't fit. You may think you can't afford to spend the time, money, and effort necessary to find the right shoes. But you really can't afford *not* to. The wrong shoes can cause serious damage to your feet.

Less painful than ill-fitting shoes, but just as aggravating, are shoes that wear out or come apart long before they've done their time on street detail. And then there are some shoes that are just plain dangerous. But before we get into that, how about seeing how much you already know about shoes?

CSK Quiz

1. True or false: No matter how well a shoe fits, it will require a period of breaking in, during which it may not be comfortable.
2. True or false: A child's foot isn't fully developed until around

age twenty. Until then, much of what eventually becomes bone is only cartilage.

3. True or false: Shoes will last longer if you wear the same pair several days in a row. That way they can assume the shape of your foot more quickly.

Now let's see how high your shoe IQ is. Number 1 is false! Forget about breaking in new shoes. If a shoe isn't comfortable when you buy it, it's going to give you nothing but trouble. So keep looking until you find shoes that feel good on your feet.

Number 2 is true. When you were born, you had far fewer bones in your feet than you have now. It takes about twenty years for a foot to develop completely, with all of its twenty-six bones in the right places. That's why parents should be very careful about the shoes—and the socks—their children wear. The wrong shoes can deform a child's foot for life. Socks that are too small are almost as harmful. According to Dr. Neil Scheffler of the Maryland Podiatry Society, children shouldn't wear shoes at all until they're ready to walk. After that they should wear shoes if they're going to be walking on hard surfaces. Going barefoot is okay on sand or grass, but nature didn't design the human foot for walking on concrete. The best shoes for babies, according to Dr. Scheffler, are those with high tops (so the baby won't kick them off) and hard soles (so the baby's feet will be adequately protected). Sneakers are fine for babies, providing the child has well-balanced feet and doesn't wear the sneakers for too many hours at a stretch. (We'll have more to say about sneakers later.)

One thing you shouldn't do is save shoes from one child to use as hand-me-downs for the next. That's fine with a lot of garments but a real blunder with shoes. The second child to wear a pair will stand a good chance of running into trouble, because the shoes have already assumed the shape of the first owner's feet.

Number 3 is false. Shoes will last longer if you give them a day's rest between wearings, so they can air and dry. Tests show, in fact, that three pair of men's shoes, worn alternately, give approximately the same wear as four pair when each is worn without change. So give your shoes a rest every other day, and the effect on your pocketbook will be the same as if you'd been given a free pair of shoes.

When you go to buy shoes for yourself or for a child, you can save yourself a lot of woe by looking at the old ones in the closet. Watch for certain telltale signs. Look first at the inside, in the toe area. If the lining is rubbed and chafed, it's a sign the shoe was too small. If it's rubbed just above the toe line, that's even worse —it means the shoe was much too short, and the wearer's toes curled up in an effort to take up less room. If seams are broken, that's another indication a shoe was too short. On the other hand, if a shoe's toes are noticeably curled up, that's a sign the shoe was too long.

Learning from your old shoes is all the more important because many shoe salespeople don't have extensive training. With the growing emphasis on high-volume sales, some shoe stores and departments are very nearly in the self-service category. You can walk into a shoe store, and have a dialogue like this:

SALESMAN: May I help you?

You: Well, I hope so. I'm looking for a pair of shoes for work. Something comfortable, not too expensive.

SALESMAN: I'm sure we can find something. What size do you wear?

You: I thought you were supposed to tell *me* that.

SALESMAN: Oh, right—well, let's find out here. (Gets a Brannock measuring device as you slip off your shoes. Begins to measure.)

You: Excuse me, but shouldn't I be standing up when you measure my foot?

SALESMAN: Oh, okay. (You stand up. Salesman measures your right foot.) Nine-and-a-half B. Okey-dokey?

You: What about the other one?

SALESMAN: The other one?

You: My left foot. One foot is usually larger than the other, you know.

SALESMAN: Right, right (Starts to measure right foot again.)

YOU: No—left, left. You already got the right one. (Salesman measures your left foot.)

SALESMAN: Well, by golly. You're right. The left one is a ten. Who would've thought that? A whole half-size.

YOU: It's only one sixth of an inch difference. A full size is just one third of an inch. Now, how about showing me some shoes. Ten B.

SALESMAN: Be right back. (Returns with several pair of shoes. You try on each in turn and reject them.) I hope you'll excuse me for saying so, but you're certainly one of the choosiest customers I've had.

YOU: Why should I excuse you? That's a compliment. Have you got anything else to shoe me?

SALESMAN: Only two pairs left. How about these?

YOU: No, I tried them at another store and they didn't fit.

SALESMAN: But maybe you had the wrong size.

YOU: No, that wasn't it. I tried a few sizes. Some styles just don't seem to fit my foot. Probably the last is wrong for me.

SALESMAN: The last what?

YOU: You know, the last—the form a shoe is made on. If it's the wrong shape for my foot, the shoe's not going to fit no matter how many sizes I try. Let me see that last pair on the floor over there. . . . Hmmm. Say! These really feel good. I can wiggle my big toes. The heel feels nice and snug, but it isn't rubbing or pinching. These are good! They grip my instep, but they're still flexible there. And you know what the most important thing of all is . . . the ball of my foot falls at the widest part of the shoe. You've made yourself a sale, my man.

SALEMAN: (Looking through boxes) I'm afraid not.

YOU: Why not?

SALESMAN: There's been a mistake. Those are the shoes you wore in here. (Makes a face as if about to cry.)

Not all salesmen are as ignorant as the one pictured in this sketch. Some are conscientious and knowledgeable professionals. If you find one, it's worth sticking with him.

Besides the knowledge to guide yourself in a store where the salespeople are untrained, you need another quality if you're going to give your feet a break. That quality is self-restraint. You'll need it if you're going to forgo the puchase of shoes that *look* very attractive but can be hazardous to your health. The leading example in the mid-1970s was the platform shoe. The thick platforms may elevate fashion—and the wearer—to new heights. But from a health standpoint the platform represents a new depth, according to many podiatrists. They have reported a rash of foot injuries directly attributable to platform shoes. A close look at the shoe shows why. Normally when you walk your foot flexes. A thick platform makes the shoe rigid; it doesn't allow foot muscles to bend at all. The strain of walking then has to be absorbed by other parts of the body not designed for that function, like the hips and ankles. This increases the danger of falling. When a falls occurs, the pressure on the anklebone is similar to that of a skiing fall. No wonder a small anklebone fracture is one of the most common injuries caused by platform shoes. The higher the shoe the greater the danger.

Platforms with no backs require a special balancing act. In order to keep your heel where it belongs, the hips are thrust forward, causing a swayback effect. That's not only unattractive, it causes pulled muscles. The greatest danger of all, though, is driving in platform shoes. National Safety Council studies have shown that the thick platform soles make it very difficult to distinguish between the accelerator and the brake. If you must wear platforms, it's a good idea to keep a pair of driving shoes in your car.

Much less fashionable than most shoes, but quite practical and economical, are sneakers. In general, sneakers are healthy for your feet—with two caveats. Number one, you shouldn't wear them for too many hours at a time. That practice causes perspiration buildup, which in turn gives fungus diseases a favorable breeding ground. Number two, especially if you're young, you shouldn't wear sneakers much if you have any deformation or imbalance in the way your feet are formed. Wearing sneakers will be more likely to aggravate such a condition than to correct it.

When you look for sneakers, there are a number of points to

watch for. The material for the upper part of the shoe should be a firm-woven fabric, like canvas, denim, or poplin. Loose weaves can stretch and tear. The soles should have a nonslip tread. The innersole, or arch support, should be cushioned to make your feet more comfortable. In the heel area the shoe should be reinforced with extra stiffening and extra stitching. That helps the shoe retain its shape and gives your heel better support. Make sure the back seam is securely stitched and squarely in the middle of the heel. Stitching throughout the shoe sould be secure, neat, and straight. Nowhere should you be able to see rough spots, wrinkles, bulky seams, or gummy adhesives. The sole should be firmly attached to the rest of the shoe, and the foxing—that's the rubber piece that goes around the base of the sneaker—should be one continuous strip, tightly attached. A toe guard is a useful feature, especially in a kid's sneaker. Fit is just as important here as with more formal shoes. Be sure to try on sneakers with the kind of socks you'll be wearing when you use the sneakers. Finally, since sneakers get dirty easily, you'll want to be sure they're machine-washable. Check the label for washing instructions or ask the salesperson. When you do wash sneakers, keep them away from chlorine bleach and direct heat, both of which can damage the rubber.

With shoes, as with other garments, the proper care will give you longer wear—which means less money out of your wallet. Most shoes should be cleaned occasionally with saddle soap or shined with a good paste or cream polish to keep them pliable. Leather does get dry, and dried-out leather fibers grind together and cause damage. Leather shoes are averse to water, also. The best thing is to keep them from getting wet by wearing galoshes. When they do get wet, they shouldn't be put in an oven or over a radiator to dry. That only stiffens and cracks them. Instead, wipe the shoes clean, pack them with paper, and let them dry slowly, away from direct heat. Then, when they're dry, perk them up again with some polish.

Before leaving the subject of shoes, let's take a moment to discuss one of the common problems that crop up inside them: foot odor. Foot odor is most likely to be a problem if you wear synthetic shoes. Most of those have far fewer pores than leather shoes. Result: Feet can't breathe. If foot odor is a problem, it may help to wear leather shoes, powder your feet, and change shoes once or twice during the day.

People often buy and wear their shoes and other clothes unquestioningly, out of habit, or as if in some sort of economic trance. Clothing is so much a part of our lives that we sometimes notice it as little as a fish notices water. If this chapter serves one purpose, it will be to get you to step back and take a fresh look at your clothing dollar and what you get for it.

SHELTER

3

Buying Your Dream House

Buying a home is probably the largest investment you'll make during your lifetime. Naturally you want to prepare yourself to make a wise choice. This chapter is devoted to helping you do that. In it, we'll examine some of the structural aspects of houses, as well as the sometimes mystifying paperwork that goes into the purchase of a house.

Let's start out with some of the structural considerations. As an introduction to these, consider, if you will, a few questions.

CSK Quiz

1. True or false: Voltage is the most important consideration in judging electrical adequacy.
2. True or false: Flushing the toilet while the faucets are on is a good way to check water pressure.
3. True or false: The seller is obligated to tell you about a structural fault in the house.

Now for a look at the answers. Number 1 is false. Voltage is not the most important consideration in electrical adequacy; amperage is. If your house has adequate amperage, you'll be able to use several appliances at once without blowing a fuse or activating a circuit breaker. It's desirable that your home be wired for at least 100 amperes. If you're looking at a house, and the present owner doesn't know the amperage, you can make a pretty good approximation by locating the main electrical cable coming into the house. Cables with a 100-ampere capacity are usually about an inch thick. If the cable's only half an inch thick, the electrical capacity may be less—30 amperes, for example, on some older houses.

Number 2 is true. Running the faucets and flushing the toilet at the same time *is* a good way of checking on water pressure. In a fair number of houses, performing this simple test will have a revealing result: The water will stop completely at one of the fixtures. This signals low water pressure, which can be a nuisance. One cause of low water pressure is the accumulation of rust in steel piping. For this reason, newer homes usually have copper pipes. You should treat copper piping as definitely preferable to other types.

Number 3 is false, with a vengeance. The seller is not at all obligated to tell you about any structural defects in the home you're buying. And he has a strong economic reason to do the opposite: to play up the home's good points and try to hide the bad.

When you go looking for a house, one of the first tools you'll encounter is the so-called multiple listing card. The term stems from a system most real estate brokers have adopted nowadays: Most homes that come on the market in an area are put in the file of ("listed" with) a large number of local brokers. This system gives buyers a wider range of homes to choose from than they would otherwise have. It also allows a faster turnover of property, giving the real estate people a chance to make more money on commissions.

The seller pays his broker a commission that usually amounts to 6 per cent of the selling price of the house. Of course, while this commission is technically paid by the seller, it comes out of the total tab that's picked up by the buyer. If you, as a buyer, are represented by a real estate agent, your agent will split the commission (usually half and half) with the seller's agent.

The multiple listing card is a description of a house. It gives you lots of information, including the location, style, number of rooms, lot size, special features. and asking price. Keep in mind that all the information is provided by the seller, who wants to present things in the best possible light.

Looking at listing cards, you can eliminate in advance many homes that won't meet your particular requirements. And you can do the same thing as you comb through the classified ads. If you need a house with three bedrooms, there's no point looking at a two-bedroom house—even if it's in "superb" condition and has a heated swimming pool. The best way to approach the great house hunt is to be methodical. Draw up a list of your requirements in a house. Your priority list should include the number of rooms you need, special features you require, and also any stipulations stemming from things that bug you about your current quarters. If, for example, you're tormented by noise, make quiet one of your absolute requirements. Then, when you visit your prospective new home, you'll pay special attention to its distance from the road, the sounds of its heating system, and so on. Don't depend on your memory to come through at a time of rushed excitement. Write your requirements down!

Chances are good that a house does contain what an ad says it contains—and that it does not include extras missing from the ad or listing form. If a description appeals to you but you're uncertain if it fills all your needs, try telephoning the real estate agency that's showing the house. They're usually glad to help you.

One part of the house's description that you should place very little stock in is the description of condition. You can usually bring it down one large notch in your mind. If a house is described as in "perfect" or "superior" condition, you can figure that probably the listing agent doesn't know of anything in particular wrong with it. The same is sometimes true when a house is described as in "excellent" shape. "Very good" can mean that the house needs some work. "Good" can mean bad. And any home described as in "fair" condition is probably a handyman's delight, if it's not ready for demolition. Of course, there are no uniform standards governing the use of these words. The translations given here can be wrong. It boils down to this: You have to evaluate the home's condition yourself.

Another part of the listing form that deserves questioning is the blank where the age is filled in. Many owners don't really know the age of their house, so they guess. Some others will just plain lie. But there's a useful trick that might enable you to ascertain the age of a house very quickly. We call it the *Consumer Suvival Kit* commode test. It's likely to work if your house was built before 1970 and if it still has the toilets originally installed by the builder. Take the tank lid off of each toilet, and check to see if there's a date engraved in the porcelain. Until the late 1960s, dates were put on almost all such fixtures (and they were almost always sold within six months of the date shown). If all the toilets in the house bear the same date, you've got a pretty close approximation to the construction date of the house.

If a house is being sold through a real estate broker, the multiple listing form will show last year's property tax total and the heating costs per month. You can verify the heating costs by asking to see a fuel bill. You can verify last year's tax bite by asking to see a receipt for payment of property taxes. What concerns you more, though, is what taxes will be in the future. In trying to gauge them, you can consider the past record of tax increases in the community, the rate at which the community is growing, and whether substantial construction of roads and sewers still remains to be done. You should also find out when the house was last assessed. If it was quite a while ago, the next assessment could bring a big jump in your tax bill.

When you go to look at a house, two of your most important tools will be pencil and paper. Bring with you your list of priorities and requirements and a list of any questions suggested to you by the ad or multiple listing form. And, while at the house, take notes. You may be seeing a number of houses, and things that seem clear in your mind as you look are likely to get blurred

later. You can't remember everything about the house, so don't
try.

Now let's consider some of the things you'll be looking for. A
useful cliché of home buying is that you should start with the
basement. That advice is hard to take literally, unless you're
going to break and enter. Inevitably, the entrance way and living
room will be among the first areas you'll see, and they'll condition
your psychological reaction to the house. But remember, much of
that reaction is to the décor and furnishings—items that won't be
there when you take over the building. So do make your way
down to the basement. It's a good place to check for leakage or
moisture. And it can be a good place to get a clue as to how solidly a building is constructed. If the interior walls are supported
by two-by-fours, it's a good sign that the house has been built in
a sturdy fashion. In case you're unfamiliar with this bit of handyman's slang, a two-by-four is a board two inches thick and four
inches wide. Solidly built homes typically have interior walls supported by two-by-fours, which are spaced 16 inches apart. Some
homes nowadays are built not with two-by-fours but with two-
by-twos. Making matters worse, the thinner boards are sometimes
placed as much as 24 inches apart. In the judgment of John
Heyn, *Consumer Survival Kit's* building consultant, the latter
arrangement doesn't provide the strength that you, as a prospective home buyer, should be looking for. (Heyn, a former custom
house-builder and general contractor, is now the head of a home
inspection firm. He holds a degree in architecture from Dart-
mouth College.)

In the basement, you may be able to get a glimpse of support-
ing boards to see whether they meet Heyn's standards. You might
also get a glimpse of the insulation used in the house. Insulation
has always been important. Today it's doubly so, with society
trying to control the use of energy resources, and *you* trying to
control the growth of your fuel bill. Heyn recommends at least a
two-inch thickness of fiberglass insulation around the side walls,
and four inches across the attic space. This will make both heating and air conditioning systems work efficiently. Some older

homes have no insulation. And belive it or not, neither do some very new homes! Where insulation is missing from a recently built house it's almost always the result of sloppy workmanship or a failure in communication while the house was under construction.

Many homes have septic tanks instead of a tie-in to a community sewer system. If you're looking at a home with a private sewage system there are several things you should insist on knowing. One is the size of the tank. Today the average family should count on having a 1,000-gallon septic tank. A second is the location of the tank and the drain field. You certainly don't want it in the front yard. And you want to assure yourself that seepage from the septic tank is not going to contaminate your drinking water in any way. You'll also want to know when was the last time the tank was pumped out and how often pumpings are necessary Last, you should find out the age and condition of the tank. Most of them are usually good for about twelve years. It cost about $1,500 to replace a septic system in 1974. So if the system for the house you're buying is old, you can add that onto the probable repair costs you'll soon be having and adjust your bid for the house appropriately.

Another important point is a home's heating system. Passion is wonderful, but you can't depend on it to keep you warm all the time. Among the more conventional heating systems, you have three basic choices: hot water, forced air, and electric baseboard. Hot water systems are usually found in older homes. The water is heated in a furnace (which runs on gas or oil) and piped into radiators around the house. Natural air currents disperse the heat around the radiators. These systems have served many homeowners faithfully for years. They do have certain disadvantages, though. Unless they're covered, radiators tend to be unsightly and pose a possible burn hazard to young children. The heat they give off is dry, leading to the need for a separate humidifying system during the winter if you're susceptible to scratchy throats. And the heat from a radiator system can sometimes be uneven: too hot near the radiators, too cold in other parts of the house.

Electric baseboard systems were touted as the ultimate in modernity when they appeared. They can be very efficient and convenient heating devices. One advantage they have is that they produce an even distribution of heat in a room. Another is that they are usually controlled by a number of individual thermostats, so you can adjust the heat level separately in different parts of the house. The chief disadvantage of electric heat in the mid-1970s was that the cost of electricity had skyrocketed in many parts of the country. As a result, some people who were the proud owners of all-electric homes suddenly found themselves faced with a nightmare of mounting costs. Some families in New York actually found that their electric bills were running higher than their mortgage payments! In the long run, though, there's little reason to think that electricity will be more expensive than the alternatives of oil and gas that are used to heat a furnace. Electricity can be generated by atomic power or the conversion of solar energy, while oil and gas are fossil fuels whose supply is ultimately limited.

The most common type of heating system in modern houses is forced air. It works pretty much as the name implies: Heated air is forced from a furnace area, passes through ducts, and emerges into each room through one or more vents. The air may be heated originally by oil, gas, or electricity. The relatively inconspicuous vents of a forced-air system avoid most of the drawbacks of radiators. If there are enough vents, and if the heat delivery system is properly balanced, you'll get uniform heat throughout the house. A special advantage of the forced-air system is that you can install air filters or humidifying equipment at the system's core, and thus have the air in your house centrally cleaned or humidified. Forced-air systems also lend themselves to the installation of central air conditioning. With a forced-air system, it's important that the furnace have adequate heating capacity. This capacity is measured in British Thermal Units, commonly called BTUs. As a rule of thumb, a furnace should provide 35,000 BTUs for each bedroom in your house. If it's a three-bedroom house, it should have a 105,000-BTU furnace. In case you're wondering how to figure out the furnace's capacity, we have some good news for you: It's usually written somewhere on the furnace. So get out your flashlight and check.

When you're looking at a house, it's a good idea to test the heating system. Raise the thermostat and see how long the system takes to respond. It shouldn't take more than a half hour for the house to reach the desired temperature. If you're sensitive to noise, you should also stay to see how the furnace acts when it's turned off. Some refuse to cease their activity without a commotion.

If you're buying a brand new home, you may not be able to inspect it physically until it's too late. So you want to do everything possible to be sure you're dealing with a reputable builder. There are several clues you can use. One, does the builder belong to the builders' association in your state? Contact the association to find out. Two, does the Better Business Bureau in your area have a file of complaints about this particular builder? Three, and possibly most important of all, does the builder guarantee his workmanship? In the past it was almost unheard of for a home builder to do so. In 1973, however, the National Association of Home Builders (NAHB) started a new and potentially valuable program. It's called a "consumer assurance plan," but what it amounts to is a warranty. Even though the warranty is limited, it's better than anything a new home buyer could get in the past. It covers faulty workmanship and defective materials for a relatively short period. Major construction defects, however, are covered for a full ten years. In 1974, as the program was getting off the ground, one large Eastern real estate firm reported that 40 per cent of the new homes it was selling were covered by the NAHB warranty. By 1975 the NAHB expected 200,000 homes to be covered. If you're buying a new home, it makes sense to give some preference to a builder offering this plan.

Suppose, however, that your new home develops problems. It's not covered by any warranty, and you need after-the-fact help. What you probably need to do in this situation is to get in touch with a good lawyer. You might end up suing the builder, or that step might prove unnecessary. Some builders become eager to rectify flawed workmanship when they see a serious possibility of a suit on the horizon. If you think your financial circumstances prohibit the costs of a good lawyer, you might be interested in some thoughts on economizing on legal fees. See page 77 of this book.

Before you resort to a lawyer, though, you might try some good old-fashioned American complaining. If your builder belongs to a builders' council or association, see if that group has a committee for arbitrating complaints. Or there may be a real estate commission in your area that serves a similar function.

As you tour through a house, you have to be alert—or perhaps "suspicious" should be the word. Watch, for example, for water marks that may indicate possible leakage or flooding. These are most likely to show up on floors or ceilings. If you notice a freshly painted, ceiling, and the room shows few other signs of having been recently redecorated, you might inquire as to the reason for the fresh paint. Remember that the owner and his agent do not have to tell you anything about the house. It's up to you to judge it for yourself.

Some people have the misconception that various lending institutions will protect them from buying a structurally defective home. It isn't so. If a bank issues you a conventional mortgage loan, it's probably made a cursory check of the house to see that it provides adequate collateral for your loan. But that check is routine and certainly carries no guarantee for you. And if the loan is insured by the Federal Housing Administration (FHA) or the Veterans Administration (VA), it's still no guarantee. These agencies approve mortgages, not houses.

A cautious buyer does not rely on building codes, either. Municipal building inspectors are few and far between, and many local building codes are simply not enforced. One way you can lessen your risk is to have a home looked over by a professional building inspector or civil engineer. Such people vary considerably in their capability and thoroughness. If you know people in the area where you're home-hunting, you might ask them if they know a building inspector with a good reputation. If that fails, you pretty much go in blind. Inspectors' fees, in 1974, ranged from less than $100 to more than $200. What you buy for that money is another pair of eyes, presumably more experienced than yours. A building inspector *can* miss the boat entirely; his work isn't guaranteed. But then again, he might spot something important—a leaky roof, perhaps, or evidence of flooding in the basement—which could cause you to adjust your bargaining posture with the current owner, or even to reject a house entirely. Incidentally, with a frame house, termite inspection is certainly called for. Some professional building inspectors include this in their service; but others don't, which means you might have to hire a separate individual to check for termites. Termite inspection usually isn't very costly, though.

Once you have a fair idea of what a home's defects are, you can take certain safeguards to be sure repairs are done before the home's title and problems become yours. One method is to incorporate a list of repairs in the contract to buy the house. In other words, you require the owner to make repairs before he gets any money. Or you could set up an escrow account arrangement. That is, some money would be held out from the sale and would not be given to the seller until the repairs are complete. It can't be overstressed that any promises from the seller must be in writing. Verbal agreements mean nothing.

Another caution: Once you sign an offer to buy the house, it doesn't matter if the roof wobbles every time you drive by. You still have to buy the house. And if you haven't got a written agreement to the contrary, *you* have to pay to fix the roof. Some buyers, incidentally, actually prefer to pay for the repairs. They figure that puts them in control of the way the repairs are done. You may feel the same way. Then you won't write any repair stipulations into your contract. Rather, you'll simply reduce the amount of money you offer for the house, leaving you the difference to pay for the repairs.

If you're shopping around for a house, you may see one you like quite a bit, but not enough to make you stop looking then and there. Clearly, you're not prepared to make a formal offer to buy; that would commit you absolutely. What you can do instead is offer the seller what's called a binder. This is a sum of money just large enough to show you mean business ($100, for example). In exchange for this sum, you ask the seller not to sell the house without consulting you. This is an informal arrangement, but often a useful one. The binder may or may not be returnable to you, depending on your understanding with the seller. Since the seller is proposing to do a genuine service for you, it makes sense to have him keep the binder, no matter what. This doesn't guarantee he won't sell the house to someone else, but it usually will assure you that he'll at least make contact with you before he does.

Let's take a closer look now at that interesting document, the offer to buy. This takes us out of the realm of evaluating a house's physical features and into the equally important—and probably more obscure—area of house-buying paperwork. The offer to buy is the first piece of official paper you'll have to deal with. If you bungle this first one, you've already made too many mistakes, and the subsequent paperwork won't enable you to make up the lost ground. The single most important thing to know is that your offer to buy is a legally binding document. In fact, when it's signed by the seller it becomes the contract between the two of you. At the top there are blanks for your name, the seller's name, and the date. Then there's a section describing the property to be sold. You should make certain that the house as you have seen it is described accurately in this section. If you want any extras left behind (such as curtains, drapes, a dishwasher, room air conditioners, attic fans, lawn furniture, garden tools, or anything of the kind) be sure to put those items in the description of the house. That way, you're offering to buy the house if, and only if, it includes those features. The worst that can happen is that the seller will say no. Then you could always prepare a new offer with fewer of those extras attached. Following the description of the house comes the sum you are offering to the seller. We hardly need comment on the importance of this figure's being correct. After that, there's a line that tells how much deposit, or good faith money, you have given the seller or his agent when you made your bid. The deposit also may be referred to as "earnest money."

After the section on the deposit comes more detail about the financial arrangements. If you're using a prepared form, be sure to read every word, and keep asking questions until you understand the meaning. If you have an attorney to advise you, so much the better. This section will specify how much money you're going to put up as a down payment; in normal times it will be about 20 per cent of the total purchase price. Your initial deposit will count as part of the down payment. If the seller accepts your offer, you'll have to come up with the rest of the down payment within a specified period, usually in a matter of days. You should make sure that this section includes specific language spelling out the mortgage terms you want and stipulating that the contract is null and void if you can't obtain satisfactory financing. For example, your offer to buy might be "contingent upon the ability of purchaser" (that's you) to obtain a twenty-five-year mortgage for at least $30,000, with interest not to exceed 7.5 per cent. (Readers in some parts of the country where, as this book goes to press, mortgage rates are higher than 7½% will be surprised to see that figure used. It seems unlikely that rates as high as 9% and 9½% will continue, and 7½% seems a realistic estimate for the average future rate.) If no bank will give you a mortgage for that much, or if you can't find a bank that will loan you money except at a higher interest rate, your offer is automatically canceled. The document should specify that if your offer is canceled, your deposit will be returned to you.

Somewhere in the offer to buy there should be a statement to the effect that if the house is substantially damaged by fire or some other casualty before the closing (that is, before the official transfer of ownership), you have the right to take back your offer. And again, if your offer is canceled, your deposit should be returned. You can also make your offer contingent on the house's passing an inspection by the inspector of your choice. The offer to buy should also include a specific closing, or settlement, date. This date can be changed later by mutual agreement of buyer and seller.

Somewhere down near the bottom, a standard contract form may say "costs of all documentary stamps required by law, recor-

dation tax and transfer tax where required by law, shall be . . ."
After that the wording can vary; and if it varies the wrong way it
can create extra expenses for you. It should say that these items
will be "divided equally between the parties hereto." It should
not say "paid by the buyer."

Now what happens, you may ask, if you sign an offer to buy
and then change your mind? The answer is simple: The seller can
sue you. And what then? He'd probably succeed in keeping your
deposit, making you pay his agent's commission, making you pay
his legal fees, and making you pay the difference between your
offer and what he actually sells the house for (if he loses money
on the sale because of your default). In short, don't sign an offer
to buy until you're sure it says what you want it to. Having a
lawyer help you at this critical stage is usually a good idea.

So much for your offer to buy. The next step is getting a mortgage loan. Most real estate agencies have arrangements with one
lending institution or another and will offer to put you in touch
with one of them. Before you accept the offer, shop around.
That's right, shop around for a lending institution just as you
would for any other product or service. Don't feel you have to
accept the real estate agent's offer of help because there isn't time
to find your own sources of financing. There's plenty of time.
Shopping around is simply a matter of getting out the yellow
pages and phoning as many lending institutions as necessary.
What you want is fairly simple—the lowest interest rate possible
from a reputable lender. Now, how much difference will this
shopping around make? Let's use the example of a $20,000 loan
over a period of twenty-five years. If you get a 7 per cent mortgage your monthly payments (combining principal and interest)
would be about $141, and the total interest you'd pay over the
twenty-five years would come to $22,390. If you get a 7.5 per cent
mortgage, the monthly payment would be $148—only $7 more.
But over twenty-five years you'd end up paying a total of $24,330
in interest—almost $2,000 more than with the 7 per cent loan. An
8 per cent mortgage would have a $154 monthly tab and a
twenty-five-year interest freight of $26,280. So one percentage
point on the interest rate makes a difference of close to $4,000!

And, of course, if the amount of money borrowed is more than $20,000, there's even more of a difference involved. The period of the loan also makes a substantial difference. A shorter-term loan requires higher payments per month, but in the long run you pay the bank less interest in total.

While you're mortgage shopping, there are a few other factors you should inquire about as well. If you want to pay off the mortgage early, can you do so without penalty? If so, get it in writing —paying off a mortgage early can be a real financial boon to you. If there is a penalty for paying it off early, find out what the penalty is. Another factor: If you should ever be late with a payment, what kind of grace period would you be given?

As a rule, commercial banks offer somewhat better rates on mortgages than do savings banks. However, commercial banks make fewer mortgage loans than do the so-called thrift institutions. Many of the mortgage loans commercial banks do make are drawn up as favors to people who have other business dealings with those banks.

While we're on the subject of mortgages, we'd better say a word about "points." Some people find points mystifying, which is unnecessary. Infuriating, yes; mystifying, no. A point is one one-hundredth of the total amount of the mortgage loan. So, with a $20,000 loan, one point would be $200; two points would be $400. Now what happens with these points? Why, they're added on to what you have to pay, of course. But instead of being paid off over the course of the years, like the mortgage loan itself, they're paid by you in advance, at the time of the closing. They may be called a "commission" or "commission fee" for the lender. By whatever name, they're a sweetener you pay to the lender for the privilege of borrowing money from him. Why, you may ask, doesn't the lender just increase the interest rate charged on the loan? A good question. The answer is that charging more than a certain interest rate is sometimes forbidden by state law or by regulations governing the particular kind of mortgage that's being issued. So the lender simply sidesteps the law by charging points. That doesn't mean that anyone charging you points is shady. Far from it—the absurdity of points has now become a standard part of real estate finance. What you do have to watch out for, of course, is the prospective lender who entices you with what seems a favorable interest rate—only to recoup by charging you more points than other lenders do. In your comparison shopping, then, you should add on the total you'll be paying for points to the amount of interest you'll pay over the years on the basic loan.

Now, aside from comparison shopping, there are some ways you may be able to get a bargain on a mortgage loan. Veterans Administration loans, better known as GI loans, are available to present or former members of the armed services. The chief advantage of a GI loan is that a veteran can borrow as much as 100 per cent of the house's value. In other words, only a small down payment—or none at all—is required. Nothing forces a bank to give a GI loan, however, and when money is tight they're difficult to get. The same is true of a Federal Housing Administration loan, commonly called an FHA loan. With an FHA or GI loan, the federal government in effect tells the bank that it will make good on the loan if you fail to do so. This promise, which is really a form of insurance, costs you something. But what you pay as a sort of "insurance premium" to have the government stand behind you is more than made up for by the liberal terms of the loan. The chief advantage of an FHA loan, as with a GI loan, is that you won't be required to make as substantial a down payment as you would with a conventional loan. The disadvantages are extra red tape and delays compared to a conventional loan, and the fact that these loans tend to dry up and be unavailable when money is tight.

Another possible bargin is a Farmers Home Administration loan. These are available to people who are buying a house in a rural area. You do not have to be a farmer or buying farm land to qualify. You must be buying in an area with a population of less than 10,000, though. You must have a maximum adjusted gross income (as of 1974) of $9,800 or less, have good credit and verification of employment, and have enough cash to pay closing costs at settlement. If you think you may qualify, look for a regional office of the Farmers Home Administration in your area.

In addition to these federally sponsored programs, some programs offering advice or financial aid to homebuyers are available on the state level. You can check into these by consulting the agency that administers housing programs in your home state. In some states, an agency can help you obtain bank financing; in some, the state itself acts as a lender.

If it's been accepted by the seller, your offer to buy becomes official once you've obtained mortgage financing. The deal's all but closed. That final step, however, is a ritual unto itself. Whole treatises have been written about the "closing" or "settlement." Really, when you stop to think of it, it's not surprising that the transfer of ownership of something as important as a house should be complicated. What you hope is that you can keep it from being brutally expensive as well.

At the closing, you, the seller, and a representative of your bank sit down together. Sometimes there's a fourth party—a person who's been chosen as an impartial official to conduct the closing. But many times the mortgage lender will conduct it. On some occasions either you or the seller will be absent and represented at the closing by an attorney. (Even if you're going to be present, it's often a good idea to have your lawyer along with you. This may not be necessary, however, if things have gone smoothly up to the closing, and you have strong reason to believe that all the other parties involved are honest and scrupulous.)

At the closing the seller gets the full sale price of the house. Part of this comes out of the down payment you've already made. This down payment, as mentioned earlier, usually comes to at least 20 per cent of the purchase price. The rest of the seller's money comes from your bank, and that's the amount you'll pay back to the bank (with interest) over the next twenty or thirty years.

So far, clear enough. But did the seller really own the home? Even if he's been living there for ten years, he has to prove that he legally owns the place. So he must produce evidence of title, and in most states help arrange for an insurance policy (called title insurance) that will guarantee your rightful interest in the property. The cost of a search of legal records to validate the title is one of the so-called closing costs. It usually runs from $200 to $500. This cost is usually split between the seller and buyer. It's fair for the seller to assume at least half these costs.

Then there are taxes. Property taxes, that is, assessed by the municipality and the county where the house is. Very few homes are sold exactly when the tax bill comes, so you and the seller will often end up splitting the cost of taxes for the year that's about to be billed. (This will often be the year before the current year, since local tax authorities typically take forever to send tax bills out. They like to get them back promptly, though.) Most banks will require you to establish a reserve fund (or escrow account) from which they will pay your county and municipal taxes as they come due. In most places, even if you prefer to pay your own taxes, you're not allowed to. The amount of the fund may be equal to a year's taxes. That means that you're going to be committing at least several hundred dollars to a fund that won't pay you any interest. But, as laws stand now, you have little choice. Banks justify the practice on two grounds. One is that it's convenient for the customer to have the bank handle the tax payment. It is, of course. But whether it's convenient enough to justify tying up all that money is a point that's been hotly argued. Banks also say they need to keep the reserve fund as a way of protecting their own investment (the mortgage loan). If your house were taken away from you because you failed to pay your taxes, the bank would be involved in a legal tangle at best, and might see its loan to you go down the drain, at worst. This rationale, too, can be argued. But at the moment it's a fact of life. Most efforts at reform are directed at trying to get banks to pay at least a modest amount of interest on the money tied up in the reserve fund.

Some banks use the same rationale to make you put money into a reserve fund out of which they will pay your property insurance premiums as they come due. After all, if your house burns down, the bank's in somewhat the same position as if it were taken away from you because of tax delinquency. However, banks are generally less firm on this requirement. You can probably arrange to pay your property insurance premiums yourself. But you will almost always have to show that you have such insurance. And you must make arrangements to obtain it prior to the closing. This is in your own best interest, since you want to be insured from the moment the house becomes yours.

As this point, if you're the pessimistic or cynical type, you might be asking, "Well, what if I die? Then the bank would really have to worry about collecting on its loan to me." That's right, and thus is born yet another closing cost—credit life insurance. This form of life insurance (which is also required by some other types of lenders) pays off what you owe to a creditor if you die while some or all of the debt is outstanding. Some banks insist you have it. If the officials at your bank are reasonable, however, you may be able to satisfy them by showing that you have enough general life insurance so that they can be confident their money will be returned, even if you die. A bank does have the legal right to make you take out credit life insurance if it wants to. But it does not have the right to make you buy that insurance from one of its subsidiaries, or from any other specific issuer.

Next on the list of closing costs are the points we mentioned earlier (see page 56). These can tack several hundred dollars onto the amount of money you have to be prepared to shell out on the closing date. Then there are various fees. Perhaps the largest of these, if you've been employing an attorney, will be your legal fee. But a lawyer may save you far more, in plain cash and in avoided grief, than the value of his fee. There are plenty of times when *Consumer Survival Kit* would advise you to go to bat for yourself without a lawyer. But when you're buying a house isn't one of them. A house is a very large investment. To begrudge a lawyer his fee for helping you make the right steps in purchasing it seems penny-wise and pound-foolish. Of course, using more of your lawyer's time than you really need just adds unnecessarily to a legal bill. Whether your lawyer should be physically present at the closing depends, as we said, on how well the groundwork has been laid in advance. If you feel shaky about how things will go, it's better to have your lawyer there with you.

Other fees that pop up at closing time will go to the government. There are "transfer taxes," "recordation taxes," "revenue stamps." The names and extent of these taxes will vary from state to state. They will constitute one of the smaller closing costs, but they'll still be annoying if you're unprepared for them. Several days before the closing, you should contact your bank or your lawyer and try to get a complete rundown on what each and every closing cost will be. Even then, you'd still be wise to show up with a little extra cash in your checkbook.

We've saved for last a discussion of one critical way you can save money when buying a house. That is to haggle with the seller over the price. Almost no seller really expects to get the price he's asking. The trick is to figure out how much you can lop off the asking price without losing a house you really want. Now, bargaining technique is an inexact science—more, perhaps, of an intuitive craft. Some factors to be considered are how long the house has been on the market, and how soon the seller has to leave for a new location. You may be able to pick up hints about these considerations from your real estate agent or from the seller himself. A seller whose house has been on the market for a while, or who has to leave for London in three weeks, is likely to be more pliant in bargaining than one whose house just went on sale and who is in no rush to move. Another factor is whether there is a serious competing bidder for the house. The seller will often let you know if there is. (Indeed, some sellers will let you know it even if the competing bid came straight out of their imagination.) Two cardinal rules can be stated. One is to make your offer formally, in writing. A seller must think twice about turning down an official offer to buy. If you make an oral offer, he's more likely to reject it and hold out for a higher price. The second rule is never to offer what the seller is asking; always make your first offer considerably less. It is possible to lose a house this way, but that outcome is unlikely. The seller may surprise you and accept your offer, in which case you'll have saved a bundle of money. Or, as happens most times, the seller will let you know that your offer, while interesting, is too low. Then the two of you will eventually settle on an intermediate price. Since every dollar you save on the purchase price will be multiplied by lessening the total amount of mortgage interest you'll have to pay, the haggle is worth the hassle.

4

Improving Your Home

Oh transient roofer, I'm looking for you.
If I ever catch you, you know what I'd do?
I dream every night, in my cold, rain-soaked bed,
Of tacking your shingles to the back of your head.

Itinerant roofer, why'd you do me wrong?
Some windstorm shingles would have lasted long.
The 210-pound type would certainly do.
Itinerant roofer, I'm looking for you.

Oh transient roofer, wait till I find you.
You sold me some shingles that just wouldn't do.
The standard shingle lasts a good twenty years.
Yours lasted a week after you disappeared.

Itinerant roofer, you told me lies.
Shingles look alike to these untrained eyes.
Now I'll get three bids from contractors true,
But, itinerant roofer, I'm looking for you!

Whether repairing or remodeling your home, you must often call in a contractor to do the work. And there are those who will do a job on *you* instead of your home. Knowing how to protect yourself could save you hundreds, or even thousands, of dollars. It's estimated that Americans are swindled out of $500 million a year by deceptive contractors in the fields of roofing, siding, waterproofing, and related trades. Though the vast majority of home improvement contractors are honest, one rotten apple can do appalling damage to your barrel.

Let's start by checking some of your existing knowledge about home improvement practices.

CSK Quiz

1. True or false: It's best to hire only those contractors who assure you the Federal Housing Administration guarantees their work.
2. True or false: Any money you spend on home improvements will be returned, usually with a profit, when you resell the house.
3. True or false: You can save a lot of money by doing business only with those companies that promise rebates for furnishing the names of other prospective customers.

Now let's look at the answers. Number 1 is false. If a contractor assures you his work is guaranteed by the FHA, he's deceiving you. The FHA is concerned with financial arrangements, not with workmanship. It does not guarantee the work of any contractor.

Number 2 is also false. On the average, a dollar invested in a home improvement adds only about 50 cents to the resale value of the house. Generally, central air conditioning, a full bath, or a remodeled kitchen has the biggest impact on resale value. They tend to add on a little bit more than 50 per cent of their cost. On the other hand, a swimming pool, a screened-in porch, or a refinished basement usually adds a bit less than half. So if you want to make one of these improvements, be sure you get your money's worth through your family's own enjoyment of them. As a rule of thumb, indoor improvements bring a better return than outdoor; and visible additions bring a better return than those that are out of sight.

Number 3 is false as well. The practice described is an unethi-

cal—and usually illegal—technique known as referral selling. If a
contractor approaches you with a deal like this, turn him down
and find a different firm to do your work.

Referral selling is only one of ten warning signals that can alert
you to the presence of a home improvement phony. These warning signals go across the board: They'll help you spot a con man
whether his specialty is roofing, siding, termite extermination, or
whatever. We've interspersed the warning signals in a hypothetical conversation that might take place between a quick-buck
home repair artist and an unsuspecting consumer.

QUICKBUCK: How do you do, Sir. Jesse Quickbuck is the name.
Listen, I just happened to have done a roofing job in your neighborhood and I have some extra materials left over. I could do a
real good job for you. (*Warning signal number one: the "*just in
the neighborhood*" pitch. If someone gives you this pitch, pitch
him out. No intelligent home improvement contractor is going to
over-order grossly on one job so he'll have enough materials left
over for an entire second job.*)

GULL: Well, I don't know. (Glances at license plate on Quickbuck's truck.)

QUICKBUCK: Oh, don't let that out-of-state plate bother you. I've
been here for quite a while now. Just haven't had time to change
it yet. (*Warning signal two: the out-of-state license plate. Of
course, not everyone from out of state is crooked. But you're
better off hiring only companies with a permanent resident in
your own area. Attorney General Louis J. Lefkowitz of New York
put it this way: "Itinerants should be avoided like the plague."*)

GULL: Yes, well . . .

QUICKBUCK: Friend, I'll be honest with you. When I look at
your roof up there, I swear I'd be afraid to sleep under it. You
may go to sleep one night and Bam! They'd be looking for you
under the rubble the next morning. (*Warning signal three: the
scare tactic. Avoid contractors who are literally trying to scare up
business. Legitimate contractors don't indulge in this practice. If
you fear there may be a grain of truth in a warning of doom from
an insistent contractor, get a second opinion from a well-known,
reputable firm in the area.*)

GULL: My, that's horrible. I mean, that sounds pretty bad. But are you sure?

QUICKBUCK: I'm sure. But I'll tell you what. I happen to be a representative of a factory which is willing to offer you a deal at a bargain price. Believe me, you'll pay nothing. (*There are two warning signals in that statement. Number four*: the factory representative tactic. *Factories rarely send representatives to individual homes. They do their selling through local stores and legitimate contractors. Number five*: the big bargain ploy. *The U.S. Department of Housing and Urban Development has written, "Reputable companies are not running giveaway businesses." When you pay next to nothing, you get next to nothing.*)

GULL: Well, what's the deal?

QUICKBUCK: I'm willing to make this a model home. You'll get commissions for everyone who sees your roof and then buys from us. (*Warning signal six*: the model home tactic. *This is one form of referral selling, discussed earlier. The model home tactic is a common, and infamous, variation. Those duped end up paying a greater quantity of money for a lesser quality of work then they would if they forgot about being a model and shopped around for a reputable contractor, established in the area.*)

GULL: Well, how much would it cost?

QUICKBUCK: Well, let's see. (Looks up at the roof.) Um-hm. Yep, yep. And then, let's see. (Scribbles a few figures on a piece of scratch paper.) Okay, I'd say $975 would do it. (*Warning signal seven*: the quick estimate. *Legitimate contractors don't scribble figures down on the back of envelopes. Get several written estimates that include the total price and specific details as to the work to be performed and the materials needed.*)

GULL: Oh, gee, I don't know . . .

QUICKBUCK: Well, look, friend. I'm going to have to ask you to decide now. With all the roofing work we have to do, I really feel compelled to offer this bargain to someone else. (*Warning signal eight*: the high-pressure tactic. *No reputable contractor will insist on an immediate decision. Chances are you'll be spending a good deal of money on the job. You should spend a good deal of time on your decision.*)

GULL: Well, could you give me the names of some people

you've done work for, so that I can see the quality of your work?

QUICKBUCK: Sir, we don't give out names. We respect our customers' privacy. I wouldn't give other people's names to you any more than I'd give your name to others. I'm sure you understand. (*Warning signal nine*: refusal to give the names of past customers on request. *Ask any contractor for the names of at least two satisfied customers. If he says no, you say the same.*)

GULL: Well, can you identify yourself for me?

QUICKBUCK: (Looks in outside mirror of his truck.) Well, let's see. (Laughs.) Yep, that's me all right. (*Warning signal ten*: a lack of proper identification. *It certainly seems logical that anyone who finds difficult the simple task of identifying himself is not a paragon of competence or honesty.*)

So much for Quickbuck. Of course, not all home improvement phonies give off such an obliging plethora of warning signals. If you are on the alert, however, you may spot a little bit of Quickbuck in a contractor soliciting your business. If you do, bid him a prompt goodbye.

How, then, do you find a legitimate, reputable home improvement contractor? Start by looking for a firm that's been doing business in your home area for a while. You can check its reputation with neighbors, the Chamber of Commerce, or the Better Business Bureau. See if the contractor is affiliated with a professional trade association. Trade groups work to uphold their reputation for craftsmanship. A contractor who pays dues to such an association probably isn't trying to squeeze a quick killing out of his work. If a contractor displaying an affiliation with a professional trade association does a job you believe is faulty, notify the association. Many of these trade groups have set up grievance committees to handle complaints and iron out disputes between their members and consumers. Don't be shy about using them if the necessity should arise. The names of some trade groups appear at the end of this chapter.

In most cases, you'll want to contact not just one contractor but several. (Three is a good rule of thumb.) Get *written* estimates from each, but don't automatically jump at the low bid. The way each contractor handles the estimate and the way he describes the work to be done may give you a valuable clue to the quality of the work itself.

When you've chosen a contractor, it will be time to sign a contract—a *written* contract. But keep a few points in mind when you do. If the job is going to run into the thousands of dollars, it's worthwhile to get a lawyer to advise you on contract details. What you save in money and aggravation will probably be worth the legal fee. In some states, contractors must be licensed by a state home improvement commission or some similar body. You can find out if your state requires licenses by calling the consumer protection agency listed in this book's Appendix. If so, then the contractor's license number, as well as name, should appear on the contract. That usually goes at the top, followed by your own name, address, and telephone number.

Next usually come the approximate starting and finishing dates for the job. This is obviously crucial information. In some states it's required by law to be shown on the contract. (Again, you can check with your consumer protection agency.) After the dates, what's called the "scope" of the contract is normally shown. This section should contain a complete description of all plans and specifications for the job. The dimensions, the types of materials to be used, and the quantity and quality of those materials should all be specified. (One way to be sure of the quality is to specify the brand.) The language should clearly state what parts of the house, rooms, or portions of rooms are to be worked on.

That's what you're going to get; now for what you're going to give—the financial arrangement. If it's a lump sum payment, it should be indicated as such. If you're paying in installments, make sure the number of payments and the amount of each payment are shown. The interest on any loan involved, should also be shown; and that interest should be shown as an annual percentage rate (APR). That's simple interest. Figures based on "add-on" or "discount" interest tend to make the loan look cheaper than it really is.

The contractor may want you to put down a large deposit in advance. That's to his advantage, not yours. You may want to put

10 per cent down, but don't pay in full until the job is completed to your satisfaction. And don't accept any open-ended pay arrangements. If the contractor can't guarantee an exact cost, he should at the very least guarantee that the cost will not overrun his estimate by more than 15 per cent. And on most jobs, the contractor who gives a flat guaranteed price is to be preferred.

It's advisable to include in the section on financial arrangements a protection clause against liens on your home if the work is subcontracted. Unless you state otherwise in the contract, subcontractors may hold your property until their charges are paid. You should withhold final payment to the contractor until he supplies you with an affidavit that all material suppliers, laborers, and subcontractors have been paid. (An affidavit is a written statement made under oath and signed in the presence of a notary public or some other official.)

Here's another clause you should definitely include somewhere in the contract: "All work will be done in a workmanlike manner." This may keep the Laurel and Hardy home improvement firm off the premises. It will certainly give you legal ground to stand on later if the job isn't done right.

You should also include a clause stating that the contractor is responsible for a clean-up of the area when the job's finished. Also, make sure any guarantees or warranties are attached to the contract and made a part of it.

For the protection of both parties, the contract should say that any changes in the plans and specifications require the written approval of both the consumer and the contractor. No alteration without representation!

At the bottom goes your signature—but only when you understand and are satisfied with the entire contract. If you find even one space blank, make sure you leave the signature space blank too. And don't let your pen get too itchy. Some contractors will hand you a completion certificate to sign, as if it were part of the contract. It's not. A completion certificate is to be signed only when the work is satisfactorily completed—never before. Don't let yourself be rushed for anyone's convenience.

Separate from the contract, but vital for your protection, is the issue of insurance protection. If a workman slips on a ladder while working on your house, you don't want him suing you. If the ladder tumbles and smashes the roof of your car, you want to be able to collect from the contractor, and so on. The point is that you want the contractor to carry adequate insurance. So get a written document from the contractor, certifying that he carries property damage and personal liability insurance, and that his workers are covered under Workmen's Compensation.

Now that you're pretty well prepared for dealing with a contractor, let's look at some of the specific jobs you might call in a contractor to do. Some of the most common are basement waterproofing, siding installation, and termite extermination.

A leaky basement can be a costly, bothersome, and smelly nuisance. Some homeowners have found, unfortunately, that fixing the situation can be even more costly and bothersome—and sometimes smelly. If a company claims it will waterproof your basement by pumping sealant around the foundation, be suspicious. Sealants are like sponges—able to soak up only a limited amount of water. Once they reach their saturation point, water then flows back into the basement. Often the contractor who pumps sealant gives a guarantee. When the leaking recurs, however, the consumer finds what's guaranteed is not the waterproofing but rather continued doses of sealant. Your best bet is to begin where many homeowners who start with sealant end up: Bring in contractors who first excavate and then install pumps and drainage tiles. Of course, you shouldn't resort to such expensive cures without trying the simple ones first. Many times, water collects in a basement because it's not draining properly off the roof. So before doing anything drastic, see if your gutters and downspouts are directing too much water at the foundation.

Putting new siding on a house can make it easier to maintain, as well as more attractive. But it's a major expense, so you want material that will last. Here are some of the major types of siding, along with some comments on advantages and disadvantages:

Wood siding has the advantage of being the same material all the way through, so nicks can be painted over. Wood does have to be treated to hold up to the weather, however, and requires fairly frequent painting.

Spray-on asphalt lasts poorly.

Real asphalt is quite inexpensive, but it gouges easily, especially on warm days. And it fades.

Galvanized steel is durable but presents a possible rusting problem. It will not rust if it's merely scratched, but it will if it's gouged.

Aluminum is popular, partly because it's easy to maintain. The main problem with it is denting. To prevent this, aluminum siding should be bought in the .024-inch thickness (not .019-inch) and should be installed with backing boards.

Vinyl is also easy to maintain. Like wood, it has the advantage of being the same material all the way through. However, it is vulnerable to temperature extremes. In freezing weather, a very hard blow (from a car bumper, for example) can shatter it. And in a fire it can melt.

Asbestos is fireproof and relatively cheap but tends to splinter.

Whatever kind of siding you decide upon, be careful about the way it's sold. One major deception in the siding business is called the "too-few-square feet" tactic." Siding is normally sold in units of 100 square feet, with the price per 100 square feet ranging from $75 to $175 at 1974 price levels. With the too-few-square-feet tactic, a firm may advertise a price of, say, $410 for 700 square feet of aluminum siding. That comes to an installed price of $58 per 100 square feet—far below the average of $125. There is a major catch, however. A small six-room house may have an area of 1,200 square feet, which means you'll be needing an additional 500 square feet of aluminum siding. Guess what the shady supplier will charge you for the extra footage? Not $58, and not $125 either, but some truly astronomical price like $200 or $300 per 100 square feet. Moral: When you're quoted a price per square unit, make sure it applies to the whole job, not just the first 700 feet or so.

Another all too frequent home-improvement job is termite extermination. Termites don't seem to understand that consumers are living on a budget. To them, dead wood is dead wood, whether it's in a fallen tree or in a house. And a termite has to eat, doesn't he? Incidentally, if you do find insect wings lying around, indicating the possible presence of termites, don't feel you're a failure at keeping a clean house. Termite infestation is not a sign of moral turpitude on the part of the homeowner; it's just a sign your house is made of wood and some termites happened to find it.

Call an exterminator right away if you think you see termites (or if you see discarded wings or a swarm of unidentified insects in the spring). A house can stand up for some thirty years with termites gnawing away at it. But delaying will just make the ultimate extermination job tougher. By the way, don't try to identify termites by their color. That method is mistake-prone. Do, however, check the critter's waistline, if you can. Ants (and flying ants) have nipped waistlines. Termites are fat.

Some exterminating firms offer free inspections, while others charge for a trip out to your home. If you think there's a serious possibility your place has termites, you might prefer a firm that charges. Such a firm should offer you a certificate saying that the house was inspected. And if no termites were found, the certificate should state that the firm will return and perform free extermination if termites show up within three months.

In picking an exterminator, one of your chief criteria should be the guarantee the firm offers if termites *are* found. The best exterminators offer a guarantee to eliminate the pests if they reappear within one year after the extermination treatment.

Whatever home improvement you're planning, get a written estimate and a written contract.

Home Improvement Trade Associations

The groups listed below are members of the National Home Improvement Council, Inc., which is located at 11 East 44th Street, New York, N.Y. 10017. The addresses of the groups' headquarters change from time to time. The names of the groups, however, are likely to remain the same, so it should normally be easy to find a local trade association in the telephone book. As mentioned earlier, some of these groups offer conciliation services to resolve disputes between contractors and consumers. *Consumer Survival Kit* believes that, in general, contractors who are members of trade associations tend to be more reliable than those who aren't. Trade associations are listed alphabetically by city.

Boston area: Eastern Massachusetts Home Improvement Council

Buffalo, N.Y., area: Home Improvement Industry Council

Chicago area: The Professional Remodelers Association of Greater Chicago

Cleveland area: Home Improvement Council of Greater Cleveland

Denver area: Association of Remodeling Contractors

Detroit area: Home Improvement Council of Metropolitan Detroit

Erie, Pa., area: Home Improvement Council of Erie

Houston area: Houston Home Improvement Council

Kansas City, Mo., area: Greater Kansas City Home Improvement Contractors Association

Los Angeles area: Los Angeles NHIC-ABCA (National Home Improvement Council and American Building Contractors Association)

Milwaukee area: Home Improvement Council of Greater Milwaukee

Mobile, Ala., area: Home Improvement Council of Mobile

Orange County, Calif., area: Orange County Chapter, NHIC-ABCA

Pittsburgh area: Approved Modernization Contractors Association

Portland, Ore., area: Oregon Remodelers Association, Inc.

Saint Louis area: The Remodeling Guild of Greater St. Louis

San Diego area: San Diego Chapter, NHIC-ABCA

San Fernando Valley, Calif., area: San Fernando Valley Chapter, NHIC-ABCA

San Francisco area: Bay Area Home Improvement Council

Seattle area: Washington Home Improvement Council
Springfield, Mass., area: Western Massachusetts Home Improvement Council, Springfield
Washington, D.C., area: Metropolitan Washington Home Improvement Council

5

Your Rights as a Tenant

When I first rented this apartment, I
Planned to pay rent, as easy as pie.
But it wasn't long after I moved in
That the heat went off and the wall fell in.
I was mad . . . incensed.

So I called the landlord very next day
Just to hear what he would say.
He said, "Oh, that furnace, it sometimes blows.
What'd you expect for so little dough?"
'Spect heat . . . and walls.

Well, the heat was off and I was cold—
The problem called for something bold,
So I stopped paying rent right then and there.
But I started to worry, I started to care
'Bout eeeeee-viction.

Well, it wasn't long before there came
A letter from the law, in my name.
It said that to court I must go—
A matter of money I did owe.
I was scared . . . depressed.

So I called a legal-aid friend I knew.
He said there's something I can do.
I said what? I need to know!
He said put the rent money in escrow.
Escrow? . . . Is that some kind of bird?

Well, I put my rent in that escrow thing
And y'know, it worked! So let me bring
A tip to you: If you want repairs
Withhold your rent and lessen your cares.
Heat works . . . wall's fixed . . . right on!

Do conditions in your apartment have you singing the blues? It wouldn't be surprising. A tenant's lot is an edgy one. As a tenant, you're constantly dependent on someone else to provide you with decent living conditions. And you always have it in the back of your mind that if you give the landlord too much grief you could be thrown out into the cold. That's no joke in today's tight housing market. As a result, many tenants live in a state of economically enforced docility. They may put up with things—like rent hikes or inadequate heat—that they never would bear, were it not for the lurking fear of eviction in the background.

Withholding your rent—or putting it, as the singer above did, in an escrow account—is a dramatic and often effective way of winning concessions from a landlord. But it's a tangled tactic, tricky and somewhat dangerous to use. The danger comes in if you don't know the rules of the game. We're going to take plenty of time now to try to clue you in on some of those rules. But they vary from state to state, and they're constantly changing. The best single rule we can therefore give you is to consult a lawyer before withholding your rent.

Now, the very first thing you'll discover if you start looking into rent withholding is that it's not permitted under your lease. That's not surprising. since leases are written for the exclusive convenience of the real estate industry, and of landlords in particular. From a landlord's point of view, a lease is as comfortable as a pair of old shoes. But from a tenant's point of view, leases pinch like a straitjacket. As a result, you can be sure the lease will say, somewhere in the fine print, that any failure by the landlord to make repairs is not grounds for a tenant's withholding rent. In plain English, leases say that tenants must pay whether or not they get what they're paying for.

This needn't stop you, however. It so happens that leases contain many clauses that won't hold up in court. The idea that tenants owe rent whether or not they get decent living quarters in return seem unjust on the face of it. And an increasing number of courts are holding that it isn't so.

That doesn't mean, though, that if the landlord fails to provide heat or otherwise makes your life miserable you can simply keep your rent money. That would be too good to be true. But by withholding your rent until a landlord calls you into court, you can sometimes get the court to order that necessary repairs be done. Once they've been done, you'll have to pay up the rent that's due. If you're lucky, the court may reduce the amount you have to pay somewhat to compensate you for the diminished value of your living quarters during the time repairs were needed but not made.

Judges won't do any such thing for you, however, unless you can show that you have the rent money on hand, ready to pay to the landlord whenever the judge says to. That's where the escrow comes in. It is not, of course, a bird, as our singer first imagined. Basically, escrow is an arrangement in which something is held in abeyance until certain conditions are fulfilled. When it is money that is being held in abeyance, there's a connotation in the word "escrow" that the money will be held by a third party. If you put your rent money in escrow, there may be a third party involved—namely the court—or there may not. Sometimes judges will ask tenants to hand over the rent money to the court. Then the court keeps it until a determination is made as to who's right, or until the repairs have been completed. Other times the court lets the tenant keep the money in a separate bank account or a safe deposit box, or even mixed with the tenant's ordinary bank accounts. These cases are not a true escrow arrangement, but the word is used anyway. The most important thing about the escrow concept is that the money is there waiting. It's not being paid to the landlord, but it's not being frittered away, either. When you withhold rent, you should always assume you're going to end up having to pay the full amount due at some point. If a judge does reduce the amount you owe, that's a welcome but unexpected bonus.

A number of states have passed laws setting up procedures by which tenants can put their rent money into escrow. Among these are New York and Pennsylvania. In other states, including California, New Jersey, and Illinois, the practice has been sanctioned by court decisions, but there's no single procedure outlined by law. But laws and court rulings are subject to change; and in the area of tenants' rights they are changing fast. So the best thing is to check with an attorney in your local area.

Most people—let's face it—are reluctant to see a lawyer for fear of high fees. But there are ways to get legal advice without going broke. First of all, there's Legal Aid. If you make less than a certain amount if money per year, Legal Aid will handle your case for nothing. The amount varies from place to place, but if your income is small it's worth checking. Look in the phone book for Legal Aid. If you don't find anything, you can call your city hall number and ask for advice on where to find a Legal Aid office.

If you make too much for Legal Aid, you might try the lawyer referral service offered by many local bar associations. If you call the county or state bar association in your area, they can tell you if they have such a plan. Where it exists, you can generally sit down with a lawyer for a half-hour discussion in exchange for a small fee—perhaps five dollars.

You can also make fee size a criterion even if you shop for a lawyer by more traditional means. You may find an attorney's name through the recommendation of a friend or relative, or by letting your fingers walk through the yellow pages of the phone book. Lawyers are permitted to list their names, addresses, and phone numbers. They are not permitted to make advertising claims, not even to advertise a specialty. So when you talk to a lawyer, ask about any experience he or she may have in tenant matters. And discuss fees openly and early. Some lawyers will resist this approach, but others won't.

If you live in a state where the legality of the escrow approach isn't clear, you may be reluctant to stick your neck out and try to break new legal ground. Then, too, there are some problems for which withholding rent is either too strong a solution or no solution at all. For example, rent withholding would be an excessive remedy for a landlord's failure to cut the grass in front of the apartment—even though that failure might be very annoying. And rent withholding doesn't offer a useful tool for problems that arise before you move in or after you move out. Let's have a look at a couple of those problems.

Before you ever move into an apartment, of course, you have to sign a lease. This is often a painful act, since the tenant has a feeling of foreboding that, down there in all that fine print, there are things that aren't good for him. What's more, the wise tenant who actually reads the lease in detail will probably have his forebodings confirmed. Nevertheless, you should read the lease. And that isn't always easy to do. Here's one common course of events, dramatized as a dialogue between a would-be tenant and an agent for the renter.

AGENT: Can I help you?

TENANT: Yes. I called, and you said my new lease is ready.

AGENT: And your name, please?

TENANT: Jackson. Harmon Jackson.

AGENT: All right, Mr. Jackson. (Shuffles through some papers.) Here it is. (Pulls out two copies, spreads them out.) Now if you'll sign here, Mr. Jackson.

TENANT: Well, I'd like to read it first.

AGENT: Oh, certainly. Take your time.

TENANT: Fine. I'll have it back to you by the end of the week. (Starts to fold up lease and put it in his pocket.)

AGENT: Oh, no. (Reaches for lease and takes it from his hand.) You can't take it out of the office.

TENANT: Can't take it out of the office? Why not?

AGENT: That's our policy.

TENANT: But I like to read things like this before I sign.

AGENT: You're welcome to read it here.

TENANT: But I'm late for work.

AGENT: I'm sorry, but you'll just have to come back when you have more time. Or else sign it right now.

TENANT: But why can't I just take it with me?

AGENT: That's our policy.

There's no law that forces a landlord (or landlord's agent) to let you study a lease properly. But if you feel you're being rushed, watch out! That's a danger signal that the landlord has something to hide.

Unfortunately, even if you have plenty of time to read the lease, you usually won't be able to change it. Most landlords have more applicants for vacancies than they need to keep their buildings filled. As a result, if a prospective tenant is too particular about lease terms, a landlord can often afford to dismiss that tenant and find another applicant who's more docile. That doesn't mean you shouldn't bother to read the lease. First of all, you might hit a lucky streak and talk the landlord into changing something. Second, you should know what you're signing anyway.

First, make sure all the blanks are filled in correctly. Especially the rent. Is it the agreed-upon sum? Secretaries usually type in these blanks, and they can make mistakes. Look out for provisions that say the rent can be increased under certain circumstances—such as a rise in the landlord's real estate taxes. And look for provisions regarding late fees. It's a terrible shock to have to pay ten or twenty bucks for a late fee when you're one day late with the rent. If you know ahead of time that such a provision's in the lease, you probably won't let it happen. And if there is no such provision in the lease, don't let the landlord charge you for it. If it's not in the lease you don't have to pay it.

It's valuable for you to know that some of the common lease provisions simply won't hold up in court. For example, there's usually a clause titled something like "Liability of landlord to tenant." It often says, "The landlord shall not be liable for any damage caused by failure to keep the demised premises in repair." Most courts will disregard this clause. Legally, the land-lord certainly *is* liable for many kinds of damage caused by his failure to make repairs. So if you've been damaged, and you want the landlord to pay you for injuries, for example, and he refuses, citing this clause, tell him you'll see him in court.

A particularly pernicious clause is called the confession of judgment clause. It gives the landlord's lawyer the right to represent you in court. And you can guess what kind of representation that would bring! In effect, the clause takes away your right to defend yourself. For that reason, the clause is against the law in many states and usually won't hold up in court in other states either. Don't let your landlord scare you into believing he can really enforce it against you.

Landlords are aware that some clauses in their leases may be illegal. That's why you'll usually find included in the lease an "illegality of provisions" clause. It states that "in the event any provision of this lease is in violation of any law, statute or ordinance, the said shall not invalidate the remaining portions of this lease." Since that's the way the game is played, here's a basic rule of thumb. If you ever have a serious problem with your landlord over a lease and what's in it, call a lawyer. He can tell you what's legal and what's illegal. Don't let yourself be intimidated by a landlord because of what's in a lease.

Here's another vignette of life as a tenant:

TENANT: (speaking into a phone) Hello, yes. This is Elmer Cartwright from Apartment 104. I'm calling about my plumbing. It's not working right.

VOICE FROM PHONE: All right, Mr. Cartright. We'll send somebody up to take a look at it.

TENANT: That's what you said you were going to do last week. And the week before. And nobody has showed up, and the sink is so bad we can't even use it.

VOICE: We'll send somebody up to take a look at it.

TENANT: (getting angry) How do I know you're going to do it?

VOICE: (getting angry) We'll send somebody up to take a look at it.

TENANT: Look, as landlord you have a legal obligation to maintain this place.

VOICE: We'll send somebody up to take a look at it.

TENANT: Well, all right. But you'd better do something about it this time. (Hangs up and shrugs in despair.)

If you feel as though your requests for repairs are being addressed to a brick wall or a recording device, you needn't give up too easily. Your ultimate weapon, discussed earlier, is to withhold rent in an escrow account. That, as we said, should be done only in consultation with a lawyer. But there are a few other things you can do yourself. Number one: You can make your requests in writing and send them by certified mail. They may have more impact that way. Number two: You can file a complaint with your city's or town's housing agency if the conditions in your building violate the municipal housing code. (In some places there's a countywide code, and your complaint would go to county authorities.) You can find these agencies in the phone book, looking first under the name of the city or county and then finding the subheading for "housing" or "health." This course has two drawbacks. It will probably make your landlord really angry at you. And it may not produce results. In some places housing inspectors can be paid off, and in many places the fines your landlord will face for code violations are fairly trivial. Nevertheless, filing an official complaint for housing code violations does produce positive results for some consumers. And if you and the landlord are already at loggerheads, you may not have anything to lose.

There's still another thing you can do: Try to organize the tenants in your building. This, too, will alienate the landlord. But it's often an effective tactic. Some landlords who are indifferent to, or contemptuous of, one person's requests will react quite differently if confronted by an organized group of tenants. A good way to go about organizing is to get the advice of a previously established tenants' group in your area. If you don't know of one, try the phone book or the library of a local newspaper. If that doesn't work, try writing the National Tenants Organization at 425 13th Street N.W., Washington, D..C 20005. When you've rounded up some members, you might consider affiliating your building's group with a citywide or statewide tenants' association. That tends to give your small organization some added bargaining power.

One good thing about a tenants' association is that it can call the landlord to account for things like not mowing the grass—issues that concern all tenants in common. If building conditions are seriously degenerating, a tenants' association can conduct a rent strike. Such an action has the same legal basis as an individual rent-withholding maneuver. But when several tenants stop paying rent at once, the landlord gets a lot more worried, since he's probably losing a sizable share of his income. Of course most problems don't call for such strong action. But a tenants' association can scale its degree of militancy to the seriousness of its members' grievances.

One step that can sometimes be taken to prevent small problems from growing into big ones is to complain to a landlords' council. Such organizations don't exist in all areas, and where they do exist they don't always have grievance committees. But in some places landlords do band together in trade associations that try to iron out tenant disputes as they arise. If there's a program like that in your area, it makes sense to give it a chance to work.

If you've built up considerable bile against your landlord, you may be eager to use the tactics we've been discussing. Before doing so, you might test your knowledge of some of the fine points of landlord-tenant law by answering the questions in this quiz.

CSK Quiz

1. A female tenant's four-year-old child crawled into the kitchen one day and turned on all the knobs on the stove. There was a skillet of grease on the stove, which caught fire. Damage to the ceiling and walls totaled $400, which the tenant declined to pay on the grounds that major repairs are the landlord's responsibility. Is the tenant right?

2. A young tenant, a bachelor, moved into a studio apartment in September, at the start of the school term. In November he met a lovely young fine arts student, with whom he became

passionately involved. In December she moved in with him, bringing with her some clothes, some books, and one favorite chair. The two lived together quietly without disturbing the neighbors. But in February the landlord brought eviction proceeding against the young man, claiming he had violated his lease by harboring an illegal subtenant. The young lady did not pay any part of the rent and therefore was not a subtenant, the young man told the court during the eviction hearing. Does the landlord have any legal ground to stand on?

3. A thirty-one-year-old tenant, an accountant by trade, makes extra money by playing the organ at gatherings in the evening and on weekends. He does not get home from work until 7 p.m., and by the time he has eaten dinner it's after 8. The rules and regulations of his apartment building state that the playing of any musical instrument after 8 p.m. is prohibited. But the man has to practice in order to perform decently, and he regards the rules as an infringement on his personal rights. He therefore continues to play, and the landlord warns him he may be evicted. Could the landlord really evict him?

Each of these three questions would be decided by a court according to the terms of a lease. (If no lease exists, tenants stay only "at will" of the landlord; that is, they can be told to leave any time—providing only that thirty days' notice is given.) The answers given here are based on what leases almost always say. (However, if a very unusual lease were in force, the answers could be different.)

In the first instance, the landlord is right. Tenants are responsible for damage that is caused by their own negligence. So the tenant would have to pay for the fire damage, unless she was prepared to argue in court that there was no negligence on her part.

In the second instance, too, the landlord is right. It makes no difference whether the young lady pays rent or not. She is still an illegal subtenant. When the landlord rented the apartment, he rented it to one person, not two. And a landlord certainly has the right to determine who lives in his building. (Landlords of sizable buildings cannot systematically refuse to rent to applicants of a given race or religion. But landlords can refuse any individual tenant they don't like.) So, if the tenant wanted his girlfriend to live with him, he was legally obligated to go to the landlord and get a new lease or a modification of the old one.

In the third instance, the landlord is right again. If the tenant finds the rule against practicing to infringe his personal rights, his only legal recourse is to move. Almost every lease provides that rules and regulations attached to the lease have the same force as the lease itself. What's more, most leases obligate the tenant to obey rules that the landlord may promulgate in the future. The better leases usually limit this duty to obeying "reasonable" future rules; or else they provide some arbitration procedure in the case of disputes over future rules. But a tenant rarely has a way out of complying with a rule that was in force when he moved in.

If you thought in any of the three cases above that the tenant was legally right, the answers given should reinforce your determination to seek help from a lawyer before attempting to confront your landlord. Tenants are beginning to win more battles than they used to. And sticking up for your rights is what this book is all about. But there's no point batting your head into a stone wall. So inform yourself about the law first; fight second.

One area that causes continuing acrimony between landlords and tenants is the security deposit. That's the money you must put down, entirely apart from the first month's rent, before you move in. It's supposed to provide the landlord with a fund he can use to make repairs if you damage the place. Of course, he can also keep money from the security deposit as compensation if you fail to pay rent. Some landlords, however, have historically viewed the security deposit not as limited to these two uses but simply as extra money to retain if at all possible.

The first thing to do about the security deposit is to read what the lease says about it. The next thing to do is to find out what the law in your state says about it. Many states have passed laws saying the security deposit cannot equal more than the sum of two months' rent. In some places, one and a half month's rent is the limit. Many states have laws specifying the amount of time a landlord can delay in returning your deposit after you move out.

A common limit is forty-five days. In addition, a few states require that your landlord pay you interest on the deposit—since, after all, it's your money he's holding. The landlord will typically have to pay you 3 to 4 per cent interest—less than you could get elsewhere, but still a welcome bonus. Now, laws governing security deposits vary widely from state to state. So here's another time when a lawyer might come in handy. You don't have to see a lawyer, though. You can inform yourself about the applicable laws by checking with local officials, a tenant organization, or a library.

In at least one state (Maryland), the law requires a landlord to give tenants a written description of all existing damage in their dwelling units at the time they move in, if the tenants ask for it. As a tenant, you should request such a description. Your state might not require the landlord to give it to you, but if he does it can save you a great deal of trouble later on. In some cases, landlords try to keep all or part of the security deposit, claiming damage that actually existed when you moved in. A written description from him when you move in would spare you that headache. Of course, you might not agree with the description. But you can then inform the landlord of your disagreement by sending him a letter by certified mail (keeping a copy for yourself). That procedure gives you evidence to use later and also gives the landlord a written agenda of your request for repairs. Some tenant advisers also recommend you take pictures showing the condition of the apartment when you move in and when you move out.

As we said right at the outset, the strongest club the landlord has in his closet is the threat to evict you. So let's discuss eviction for a minute. For a landlord to evict you, he must follow standard court procedures. So-called self-help evictions are frowned on by courts almost everywhere. So a landlord can't just toss your furniture into the alley and padlock your door. If he did, you could sue him for damages and win. And he knows that, so if he threatens to just kick you out without getting any court documents, it's a pretty good bet he's bluffing. To evict a tenant legally, a landlord must obtain certain papers and pay certain fees. The papers must be legally served on the tenant, and a hearing must be held. Both sides may request delays. And whoever loses may appeal. Even if the landlord wins, there are still more papers and procedures before he can get you out of the apartment. So just because you get an eviction notice, it doesn't mean you are going to be out on the curb with your furniture by nightfall. If you are served with eviction papers, don't panic and don't do anything hasty. Do seek out legal help promptly, however. If you wait until the last minute, you might not get as good a lawyer as you otherwise could, or you might not be able to inform the lawyer fully about your case. Remember that Legal Aid lawyers often do work of a high quality and that they often know landlord-tenant law better than many lawyers who charge higher fees. Never ignore a summons or directive to appear in court, as some frightened or uninformed tenants do. That's a sure way to give the landlord victory on a silver platter. If a court date set is inconvenient for you, either you or your lawyer can probably arrange a delay. But if you're supposed to be in court on a given day, be there.

Some surveys have shown that judges tend to be predisposed to favor landlords in disputes with tenants. There are some possible reasons why that might be true. Most judges are not tenants, and some are landlords themselves. Landlords tend to be wealthier and sometimes more articulate than tenants; as a corollary, they can sometimes afford to hire impressive-sounding lawyers. Tenants who are poor, black, or Spanish-speaking have the hardest time overcoming these barriers, according to some experienced court observers.

Nonetheless, these obstacles have often been overstated. Most judges want to be fair. And the right courtroom behavior can help you, as a tenant, to turn around any odds that may weigh against you. A survey done in Brooklyn by court observers found that tenants got the best results when they spoke up forcefully in presenting their viewpoint. The survey also found that tenants did better when they had lawyers than when they didn't. (Interestingly, landlords represented by lawyers fared no better than landlords who represented themselves.) Judges, not surprisingly, also tended to favor tenants who were neatly dressed and who showed familiarity with the details of their cases and with the laws applying to their disputes. You might think that the worst possible approach would be belligerence. And the survey did show that the best results were obtained by tenants who were firm and forceful, yet controlled and polite. However, tenants who showed belligerence fared better than those who were meek or impassive. So, if you're in court in a landlord-tenant dispute, speak up!

Although thousands of eviction suits are filed every year, relatively few persons are actually evicted. Some tenants just move out if the landlord wants them out. But usually the tenant works out some arrangement with the landlord, and the landlord ends up getting his rent. Your task as a tenant is to make sure you've caused enough of a stir so that you get your money's worth for that rent in the future.

6

Alternate Housing Styles

Mobile Homes and Condominiums

When is a house not a house? Answer: When it's a mobile home or condominium. Both of these alternate forms of housing offer valuable advantages. Either is likely, however, to disappoint the buyer who purchases one as if it were a conventional home. The satisfied owner of a mobile home or a condominium will be the buyer who has recognized and avoided the special hazards of his chosen form of housing.

These two special situations fall between the more common alternatives of apartment renting and house ownership. Nowadays, mobile homes are chosen largely by people at the lower end of the income range; condominiums by people in the middle or at the upper end. The possible pitfalls of the two—while sometimes overlapping—are different enough to merit our considering these two housing alternatives separately. We'll start, then, with mobile homes. (If your interest in this chapter is limited to condominiums, you can turn directly to page 96.)

Since time began, man has been envious of the turtle, the snail, and the hermit crab—all able to move about freely and yet, wherever they go, able to take their homes with them. Nature designed these creatures' mobile homes. They're utilitarian and maintenance free, and the price is right. Unfortunately, we can't always say the same about *our* mobile homes.

Mobile homes are the subject of a number of misconceptions. To see whether you share any of these common erroneous beliefs, try the quiz below.

CSK Quiz

1. True or false: Mobile homes are mobile.
2. True or false: There are federal standards to insure the quality of mobile homes.
3. True or false: Trailer park tenants have the same rights as apartment tenants.

Now for a look at the answers. Number 1 is false. Mobile homes are not always mobile. About 75 per cent of all mobile homes are put on permanent home sites and never moved again. If they *are* moved, damage is often the result. Walls are sometimes twisted, and doors and windows often jam. Wiring can also be damaged, causing a serious fire hazard. So when mobile home owners relocate, most of them find it more convenient to sell their "mobile" home than to move it. Our present-day mobile home stems from the old Travel Trailer, an 8-foot-by-32-foot box pulled behind your car for weekend trips. Today's mobile homes can be 14 feet wide and 72 feet long—quite a different animal. In truth, the term "mobile home" today is almost a code word for "low-cost house." Of all living units built in 1973 that cost $15,000 and under, about 95 per cent were mobile homes. Those of us who own them are no more mobile than the rest of the population, just more interested in an economical dwelling.

Number 2 is also false. About 8 million people are living in mobile homes, yet this booming business has no federal regulations to insure the quality of their construction or their safety. One industry group has established a self-regulatory standard. All subscribers to the Mobile Home Manufacturers Association (MHMA) are required to build in accordance with certain minimum guidelines. Even though some call their standards weak, vague, and incomplete, they're better than nothing. The trouble is that only 30 per cent of all makers of mobile homes belong to the MHMA.

If you buy a mobile home from one of the 70 per cent who don't subscribe to the MHMA, you may not even have the benefit of minimum standards.

Number 3 is also false. Mobile home park tenants have very few legal rights in most states. Almost everywhere, their rights are more limited than those of tenants in apartment buildings (see Chapter 5). We'll discuss that aspect of mobile-home living in more detail later.

Right now, let's consider some features to look for in the construction of a mobile home. To begin with, the insulation should be adequate to cope with the climate in your region. In northern climates, Batt insulation is best. It consists of bags of insulating materials quilted to prevent shifting. In other parts of the country, a lower quality of insulation may do nicely. Mobile homes also vary according to how much pressure they're designed to take from ice, snow, and wind. So the MHMA standards vary according to the region in which the home is intended to be sold. Be sure the home you buy meets the standards for your region.

Remember that roofs and floors must be insulated, too. The sun beating down on a metal roof without proper insulation can make things pretty warm. And even though there is skirting around the bottom of the trailer, the floor can still get cold without proper insulation. Be sure to see that there is weather stripping around the doors. Also look for a storm door. Not only is it a safety factor (you can see who's there without completely opening your home) but it's also additional insulation. Wood backing underneath the metal siding also improves insulation—and adds strength to the walls.

Windows are important for both light and ventilation. As a minimum, the window space in each room should equal a tenth of the room's floor space. Storm windows cost extra, but they'll save you some heating and cooling costs. There must be at least one window in each bedroom that can be opened without tools and is no more than four feet off the ground. Such windows can be used as emergency exits. And, unfortunately, emergency exits can be important in a mobile home.

Many mobile homes are furnished when you buy them. There's a wide range of furniture prices, a fact that may or may not be obvious, depending on whether the cost of the furniture is shown separately or lumped in with a total cost figure. If you choose to buy your home already furnished, never settle for a model whose décor you don't really like. Replacing a good portion of the furniture is an expensive proposition. So it's better to keep shopping around until you're satisfied.

A final point on construction: Note the location of the furnace. Think of it as a possible starting point for a fire. That should make you think twice about buying a mobile home with the furnace in the hallway. If a fire were to start there, the hallway that normally provides an escape route would be the first area to fill with smoke and flames.

The subject of fire safety in mobile homes has attracted considerable attention. According to Lillian Jarmon of Ralph Nader's Center for Auto Safety, "Just about everything about mobile homes contributes to their flammability." Wood paneling, only five thirty-seconds of an inch thick, often carries a fire rapidly from room to room. Furnaces are often placed near this paneling, with no fire-retardant barrier in between. Bulit-in furnishings are often made of polyurethane or polystyrene—plastics whose flammability has attracted considerable attention in the media. Ceilings and floors are still more fire-prone. Ceilings are often made of a highly flammable blend of wood pulp and plant fibers. Floors are often so constructed as to provide what Ms. Jarmon has called "practically the best kindling in the world." Glossy paint finishes, sometimes called "Alabama flash," have been criticized for putting a final touch on the flammability problem. Mobile homes made between 1965 and 1972 may also have aluminum wiring. Aluminum seemed like a good idea to those who were impressed by its cost—about 60 per cent below the cost of traditional copper wiring. But in practice aluminum wiring has proved prone to frequent fire-producing accidents. For that reason, it's no longer used.

If you live in a mobile home, there are a few things you can do to cut down the fire hazard, though it will always remain greater than it would be in a conventional home. According to Ms. Jarmon, two or three dry-chemical fire extinguishers and two or three smoke detectors (they're not too expensive) should be placed strategically around the house. Use fire-retardant fabrics for your curtains and bedspreads. Be extra careful about smoking. And, if you have aluminum wiring, have it checked at least once a year.

Besides fire to worry about, there's also wind. When there's a flurry of tornadoes in the Midwest, news reports often carry a tally of injuries and deaths, with a disproportionately high number of them occurring in mobile home parks. The reason is that mobile homes, being lighter and less securely anchored than conventional homes, are particularly liable to be smashed, bashed, and tossed by severe winds. On the Eastern seaboard mobile home owners often suffer more severely in hurricanes than do occupants of conventional housing. There is a way to minimize this problem. It's called "tying down," a relatively simple procedure that gives the home a more secure anchor than it otherwise would have. Beware of being bilked when you hire a contractor to do this job, though. Some contractors charge as much as $250, even though (at 1974 price levels) you should be able to procure a good job for less than $100.

Next to the big dangers of fire and wind, the worst potential problems of mobile home ownership are the hazards of inadequate workmanship. The mobile home industry has never really decided who's responsible for repairs, the dealer or the manufacturer. Many buyers get trapped in an infuriating revolving door treatment. They call the dealer with a problem; he refers them to the manufacturer; the manufacturer refers them back to the dealer, and so on. One study has reported that fully half of all mobile home owners experience some maintenance problem on moving in. About 34 per cent of these people had to wait at least a month for repairs, and 20 per cent ended up repairing the fault themselves.

Well, you may ask, where are the warranties? That's a good question. Believe it or not, some warranties require the owner to send the home back to the manufacturer for repairs. And to send it back with all cost *prepaid*, yet! Those, of course, are the worst warranties. But they illustrate the need for checking warranties carefully before you buy.

As a rule, the warranty on your mobile home covers only manufacturing defects in the home itself. It does not usually cover any appliances, fixtures, furniture, or, for that matter, the furnace. These are all covered by their own warranties. When you move into a new mobile home, some of your first moments should be spent filling out all of these warranties. This will give you some protection from the beginning. The quality of that protection isn't all it might be, however. Let's say the roof of the mobile home falls in. Many warranties have a neat clause that says the home's maker disclaims *all* implied warranties, including the warranty of fitness or merchantability. This means you have no guarantee that your home will even be livable. So if the roof falls in, the manufacturer is obliged only to repair the roof. If anything or anyone was hurt, well, that's too bad. What's more, if the manufacturer blames the cave-in on poor maintenance or improper setup, he may not even have to fix the roof!

And what, you may ask, is "setup?" Another good question. When the home comes from the factory to your home site it must be taken off the axles and placed on a sturdy foundation or slab. It must be perfectly level, or some very interesting things happen: The walls, partitions, siding, ceiling, floor, or doors can buckle. This causes leaking windows, split roofs, and trouble in the siding. Expensive trouble. And guess who pays the bill? You, the owner, because the manufacturer says you've had your home badly set up. Setup (also called blocking) is the most important aspect of mobile home care. And yet only one state, Arizona, licenses the men who set up mobile homes. So there you are with a leaking roof. You call the dealer or manufacturer, and he can claim improper setup, leaving you to foot the bill.

If this discussion begins to sound like a scare story, it is. Mobile home living can be extremely pleasant and economical. But that doesn't happen automatically. It will work out that way for you only if you're very careful—or very lucky. And there's one more pitfall that remains to be discussed. It's the landlord-tenant aspect of mobile home living. Of course, this needn't concern you if you can buy your own land and put your mobile home on it. (Even if you can afford the land, you may discover that's not so easy. Many areas have severe zoning restrictions on where mobile homes can and can't go.) So many—probably most—mobile home owners live in what used to be called trailer parks. These are privately owned, and the person who owns the park is your landlord —even though you own your own home.

We examined, in Chapter 5, some of the hassles that can erupt between landlords and tenants. In mobile home parks, many of the same volatile factors are present. But generally speaking tenants in trailer parks have fewer protections under the law than other tenants. The reason: Leases are practically unheard of. Without a lease, you're a tenant "at will," which means the landlord can kick you out when he pleases. A number of states— among them Delaware, Florida, California, New York, New Jersey, Maine, Wisconsin, and Minnesota—have passed laws protecting tenants against arbitrary evictions and certain other abuses. But these laws are uneven in the amount of protection they provide, and some states have no protection for mobile home park tenants at all.

The first problem may arise before you even enter the park. About 60 per cent of park landlords own or have an interest in a mobile-home dealership as well. They may require you to purchase your home from their particular dealership in order to live in their park. This practice is illegal in many places and should be illegal everywhere, but it continues nevertheless. So ask about any such restrictions before renting space in a park.

The next problem is that there may be an entrance fee. These resemble security deposits only in that they are paid in advance and are separate from the rent. Unlike security deposits, they aren't refunded when you leave. In fact, some parks actually charge you an "exit fee" when you depart. These fees range from $200 to $2,000, so always ask about both entrance and exit fees before you take space in a park. And try to get the landlord to put his answers in writing.

From walking around the park, you can get a pretty good idea of how the landlord is at paving and general upkeep. Don't forget to check also into the question of how utilities are provided (including sewer service, as well as fuel, electricity, water, and telephone service). Some landlords will charge you hook-up fees for connecting your home to these utilities. Some landlords will direct you to certain vendors for the utilities, or for skirting around the bottom of your home, or for setup or tie-down services. Sometimes the vendor the landlord will direct you to is none other than the landlord himself! Sometimes it's a friend of the landlord. Of course, it's fine for the landlord to *suggest* a vendor. But if he *requires* you to obtain services from a particular vendor, you can bet you're going to pay an inflated price. And you can bet that, one way or another, some of that money is going to end up in the landlord's pocket.

Not all landlords are like that, of course. Quite the contrary, most are honest. Even honest businessmen like to make money, though. And, with the shortage of mobile home park space in most areas, landlords can charge whatever they choose for their space. Where there are no leases, rent can be raised often. So ask around among the tenants as to what the pattern of rate increases has been before you commit yourself to renting in a mobile home park. Once you're settled, you probably won't want to move. So it's worth taking the time to pick a park very carefully.

One aid in choosing a park is *Woodall's Mobile Home & Park Directory*. Published by the Woodall Publishing Company of Highland Park, Illinois, the directory is a sort of bible for the mobile home community. It rates some 13,000 mobile home parks and communities, giving each an evaluation of from one to five stars (unrated communities are alleged to be less good than one-star parks). Criteria for rating include a park's general appearance, the condition of its streets, its ability to accommodate large mobile homes, its requirements for home owners to equip their trailers with skirting and awnings or cabanas, its landscaping, the adequacy of its parking, the quality of its recreational facilities, and the availability of its management personnel (among other criteria). Use *Woodall's* to help you pick a park, along with your own careful observations. Despite the perils of fire, wind, landlords, and unguaranteed workmanship in the homes themselves, mobile home living can be safe, economical, and fun—if you take the trouble to make it that way.

Some of the problems of mobile home owners also affect buyers of condominiums. Both own their own homes, but both may face hidden costs and may end up having a landlord after all. The origin of the word "condominium" is Latin. In fact, the condominium form of housing was introduced by none other than Julius Caesar. What the buyer must be concerned about today, though, is the fact that some sharp condominium developers are still having a Roman holiday.

Some 2,000 years after Julius Caesar, condominiums have been enjoying a burst of popularity. Experts estimate that about half the housing units built in this country during the mid-1970s were condominiums. Buyers are interested in condominiums because they can offer an advantageous blend of house and apartment living. Sellers are interested in them because they're profitable.

If you buy a condominium, you don't have to maintain the exterior. Usually you pay a monthly fee to cover maintenance. No more puttying windows and cutting grass. Frequently, this means more time to enjoy the swimming pool, tennis courts or other recreational facilities. For many people, especially young couples, the purchase of an apartment condominium is a stepping stone to eventual purchase of a house; in a condominium you can start accumulating equity for later use as a down payment on a house. The fact that you own your unit has definite advantages. No lease, no increasing rent. You can deduct property taxes and mortgage interest on your income tax return. Despite these rosy aspects, there are hidden hazards. Before we get into that subject, let's see how much you know about condominiums to begin with.

CSK Quiz

1. True or false: If you live in an apartment building that is being converted to condominiums and don't want to buy one, there's nothing you can do except move out.
2. True or false: In some condominium developments, if you sell

your unit at a profit, a part of your profit goes to the owner's association.

3. True or false: If you buy a condominium in a popular resort area, you can usually count on rental income to defray your costs.

Now let's look at the answers. Number 1, unfortunately, is true. There's not much you can do if your apartment is converted to condominiums and you don't want to buy. When your lease expires, you just have to leave. Some renters have even complained about being harassed to leave *before* their leases expire. If condominiums do take over the rental market, as some experts predict, this could create a whole new housing crisis for people who can't afford to shell out $20,000 and up to buy a condominium. The only state, as of mid-1974, that had any protection for tenants in this bind was New York. There, an apartment building couldn't be converted to a condominium unless at least 35 per cent of the current occupants went along with the plan.

Number 2 is true. Some agreements do stipulate that, if you sell your unit at a profit, a percentage of that profit must be turned over to the owner's association. Although this is rare, the mere possibility should illustrate the need for approaching a condominium purchase very cautiously.

Number 3 is false. One of the biggest mistakes you can make is to expect to rent out your unit easily to defray most of your expenses. In order to rent it out, you'll have to avoid using it yourself during peak seasons. If you do rent it out, all the better. But the experts are unanimous: Don't expect to and, above all, don't do your financial planning with the expectation of large rental income.

Before we go any farther, we should take a look at exactly what a condominium owner owns. Let's use an imaginary example, Superswell Estates. It's a development of 200 condominium units with a swimming pool, tennis courts, and a playground. If you bought a townhouse condominium here, you'd get a mortgage, just as if you were buying a house. You'd have monthly mortgage payments, and you would own the interior of your townhouse. You'd also own, in common with the other 199 unit owners, the swimming pool, the tennis courts, and the playground. Now, it costs money to maintain and manage those common areas, so you would have to pay one two-hundredth of those expenses. There are many variations of this setup, but that's the basic idea.

Then again, it's not always quite as simple as it sounds. Here's what happened to one young couple living on Superswell Estates:

HE: Well, honey, it's not a house, but we do own it.

SHE: Look at it this way darling, it's the first place we've had that's really all our own. (Picks up a hammer and nail and starts pounding the nail into a wall.) I think this painting will look good over here by the sofa, don't you?

HE: Yeah, sure, it'll look great.

(Loud knocking on door. She opens it, and a burly man with a policeman's cap enters. He wears a t-shirt reading "condominium patrol" and carries a putty knife and spackling compound.)

PATROLMAN: Sorry lady, you can't do that.

SHE: Can't do what?

PATROLMAN: Can't drive nails, screws, or anything else into the walls.

SHE: I can too! We own this place. This is *ours*. We can do anything we want to it.

HE: That's right. We own it, just like a house. You can't tell us what to do.

PATROLMAN: You're wrong, fella. Look at your contract. You own all the enclosed space here. . . .

HE: (interrupting) And the walls. The walls are ours!

PATROLMAN: You own the *surface* of the walls only. Read your contract. And don't go trying to stick anything beyond the surface into *our* walls. (Uses the putty knife to slap spackle on the nail hole and walks out.)

As you can see, the definition of what you own, which you'll find in the legal papers you have to sign, should be one of your primary concerns. Of course, it would be a rare condominium that had a patrolman. And as a practical matter, our young couple will probably solve their problem as most people do. They'll stick up the pictures anyway. Any rule preventing it is a hard rule to enforce. But you should remember to pay attention to how much of your unit you really own.

There are other pitfalls in the ownership agreement. Let's look in on the same couple after fifty years:

She: Say, Henry. What's going on out there?

He: What is it, Martha?

She: Something strange going on outside.

He: (comes to window) Looks like a wrecking crew. I wonder what they're going to wreck.

(*A wrecker's ball comes slamming in through the window. Henry and Martha both fall to the floor. Furniture is flying everywhere.*)

He: We're getting wrecked.

She: Henry, I never used to mind getting wrecked with you, but this is ridiculous! (Grabs a curtain rod, ties on a white shirt, rushes to the window, and waves the improvised white flag.) Hey, you idiots. You can't do this! This is our place. We own it. We paid it off twenty-five years ago!

Well, that scenario may be a bit exaggerated. But our old couple did forget one important factor. Who owns the land? In some condominium developments, the land is owned by the developer or an affiliate of the developer, who *leases* it to the owners' association. When that lease runs out, you can be out of luck. Here is a quote from the prospectus for one condominium development: "The land lease procedure is being used to avoid problems 65 to 100 years hence, when substantial remodeling may be required to keep the [condominium] in first class shape. Though properly maintained and repaired, any resort hotel facility suffers from functional and socio-economic obsolescence. Such obsolescence requires that after 50 to 70 years, the facility be gutted and renovated to keep pace with building technology and resort visitor tastes." Unquote. There is no mention of compensation to unit owners for the gutting of their units. You should be careful to note whether there is a lease hold arrangement. It is far preferable for the owners' association to own the land.

The owners' association should also own the common areas, such as parking lots, tennis courts, pool, and so on. In some condominiums the developer retains title to these areas. Then he, or some firm to which he has sold his rights, leases them back to the owners' association, charging whatever the traffic will bear. In a few years he's collected what all the common areas are worth. And he can keep collecting, under some leases, for ninety-nine years. As this book went to press, such practices were under legal attack in some areas, notably Florida. But nothing had happened yet to keep developers from engaging in this sort of milking procedure.

Of course, at the outset the developer owns everything. But at some point there must be an arrangement as to how he transfers ownership of the common areas to the owners of the individual units. If you're going to buy one of those units, then the sooner that transfer takes place the better it is from your point of view. One year would be a good rule of thumb. It is not necessarily a bad idea for the developer to *manage* the common areas, at least for a while. But the association should own them. By the way, if you plan to buy a condominium, be prepared to play an active role in the owners' association. And make sure the bylaws allow you to play an active role.

Developer ownership of common areas is only one of several hidden costs that can be entailed in condominium ownership. Another is maintenance. You may not think maintenance is a hidden cost, because when you buy they tell you what the monthly maintenance cost is. True. But if you were trying to sell units (and you were less scrupulously forthright than you are), mightn't you be tempted to understate the cost of maintenance? At the beginning, the developer is maintaining the place, and if he loses money on maintenance he has a tax write-off. So he might tell you that maintenance will cost you, say, $25 a month. But when the owners' association takes over, you may find that it will cost a lot more. The best way to guard against this peril is to check out carefully the reputation of the developer.

Another possible hidden cost is land rent. If you don't own the land, you've got to pay rent to whoever does. And that rent can go up. So fear of the wrecker's ball isn't the only reason you should check carefully who owns the land.

There's also a possibility of membership fees. Many times, you'll have to pay a fee to use the golf course, the swimming pool, or what have you. Those fees can increase. One executive found out too late that he had to pay $1,200 a year to use the golf and swim club. Even if you're wealthy, that kind of news can come as an awful shock. This hazard is tied in, of course, with ownship of the common areas, which we discussed earlier. But even if the owners' association holds title to the pool or golf course, fees would still have to be charged in many cases.

Then there's furniture rental. In some condominiums, you lease the furniture for your unit. This can cost as much as $100 a month. If you want to furnish your place yourself, you must sometimes get the approval of the developer. And if you buy a condominium in a foreign country, like Mexico, there may be stipulations that say you cannot bring furniture over the border for your place.

One more semi-hidden cost: property taxes. It's no secret that you have to pay them. What some people forget is that they can go up every year and often do. Of course, that's true for a house, too. But it ought to be considered in your financial planning.

Whatever hazards may lurk in existing condominiums, unbuilt ones have more. Some experts simply advise against purchasing an unconstructed condominium no matter what. They point out that there's many a slip between the artist's rendering and the final reality that you have to live with. But there are certain protections for you, if you decide to go this route. One of them is called a property report. If you're purchasing a condominium unit in an unbuilt development, the developer is required to give you a property report. It will spell out in some detail what is going to be built and what it will cost you. It will tell you whether you'll have to pay high hook-up charges for sewers and electricity and what it will cost to join the golf club, beach club, or whatever. What would you do if you bought an unbuilt condominium and then found out there was no water for 100 miles around? Don't laugh—it has happened. But it won't happen to you if you read the property report. Another thing that document will tell you is whether the developer has been in any trouble with the law. That's very useful information. In short, read the property report carefully before you sign anything.

A second possible aid is a prospectus. If a condominium is sold with emphasis on the economic benefits to be derived by the buyer, then it's classified as a security. That makes it subject to jurisdiction of the Securities and Exchange Commission (SEC), which requires that a prospectus be issued. These documents are quite detailed and make fascinating reading, once you get past the sometimes turgid style. For example, a prospectus for one particular condominium colony in Mexico states the following: that foreigners are not allowed to own property in that part of Mexico; that there is a land lease arrangement which expires in thirty years; that the condominium is an active seismic region (which means earthquakes are to be expected); that you must give the developer 120 days' notice if you plan to use your unit yourself; that there is a fee for the use of the golf course, tennis courts, and health facilities; that, if your unit is rented out, you will receive only 50 percent of the proceeds; and so on.

Some condominium developments, especially those in resort areas, offer what's called a rental pool arrangement. It sounds like a good deal. When you're not using your condominium, the developer will act as your agent and rent it out for you. He'll advertise it, and through his contacts in the real estate business he'll find people to rent it. Of course, he gets a cut of the rent, which seems only fair. But then, there's a question of how big the cut should be. We took a close look at the prospectus for one condominium development in a popular ski area, where the rental pool arrangement is offered. The units sell for $36,000. If you want to enter the rental pool arrangement you have to put down $500 more right off the top. The company agrees to rent out your place if it can and consents to keep a modest 40 per cent of the proceeds to cover operating expenses. You get 10 per cent to cover "wear and tear on your unit." And what happens to the remaining 50 per cent? It goes into a pool. At the end of the year, you get a cut of the pool, depending on how many days you made your unit available for rent. (It doesn't matter whether it was actually rented or not; you still get a cut of the rental pool money).

Now, how will your total rental income compare with the annual costs to you as the owner of a condominium unit? In the front of the prospectus is a warning in large letters. It says that you'd better be ready to pay all the expenses of keeping up your unit, because "rental income from the agency arrangement may be insufficient to cover these items." That may be the understatement of the year. In this particular condominium, you'd pay more than $1,500 a year to the owners' association (for maintenance and insurance), $300 to the developer for land rent, $1,150 to the developer for furniture rental, $850 in property taxes, and $2,650 for mortgage payments. That's a grand total of more than $6,500. Under the rental pool arrangement we've just described, you couldn't possibly collect more than $2,500 from rental income— less than half the amount needed to meet your annual expenses. So we repeat what we said in our quiz segment: Don't count on rental income to defray the costs of owning a condominium.

What we've said up to now still doesn't cover all the strings that can be attached to your contract. For example, like tenants of mobile home parks, you as a condominium owner may be limited to certain purveyors of services, ranging from garbage collection to the vending machine concession. And, as we said in the case of mobile home parks, these local monopolies tend to take advantage of you by charging extra-high prices.

When you're looking for a new home, it's hard to keep cynical, practical details like this in your mind. You may wonder how you'll remember them all. The answer is you won't; you'll forget. So, before buying a condominium, always consult a lawyer. That way, if you choose this Roman-initiated form of housing, you'll end up being more of an emperor in your own home. And the developer will have less of a Roman holiday at your expense.

7

It's Your Move

Fifty-fifty—according to a recent survey, those are your chances of having a mover do a satisfactory job of moving all your possessions from one place to another. This chapter is devoted to helping you improve those odds.

To begin with, let's see how much you already know about certain aspects of moving.

CSK Quiz

1. True or false: If your goods are delivered more than a week late, you don't have to pay the full cost of the move.
2. True or false: The bill for your move cannot exceed the estimate by more than 10 per cent.
3. True or false: You are allowed nine months to make a claim against a company for damaged goods.

Now for the answers: Number 1 is false. You have to pay the full cost of the move regardless of when your goods are delivered. In a recent survey of people who had just moved, 16 per cent said their shipment had been picked up late and 33 per cent reported a late delivery. Unfortunately, if that happens to you there's very little you can do about it. However, you can lessen your chances for a late delivery by avoiding the peak moving season. Three quarters of all moves in the United States are made in the summer months of June, July, and August. Most of them are made around the first of the month, so that people can avoid another month's rent. If you must move during the summer, try to do it around the middle of the month. Even paying another month's rent might be cheaper in the long run than paying for lodging and meals while you wait a couple of weeks for your goods. This kind of scheduling will also cut down on damages caused by overworked and undertrained moving men.

Number 2 is also false. The final bill can and sometimes does exceed the estimate by much more than 10 per cent. It's not unheard of to end up paying double the estimate. To protect yourself, you should get numerous estimates. Make sure an agent of the company comes to your house and looks at your goods. And be sure he sees everything you plan to move. Beware of extra-low estimates. They may be "lowballs" designed to grab your business, rather than an accurate reflection of what the move will really cost. It's likely you'll be safest if you pick one of the medium-priced companies. On delivery day, you must be prepared to pay for the move with cash, a money order, or a certified check. Personal checks are almost never accepted. Until the movers receive payment, they won't unload the van. However, the amount you're obligated to pay on delivery day is limited to the estimated cost, plus 10 per cent. If the final cost exceeds the estimate by more than 10 per cent, you don't have to pay the balance right then; you have fifteen days.

Number 3 is true. You do have up to nine months to file a claim. But the sooner you do it the stronger your case. You must prove that the damage was the mover's fault. That's difficult to do if you've had possession of the item for some time after the move.

One of the first things you should learn, if you're going to move, is not the ABCs but what might be called the Ms, CHs and Gs. Those are some common abbreviations used by moving men, and it pays to know them, plus a couple more. M stands for "marred" —roughly the condition you'd get if you rubbed a little sandpaper across a finished piece of furniture. CH stands for "chipped," and it means pretty much what it says. G stands for "gouged." Of course, one man's CH is another man's G. Other common markings are SC for "scratched," T for "torn," and BR for "broken." Rarer is BU, which stands for "burned." The point of all this abbreviating is its use on the inventory form. In any interstate move (that is, a move between states, and not within one metropolitan region), the mover must fill out a form describing every item that is to be transported. Each item is tagged with a number, corresponding to its place on the inventory list. And on that list the condition of each item is noted according to the shorthand we just looked at.

We forgot to mention one abbreviation—OK. It stands, as you might suspect, for okay, or in perfect condition. The sad fact is that you're not very likely to see it on your form. Movers seem to have highly refined sensibilities: They can detect a tiny scratch or scrape on almost any piece of furniture. What's important is that you check to make sure their high standards don't get stretched into outright misrepresentation. You should check the condition marked for each item. If you disagree with the mover's judgment of an item's condition, say so—in writing, right there on the inventory form. That way, if an item is damaged in shipment, the mover won't be able to claim that it was that way all along.

Once you've made the decision to move, your first step is to call several companies for estimates. Which companies should you call? There's no hard and fast rule. If you know people who have moved recently, or who move a lot, ask them for recommendations. The Interstate Commerce Commission, which regulates the moving industry, has been less than a fountain of information for consumers. It does, however, require companies to submit information on what percentage of damage claims they pay, how long they take to pay them, and how often their estimates are below the actual cost of the move. *Consumer Reports* magazine collected and printed that information for twenty major companies in its May 1973 issue. You can find back issues of *Consumer Reports* at many libraries.

Although it won't help you pick a mover, the ICC has also printed a helpful pamphlet called "Summary of Information for

Shippers of Household Goods." When you're making a long-distance move, the law requires that you be given a copy of this pamphlet. If you're making a shorter move, it wouldn't hurt to ask for a copy from your mover before you move. It doesn't take long to read from cover to cover (it's seventeen pages long), and it's worth having around.

When someone comes to your home to give you an estimate, feel free to ask a lot of questions. And expect direct, honest answers. If you don't get them, call another company. Many estimators get a commission based on the number of people they sign up. Keep that in mind when they tell you grandiose stories of their highly trained and experienced moving experts who treat every piece of furniture with tender loving care. During the peak summer season, your experienced mover may be a hitchhiker that your driver picked up a couple of blocks from your house.

Another thing about the estimate: Most of the cost of a move is based on the weight of the shipment and the distance it must travel. All the big moving companies adhere to a uniform formula for this basic charge. It's the special services that may differ. These include any packing the mover does, the use of his cartons, and the unhooking of your appliances. Make sure you understand exactly what is covered by the estimate price. And even then be prepared for a bill bigger than the estimate. One study found that the twenty biggest carriers underestimated the bill 23 per cent of the time.

Along with your estimate, the company will prepare what's called an "order for service." This will specify the agreed-upon pickup and delivery dates. It will also give the location of the scale to be used in weighing your shipment. The dates, alas, are only target dates as far as the mover is concerned. As stated before, a third of all deliveries are made late. So brace yourself for that and be prepared to find temporary accommodations.

Now, let's get back to that scale mentioned on the order for service. You should familiarize yourself with its location so you can go there yourself on moving day and see your goods weighed. On your official moving document (the bill of lading), the mover must show the "tare" weight of the van. The tare weight is simply the weight before your goods are loaded. (Thus, it might include the basic weight of the van plus the weight of another shipment of goods loaded before yours.) After your goods are on board, the movers weigh the van again, and you're legally entitled to be there when they do. You can check the reading and be sure they don't tip the scales by putting some crew members on the van. The basic charge for your move will be based on the net weight, which is simply the difference between the tare weight and the gross weight after your goods are aboard.

You may wonder how you can know that the tare weight given to you is accurate. There's a fairly simple answer to that. The driver carries what's called a manifest. It shows the weights for the previous households on his route. So you can check the gross weight of the last household pickup, and that should be your tare weight. If you're still suspicious that something's wrong with the weight picture, you have one more recourse. You have a legal right to request, prior to the delivery date, that the shipment be reweighed in your presence. This is done at the destination. First the loaded van is weighed again, then another reweigh is preformed after your goods have been unloaded. The charge for this will typically run about $20. However, if you've been gypped, there's no charge. The ICC says you can't be charged for the reweigh if it shows the previously billed net weight was more than 120 pounds too high. The reweigh is also free if the billed net weight was 25 per cent or more above what the company estimated the net weight would be.

Earlier we mentioned a document called the bill of lading. It is, as we said, your official moving document. For one thing, it serves as a receipt for your goods. For another, it is the closest thing you have to a contract with the mover. Needless to say, you should be sure your mover has given you a bill of lading before your shipment leaves its point of origin. Then examine the document carefully. Be sure your destination address is shown correctly on it. Make certain that it contains the name, address, and phone number of the party through whom you can be reached during the move. Otherwise, the mover has no way of notifying you if there's a delay or of confirming that delivery will be made when you've planned. The bill of lading also spells out the insurance provisions covering your belongings while they're in transit.

There are three basic ways of insuring your goods. If you don't specify your preference, your belongings will be insured for $1.25 times the number of pounds in your shipment. For example, if your shipment totals 5,000 pounds, your goods would be insured for $6,250. If something breaks—say, a lamp—you can collect its full value. Of course it would be the present value, not the cost of the lamp when it was purchased. And the total you collect cannot exceed the limit (in this case, $6,250). The cost of this standard coverage, in 1974, was 50 cents per $100 of protection. So, for a 5,000-pound shipment, your $6,250 of insurance protection would cost you $31.25. You'll automatically be billed this amount unless you specify you want a different type of coverage. And the charge will appear on the bill of lading.

Let's suppose you want to save money and get less insurance protection. Then you can specify that you want "60 cent per pound per article" coverage. This gives you very little insurance protection, but it's free. All the movers have to pay you if they break something is the weight (in pounds) of the article broken, times 60 cents. So, if a 10-pound lamp is broken, the most you can collect for it is $6.00. If the value of the lamp is less than $6.00, you'll get only the actual value. But if the value of the lamp is $50, you'll still get only the $6.00, based on the formula of 60 cents times 10 pounds. To get this cheaper kind of insurance, you must write "60 cents per pound per article" on the bill of lading. But we don't recommend you opt for such meager protection unless you're positive your goods are covered by other insurance policies that you own.

Let's suppose, now, that your 5,000 pounds of belongings are worth more to you than $6,250, as might well be the case. You could then choose the third type of insurance protection. You could sign up on the bill of lading for extra coverage—enough to produce a valuation you consider adequate to cover your shipment. The cost would again be 50 cents for each $100 of valuation. So if you figure your goods are worth $10,000 it would cost you $50 to insure them for that amount.

To sum up, then, the bill of lading is your receipt for your belongings, your contract with the movers, and your insurance document protecting your goods while they're in transit. So read it carefully before signing, following the guidelines suggested here. It pays—even if you have to spend some uncomfortable moments with a husky, impatient mover at your elbow.

That same advice holds true on the other end of the line when your goods are delivered. In fact, it's doubly true. The movers will be in a rush to unload and depart. To do that, they'll shove a copy of a release form in front of you and ask you to sign on the dotted line, certifying that all your goods have been received in good condition. How are you supposed to know they're in good condition? The answer is to make the movers wait as long as necessary for you to check for damage. The movers won't like it. But the moving industry sets up the rules. You're just playing their game and trying to protect yourself.

Back when the inventory was made, you were given a copy. You should have it on hand when the goods are delivered. Check each item to be sure it's in good condition. That means checking every lamp, every piece of furniture. If you have a lot of boxes, you don't have to check every box. If none of the boxes appears to have been banged up, it should suffice to check the one or two boxes you know contain really fragile items. If those are all right, it's a pretty good bet that the less fragile objects in other boxes survived the trip in good shape.

Before signing the delivery receipt, the inventory, or any other release form the movers give you when your goods are delivered, be sure that at least one of these forms has been marked with a notation of any damaged or lost articles. If the driver won't make such notations on the forms, make them yourself. Telling the movers orally about damage or loss isn't enough. Going through all this careful checking and noting won't come naturally. You and your family are likely to be impatient and excited. You can't wait for the movers to leave so you can start putting your new home in order and enjoying it. Nonetheless, careful checking at the time of delivery can save a lot of grief later. And it certainly makes it easier if you have to collect a claim.

It's worth noting that movers are not responsible for exceptionally valuable things such as money, watches, jewelry and heirlooms. You should always transport those items personally.

If you do have to file a claim, remember to do it as soon as possible. It has to be done in writing, on a special claim form the company provides. So the first thing to do—either the day of delivery or the next day—is to call the local agent for the moving company and arrange for the form to be sent to you. If you don't know who the local agent is in your new home area, be sure to find out from the moving men. When you file a claim, give as much information as possible about the lost or broken item. This would include the date and place where it was purchased, the price you paid, the exact nature of the damage, and any estimates of repair costs you've obtained. Some companies require that you provide documentation for this information.

If there's any fundamental rule about moving, it's Murphy's law: If something can possibly go wrong, it will. One might add a corollary: It will happen at the worst possible moment. And moving can be a trying time, anyway. A study done at Yale University found that among a group of women suffering from severe depression, moving was often a recent experience.

That isn't surprising, according to Dr. Chester Schmidt. A psychiatrist with Baltimore City Hospital, Schmidt has studied the effects of various transitions in life, including moving. Moving, he points out, is a kind of uprooting of the human organism. People's roots, as Schmidt sees it, are a series of "sustaining relationships that have some depth to them." People may form sustaining relationships with friends and neighbors and also with activities that they find meaningful. When a family moves these are torn apart, and new ones must be slowly rebuilt. Often the breadwinner—typically the father—finds the transition the least difficult. That's because he experiences the least discontinuity, as he quickly "reinvests" his emotional energy in his job.

For the wife and children, it's often a lot more difficult. The core family alone, Schmidt finds, is hard put to provide for all of its members' emotional needs. "People need outside relationships." Husbands often find them at work, children at school. So it's wives and mothers who have the hardest time. This is all the more true because many times the wife gets saddled with the detail work on the move.

It's not necessarily easy on the kids, either. Infants, of course, will make the transition fairly easily, since they have no extended ties to be broken. But once children reach the age of five or so, moving means leaving behind friends—often the only friends the child has known. A child may respond by becoming crabby or morose, by crying an unusual amount, or by having bad dreams for several weeks or months after a move. Adolescents often suffer severely for a short time. But they are usually resourceful and resilient enough to bounce back quickly.

How do you go about coping with these psychic dislocations? Schmidt recommends, first of all, that you talk about them openly. Letting feelings of loneliness, or even resentment, be expressed will prevent them from building up and festering. Second, every family member should, if possible, have some job to perform in connection with the move. This will not only spread the work out but also keep children occupied and involved so that they're less likely to brood. When you arrive at the destination, the family should deliberately plan a lot of recreational activities together. And they should deliberately set out to re-establish outside ties by joining community organizations or participating in their activities. Of course, each family will vary Schmidt's advice to suit its own members' needs. But knowing that a post-move depression is not abnormal will help you roll with the punch, and Schmidt's suggestions may help a family regain its balance more quickly. Another idea some families have found useful is to subscribe in advance to the local newspaper of their new town. This helps them know the community and feel a sense of familiarity and recognition when they arrive.

So far we've been talking about how to deal with the movers and how to deal with your own reactions to the move. That might seem like a large enough order. But the truth is that moving involves dealing with dozens of other people and organizations as well. Sometimes it seems that there are hundreds of people who don't care about your whereabouts until the time comes to change it. Then they must be notified, paid, dunned for money they owe you, solicited for information, registered with, withdrawn from, said goodbye to, or invited over for dinner. The list of miscellaneous tasks associated with moving is enough to make any family feel it's plunging into chaos.

A number of moving companies offer you booklets or checklists to help you deal with this chaos. Often the information is put in the form of a timetable—things to do four weeks before the move, two weeks before, a day before, and so on. That seems to be a reasonable approach, so we've adopted it here. Most of the suggestions that follow are culled from material put out by commercial moving companies.

You should start getting estimates from moving companies six to eight weeks before you plan to move, if you possibly can. Then you can make an informed choice—and improve your chances of getting the moving dates you want.

About a month before moving day, you should choose a moving company and sign an order for service. Start combing your house or apartment, looking for things that should be thrown out, given away, or sold. Transporting items you don't really need adds unnecessarily to your cost. And those items might come in handy for a friend or bring you a little money if you sell them. You can also give them to charity and get a tax deduction. Your search of the premises should definitely include any basement, attic or garage you may have.

About a month in advance is none too soon to find out how much of your moving expenses, if any, will be paid by your company (either your present employer or one you'll be working for at the new location). This is the time, too, to decide how much packing you'll do yourself and how much you want the movers to do. We'll discuss hints for packing items yourself a little bit later.

Many people find it helpful to buy a little notebook (or rescue one from a drawer), and use it to jot down notes and lists of chores for the move. You should prepare a list of people and organizations to which change-of-address notices will be sent—and start sending them out now. Magazines like to get at least four weeks notice; they often prefer six. It's good to send all your friends change-of-address cards, even if you've told them about the move before. The cards make a handy reference, and your friends might have forgotten to write down the new address the first time you told them. As for organizations that must be notified, you'll make your own list, of course, but the one that appears on page 115 should provide some ideas. Don't forget to let the post office know you're moving and to fill out the official form that enables the postal service to forward your mail. You can get this form at your local post office; it takes only a minute to fill out.

The closer you get to moving day, the more hectic things tend to become. So the more things you can take care of a month or more in advance the better off you are. Arrange at work to have your W-2 or other tax forms forwarded. Arrange with your doctor or doctors to have all the family's medical records transferred. If possible, try to get a copy for yourself and one for the new physician. These records should include a history of past illnesses for each family member, a history of vaccinations, the date of each family member's most recent examination, and the names of any current prescription drugs. (Be sure you have filled all prescriptions with an adequate supply of drugs before leaving. It could take a while to get the prescription refilled at your destination.) The same kind of check should be done with dental records. This is the time, too, to talk with the family's insurance agent or broker and find out who will service the policies at the new location. If you're a homeowner, make sure there are no unpaid taxes on your home (including special assessments, like sewer assessments). You can do this with a quick call or visit to city hall. If you're going to need letters of introduction, now's the time to ask people to write them. If any member of the family is subject to the draft, a note should be dropped to his draft board notifying it of the change in location. If you have school-age children, arrange for the transfer of their records to the new school they'll be attending.

Because movers are prohibited from carrying items of extraordinary value, such as jewelry, money, or precious stones, you have to decide how you're going to transport these items. If you're going to carry them along, think about the safest way to do it.

(Carrying travelers' checks, for example, is safer than carrying large amounts of cash.) Some items can be forwarded by registered mail or through a private insured forwarding agency.

If you have charge accounts with stores that don't exist at your new location, you'll want to close them out. You can arrange for the final bill to be forwarded to you. Or you may find it simpler to be sure the account's paid up.

Whom to Notify When You Move

Friends and relatives
Post office
Magazines and newspapers
Draft board (if any family member is subject to the draft)
Insurance companies:
    Life
    Health
    Homeowner's or renter's
    Auto
Utilities:
    Phone
    Electric
    Gas
    Water
    Fuel
Organizations and clubs (including book and record clubs)
Schools and churches
Businesses where you have charge accounts
Veterans Administration (if anyone in family is a veteran)
Professional Services:
    Doctors
    Lawyers
    Dentists
    Brokers or financial advisers
Banks

Pets present a special problem. Some families solve it by giving pets away, but others would find this course heartrending. Federal regulations prohibit your mover from taking your pets on their van. So you have to either take your pet along with you in your car or make some special shipping arrangements. By the way, pets, like children, should have their immunization records rounded up before departure.

If you're going to be traveling during a busy season, it would be wise to make any hotel reservations you'll need well in advance. One good way to do it is to make reservations about a month in advance and to reconfirm them a day or two before leaving.

It hardly needs to be mentioned that if you're selling a house you should get it on the market as soon as possible. You certainly don't want to take a loss (or even an unreasonably small gain) because you were forced to sell in a hurry. Some apartment renters will be responsible for securing a new tenant, especially if this is the deal they make with the landlord in order to break a lease. If you're in that situation, a newspaper ad is probably the best course. It may cost fairly much, but it will bring you more prospects to look at the apartment than any other method. Here, too, it pays to start early.

Around a month in advance, you'll change your shopping habits. From now on, food is bought only in small quantities, and meal plans start being tailored to the goal of emptying the freezer and the refrigerator.

Keep in mind what Dr. Schmidt said about the traumas of moving. Talk with the family about the move and the reasons for it. Get the children occupied with small but meaningful tasks related to the move.

Although this is a busy time, it's a good one for checking your credit rating through your bank or a local credit bureau. If it's good, ask to have it forwarded to a credit bureau in your destination area. This will help you if you want to establish credit quickly. If you find there's something wrong with your credit rating, read Chapter 13 of this book for some hints on what to do about it.

About two weeks prior to the move you may feel the clock is

beginning to tick a little more loudly than usual—or perhaps faster. This is the time to hold farewell parties: You may not have time at the last minute. Make your final travel plans and have your car prepared for the trip, if it's going to be a long one. That could mean a tune-up and oil change. Definitely check to be sure brakes, tires, and windshield wipers are in good condition.

Check the insurance policy that covers your household goods to see if it covers them in transit. If not, now's the time to make final arrangements for any rider or "floater" providing that coverage. If you don't have this kind of protection through your insurance company—and most people don't—then you should definitely consider buying extra insurance from the mover, as discussed earlier. Be sure this coverage gets written onto the bill of lading. And arrange for fire or property insurance at your new home. There shouldn't be a gap.

If you have clothing or rugs to be cleaned, now's the time. Leave the clothes in their cellophane bags when they're ready, and the rugs rolled up, for easy transportation by the movers. If you're doing some packing yourself, start now if you haven't already. Return any borrowed items and get back anything you've loaned out.

Talk with your utility companies: gas, electric, water, and phone. Give them your new address and arrange for the return of any security deposits you've put down. Set a definite date and time for the cutoff of utility services. Then confirm the arrangements you've made by letter and keep a copy of the letters for yourself. If you're going to take any appliances along with you, talk with your mover about how this will be done. Some appliances require expertise to disconnect safely; others require servicing before they can be moved without damage.

If you've been able to keep up with the pace suggested here so far, the last week shouldn't really be much of a problem. Much of the work will already be behind you. About a week before moving day is a good time to start packing suitcases containing family necessities and to set aside a box or bag containing games or toys to entertain the children during the trip. This is the time to get rid of all flammable or explosive substances you have around the house or garage. You may want to keep a list to enable you to replace these.

A day or two before the move, things will inevitably start getting a bit hectic. You should finish packing, defrost the refrigerator and freezer (let them air out for at least twenty-four hours), and remove any breakable or spillable items from drawers. It's fine to leave clothing or other light items in drawers, but heavy items make it tough on both the movers and the drawers. If you have a power mower or some other piece of machinery, drain the fuel and the oil out of it. If you must move any container with liquid in it, be sure it's tightly covered and placed in a separate (preferably waterproof) package. If you spend your last night at home, plan for a moving-day breakfast that requires no preparation and can be eaten on paper plates (or at a local restaurant). Take down your curtains or draperies. But, as a rule, you needn't take beds apart or roll up rugs. Movers usually do this free of charge. Reconfirm your hotel reservations and check the tire pressure on your car's tires. The night before the move will probably be spent with friends or relatives or in a motel, since your home will probably have reached the point of uninhabitability.

Then comes moving day itself. The first thing to do is pray for the arrival of the van at a reasonable hour. Have a good breakfast, since some meals may be disrupted or eaten at unusual hours later in the day. It's usually a good idea to have someone watch the chidren at one location while you are on hand at the point of departure to direct things and answer the movers' questions. Make sure everything you own is inventoried, and check to see that the condition of your items is not mistaken on the inventory form. Check the bill of lading carefully: Be sure that all addresses are correct, that you have registered for all the insurance you need, and that you've given the mover an accurate phone number where you can be reached before delivery day. Be sure your traveling kit inclues a flashlight, sun glasses, a first aid kit, and any necessary baby items, such as diapers. Before you actually leave, check to be sure every nook and cranny (including every closet) is empty. Turn off the lights, if they haven't already been shut off. Leave the key with a responsible person at a prearranged location.

Sometime later—not too much later, if you're lucky—will come delivery day. An adult should be free to supervise the movers and to tell them where each item of furniture should go. Check the condition of everything as it's delivered, and make written notations of any damage, as described earlier. Give the children tasks to do, such as unpacking their toys or helping to clean up. If you haven't already done so, phone utility companies to make arrangements for service. Don't try to do too much the first day. The long business of settling in and rearranging your new home is bound to take some time. But, as we said earlier, do take some time to examine fragile items in boxes to make sure they're okay.

If the movers have done all the packing, they're responsible for any breakage that occurs. If you've packed some boxes yourself, the movers aren't responsible for damage unless the boxes themselves have been harmed. But don't let that discourage you from doing your own packing. You can save a lot of money by doing it. In fact, it's one of the few places where you *can* save on a move, since most of the basic charge is fixed according to weight and distance. And you needn't fear breakage of items you've packed yourself if you use a lot of padding and follow some simple rules. Pack books upright, and alternate them so that the binding of one book faces up, while that of its neighbor faces down. Use small cartons for books, so that no carton weighs more than 50 pounds. Plates and phonograph records should also be packed on their edges. The chances of breakage are much greater if they're flat.

Very fragile items, like mirrors and glass table tops, should probably be left for the movers to pack. You can pack glassware yourself, though, if you want. Wrap it carefully in paper and place each glass or cup on its rim (upside-down) in a carton, with crumpled newspaper for padding between items. Be sure the carton is packed tight and that nothing rattles. If you do hear a rattle, count to ten and pack the whole carton over again. When using newspaper for packing, remember that it's best used only as outer wrapping. If you use it to wrap an item directly, you always run the risk that ink will come off and leave a stubborn smudge.

Cartons can be obtained from the mover, as can sealing tape. But you have to pay for them, and the charge usually isn't particularly modest. So, for at least some of your packing boxes, consider using boxes that are discarded by local merchants. Liquor boxes, because they're strong, are particularly suitable. Be sure to select ones that still have lids, so they can be sealed And when you're packing yourself, be sure to mark each box with the name of the room where the contents will go in the new house and with some indication of the contents. For example: "toys for baby's room" or "glasses for dining room." This practice will save the movers time in unloading, save you time in unpacking, and help you locate vital items quickly.

Despite all the thoughts you've absorbed from this chapter on making your move go as smoothly as possible, things may *still* go wrong. If they do, thre are two agencies that can help, in most states. The first to try is a local office of the Interstate Commerce Commission. The ICC has offices in eighty-two major cities around the country. If that fails, try your state consumer protection agency (listed in the appendix at the back of this book). That agency should be able to help you or steer you to someone who can.

TRANS-PORTATION

8

Flying on a Down-to-Earth Budget

There's nothing so exhilarating, if you're in the proper mood, as the roar of a jet engine and the smooth feeling of a plane lifting off the ground. For many travelers, that exhilaration persists as the plane zooms over awesome clouds and lands them safely, and on time, at their destination. For other travelers, however, the exilaration is muddied by other emotions, ranging from annoyance to disgust. Lateness, bumping from flights, baggage mishandling, and ticket overcharges are some of the ills that spoil the friendly skies of any airline for those passengers affected by them. This chapter won't make your plane land on time. It won't necessarily keep your luggage from ending up in Kalamazoo. But it will tell you some of your rights as an air traveler and give you some hints that may help you avoid problems—or win compensation for any mishaps that befall you.

In an average week, regularly scheduled airlines in this country carry three and a half million passengers. The average trip is 800 miles. More than 75 per cent of travelers going from one city to another on common carriers go by airplane. So air travel affects plenty of people. If it hasn't already affected you, it probably will. Let's start out with a few basic questions about this popular form of transportation. The way you answer them will show how experienced—and how savvy—an air traveler you already are.

123

CSK Quiz

1. True or false: Airlines can and do advertise low airfares that do not exist.
2. Travel agents must be licensed in order to do business.
3. The airfares posted by the airlines with the Civil Aeronautics Board are almost all the same.

Now let's take a look at the answers. Number 1 is true. Airlines can advertise airfares that don't exist. In fact, three large airlines recently advertised a reduced fare from New York to Miami. Unfortunately, the fare had not yet been approved by the Civil Aeronautics Board (CAB), the federal agency that must approve all interstate airfares. As it turned out, the CAB rejected the proposed fares. Meanwhile, tickets had already been sold on the basis of the low fares advertised. When the passengers arrived at the airports for their flights they were charged extra—up to $60 extra— for their tickets. This was not an isolated incident. So if you see an enticing ad for a very low airfare, look for some fine print. Somewhere in the ad (and you may need a magnifying glass to find it), you may find the words, "pending CAB approval." If you want to be ultra-cautious, ask the airline whenever you buy tickets whether the fare has been approved by the CAB. (Of course, this precaution doesn't apply if you've already flown the same route before for the same fare.)

Incidentally, the CAB has a rule that states you must pay the fare in effect the day you fly—not the day you bought your ticket. If you buy a ticket in April for a flight in June and prices go up in the interim, you'll be charged extra at the gate. By the same token, if fares have gone down, you should get a refund.

Number 2 is false. There is no licensing or testing of travel agents, so anyone can claim to be an agent. In fact, a Baltimore woman calling herself an agent collected thousands of dollars from unsuspecting consumers for nonexistent tours of Greece. Before you put your faith, and your vacation, in a travel agent's hands, you should check that person out as much as possible. Find out if he or she is a member of the American Society of

Travel Agents, the industry's professional organization. Check with the Better Business Bureau in your area and with the consumer protection agency in your state (see Appendix) to see if there have been many complaints lodged against the agent or the agent's firm. Most are reputable and honest, but it's worth taking precautions to avoid the ones who aren't.

Number 3 is true. The rates posted with the CAB are almost all the same for flights between the same cities. The only exception is with joint fares, which we'll talk about a little later. This doesn't mean, though, that the price you'd be charged for a trip will always be the same. Far from it. The fare structure is very complicated, and it's not unusual to call different airlines and get different prices. Sometimes you'll even get different prices from different ticket agents at the same airline. Buying an airline ticket is not necessarily simple. It can be almost as complicated as itemizing deductions on your tax return. There are so many special fares that even the agents have trouble keeping track of them. For example, there are some 113 different round trip fares between Baltimore and Miami. Some of them are affinity group; Tuesday through Thursday daytime; Tuesday through Thursday night; weekend daytime; weekend night; accompanying spouse; accompanying member of family (which breaks down further by age); first class; coach; "Discover America;" "Visit U.S.A.;" military reserved; military standby; in season; out of season; winter group inclusive tour—you get the idea. With such a complicated fare structure, overcharges arre not surprising. (Incidentally, the CAB is working on persuading the airlines to get rid of a large number of these special fares.)

In May 1972 *Consumer Reports* published the results of a survey it had conducted. Buying thirty-one tickets, investigators from the magazine found they were overcharged twenty times. The overcharges averaged $12. In January 1973 the magazine published the results of another survey. Again, overcharges were documented. We asked a CAB official if overcharging is common. He said no. We then asked if it was rare. The answer; "No, it's not rare by any stretch of the imagination." So, by the CAB's own admission, that puts the incidence of overcharging somewhere between rare and common.

To avoid being overcharged, you should understand something about the Byzantine workings of the airfare structure. To begin with, there is such a thing as a tariff book. It contains published fares. But not all fares are published. For example, there is no direct flight or published fare from Baltimore to Chattanooga, Tennessee. In order to tell you the fare, an agent would have to use what might be called the "nearest-farther-point principle." That principle states that the fare charged to take you to one destination cannot be greater than the *published* fare for the nearest point beyond that destination. In this example, the agent would have to find the nearest point beyond Chattanooga for which there *is* a published fare—in this case Huntsville, Alabama. The published fare from Baltimore to Huntsville in 1973 was $54. That means that (in 1973) $54 was also the highest legal fare to Chattanooga.

The nearest-farther-point principle is an official part of the regulations under which airlines operate. But some ticket agents don't really understand it. Others simply forget it when they're rushed. And perhaps some eager-beaver ticket agents ignore it, thinking that bringing in extra revenue for the company will win them favor. What agents under any of theses circumstances do is figure the fare point to point. In the example used here, they take the fare from Baltimore to Atlanta ($50), and the fare from Atlanta to Chattanooga ($19) and add them together. That's the route you'd actually fly, but that's not the way you should be charged. You'll note that the point-to-point fare of $69 is a full $15 more than the highest legal fare you should be charged.

Are you ready for another complication? Ticket agents using the point-to-point method are supposed to deduct $4 from the price of the ticket resulting from their calculation. But one airline official told us that this deduction, too, is often forgotten. In the example given, even deducting $4 would still have left the point-to-point fare $11 higher than the nearest-farther-point principle permits. Remember, you have a right to demand that the fare be calculated according to the nearest-farther-point principle and to be charged no more than the fare to the nearest farther point.

Another trick in the airfare game involves joint fares. Most big airlines have arrangements with small feeder airlines for joint fares to smaller cities. For example, if you were flying from Baltimore to Flint, Michigan, the cheapest and fastest way to go is to use the joint fare offered by United Air Lines and North Central Airlines. You'd fly United to Detroit and North Central to Flint, paying one fare for the package. However, you could do that only if you knew you could—and probably wouldn't know it unless the ticket agent told you. To find this joint fare, the agent has to do some digging in the joint fare tariff list. Agents don't always do that. So you could end up paying more—and going miles out of your way if the agent routed you through another city. So, if you fly a route that involves a connecting flight, *ask* the agent if there is a joint fare published for that route. It may save you some money.

There's one more wrinkle you should know about. It's called the "fictitious point" or the "hidden city." We surveyed a trip from Washington, D.C., to San Juan, Puerto Rico, and on to Montego Bay, Jamaica, then back to Washington. As it turned out, the lowest possible fare involved a hidden city or fictitious point, namely Port-au-Prince, Haiti. You see, there is a published fare in the tariff books to Port-au-Prince. This fare allows stops in San Juan and Montego Bay. Believe it or not, it does *not* require that you ever go to Port-au-Prince. A good agent would construct the fare using Port-au-Prince as a hidden or fictitious city and would charge $188. That's far below the point-to-point fare, which is the sum of the fares for the individual legs of the trip. The prices quoted to us ranged from $260 to $348. If we had simply accepted what the ticket agent offered, we would have paid an overcharge of as much as $160 compared with the most economical fare available. The moral: If you're flying a route that's the least bit complicated, ask if the fare can be constructed using a hidden city for the lowest possible cost.

To sum up, the first question to ask when buying a ticket is whether the fare is published. Second, would it be cheaper using the nearest-farther-point principle? Third, is there a joint fare published? Fourth, can the fare be constructed using a hidden city? Asking these questions can save you quite a bit of money.

And if you don't ask them, don't count on the ticket agent to take care of things for you. It's not necessarily the agent's fault either. John Galloway, a transportation specialist for Consumers Union, told Consumer Survival Kit that many of the agents are inadequately trained. Said Galloway: "The airlines emphasize the wrong things. Eastern Airlines, for example. has a very elaborate dress code for employees. It goes into such things as the number of rings that a woman agent may wear, the color of her earrings, the type of slip, the color of her lingerie (beige or nude). . . . Agents are inspected three times a month for their personal appearance, but there is no program to inspect the tickets that they write."

Galloway believes the airlines could make greater use of their computer facilities in seeing that consumers get the lowest fare for which they qualify. "United Air Lines, for example, has a very elaborate, sophisticated computer," he notes. "According to a recent full-page ad in the *New York Times*, their computer can remember 'where you are going, that you can't eat salt, and that your pet poodle detests being called poochie.' That's all very nice, but that computer can't tell you the fare from New York to Dubuque, Iowa."

Another place where airlines have drawn criticism is with regard to the practice of "bumping." For the uninitiated, "bumping" has nothing to do with roller derby, or even with unexpected air turbulence. It's the practice of denying a seat to a person who holds a confirmed reservation. Why would an airline do such a thing? Well, it works this way. Suppose a plane has 100 seats. The airline may sell 120 tickets, because they know some people are going to make reservations and not show up. It's the airline's way of protecting itself. But of course the hitch comes if more than 100 people show up. Then a game of musical chairs, airline style, ensues. Up to twenty people have to be told they've been bumped off of the flight. In theory, the first people bumped are airline employees riding on greatly reduced fares. After that, people are to be bumped on the basis of the validation date on their ticket. The later you validate, the greater the chance of your being bumped. But in practice, one agent told us, people are often bumped on the basis of how much trouble the airline employees think they will cause. If you look like the type to take it lying down, you're more likely to be bumped. But if you look like the type to make a stink, they'll think twice. If you're inherently a gentle person, perhaps the best you can do to protect your own interests is to *look* mean. It may help.

If you do get bumped, you have certain rights. First of all, the airline is obligated to help you make other arrangements to reach your destination. If they get you there within two hours of your originally scheduled arrival time, they have no further responsibility. But if they can't, they must give you compensation—the official term for it is "denied boarding compensation." This equals the cost of your ticket, up to $200, plus your original ticket back. The original ticket can be used at a later time or turned in for a cash refund. So you can get double your money back, if the original ticket cost $200 or less. Or you can get a monetary penalty, plus a substitute flight. The choice is yours. If you're bumped and can't get to your destination within two hours of your original flight, you should *demand* your denied boarding compensation.

You also have rights if your flight is delayed for more than four hours. You should be given meals during normal eating hours, hotel accommodations if the delay occurs during normal sleeping hours, and transportation to the hotel. If for any reason an airline refuses you these amenities, ask to see its tariff book. By law, they must let you see it. Look under "delayed flights" and see what they are legally obligated to do for you. Then demand that they do it.

Some 83,000 passengers were bumped in 1973. Long flight delays presumably affected more than that. But probably the most commonly heard gripe from consumers when it comes to airlines is mishandling of luggage. With millions of pieces of luggage being flown every week, it's not surprising that some get lost or banged up. But it is infuriating if it happens to you. There are some ways you can help prevent such a disaster from occurring. First of all, travel as light as possible. If you can get by with a small suitcase that can be carried aboard and stored under a seat, you're ahead of the game. (Carrying only on-board luggage also saves you time that would otherwise be spent at the baggage claim area.) If you have a large bag, you'll have to check it, of course. But remember that the farther you are from the plane when you check in, the more people must handle your bags, and the more chance for error. If you check your bags at the curb, more people will handle them than if you check in at the counter. And if you check in your baggage at the gate, it goes directly on board. So, if the airline will allow it, checking in at the gate is usually the safest course of all. Some people are reluctant to check in at the gate because they have the notion their bags will sit by the gate and get water all over them if it's raining. The fear has some validity, but the truth is that your bags stand a chance of getting wet on a rainy day no matter where you check them.

Your luggage is less likely to wind up on the other side of the continent from you if you get to the airport reasonably early and avoid split-second connections between flights. Like anyone else, baggage handlers make more mistakes when they're rushed than at other times. Do check to make sure the tags put on your luggage show your correct destination. If you don't know the abbreviation used on the tags, don't be shy—ask. And do remove any old tags from your luggage. If you want to save them as souvenirs, keep them in your coat pockets until you get safely home.

The CAB suggests that you put your name, address, and telephone number on both the outside and the inside of your luggage. That way, if the outside label should be detached or damaged, airline personnel could identify it from the inside label. Some people are reluctant to use identifying tags for fear burglars will obtain their address and burglarize their house while it's unoccupied. That's not unheard of, but it's a less likely risk than that your luggage will be misplaced. If you're worried about burglars, you can use a tag that can't be read at a glance—one that needs to be unfolded to be read, for example.

To avoid breakage, don't pack your bags too full. That puts pressure on the contents. And airlines are reluctant to pay for damage they believe was caused by a passenger's overstuffing his luggage. Don't pack glass or other fragile items. They aren't covered by the airlines' insurance policies, and the airlines won't reimburse you if they break. As a rule, soft-sided luggage lasts better and does just as good a job of protecting contents as the more expensive rigid-sided kind.

If a bag of yours is lost or damaged, report it immediately. Don't wait around at a deserted baggage claim area hoping your bag will straggle in. If you report a missing bag promptly, a search of the plane can be made before it takes off again. If your bag still doesn't show up, or if it's damaged, or if its contents are damaged, file a complaint *immediately.* Airlines are much more likely to pay a claim if it's filed promptly after the loss or damage is discovered. Don't just make an oral complaint; make sure you fill out an official loss or damage report. Don't give anyone your baggage check. Hold onto it until you get either your baggage or your compensation for it. If you have to buy or rent clothes or other items to make do until your missing luggage is located, present the airline with a bill for the tab. If you're going to do this, it would be wise to read the airline's staff tariff book to see what they're legally obliged to do for you.

An airline's total liability for missing luggage is limited to $500 per passenger. That means $500 is the most you're likely to get on any claim, no matter how many of your bags were lost. If you know the belongings in your baggage are worth more than that, you can buy extra insurance from the airline before you check the bags. The usual cost for this extra insurance is 10 cents for each $100 of insurance. Needless to say, if you're going to need extra insurance, you don't want to show up at the airport at the last minute. Give yourself plenty of time.

A last, and very important, precaution: Never carry anything that's absolutely vital to you in a suitcase you're going to check. Medicines, eyeglasses, manuscripts you've been working on for months, million-dollar contracts . . . all these belong in your carry-on luggage.

While we're in the area of the baggage compartment, let's consider some living creatures who ride there—pets. According to Galloway, the death of pets in the cargo holds of planes is an "all-too-frequent" occurrence. Exact figures are unavailable, because the airlines don't keep them. Some recent estimates have suggested that about 300 pets a year die in planes, but Galloway believes that is a conservative estimate. "There's a problem with temperature," he says, "there's a problem with lack of oxygen, and sometimes there's a problem with just the way these animals are handled. The hold *is* pressurized. If it weren't pressurized, your shaving cream would go all over your suitcase. But the oxygen is limited. It's limited in order that, if a fire starts, the fire would die for lack of oxygen. The problem is that there are animals that die for lack of oxygen—especially in a crowded baggage compartment where there are a number of animals."

Another issue that has concerned Galloway, and Consumers Union, is the pricing of package tours. These are tours in which a plane fare is lumped in with other goods or services, such as a hotel room, car rental, and tickets for entertainment. The trouble with package tours, from the consumer's point of view, is that they're difficult to evaluate. To tell whether a package deal is economical or not, you have to know the separate value of each component going into the package. Consumers Union performed such a breakdown for an Eastern Airlines vacation package tour to Disneyland. The result, published in *Consumer Reports* in its January 1973 issue, was that the package cost $175 more than the separate costs of the parts (for a family of four staying at Disneyland one week. To do that kind of detailed evaluation would require more time and effort than most people have available. But you can do roughly the same thing on your own by consulting with a travel agent and doing some checking yourself. Really, you *have* to do it on your own; the airlines certainly won't do it for you. Sometimes a package tour turns out to be a good deal, sometimes not.

A deal on which you're more likely to save money is the charter flight. A charter flight is set up to carry a specific group of people to one destination—or a series of them—on a one-time basis. Such flights are to be distinguished from regularly scheduled flights; in fact, they're often flown by non-scheduled airlines. It used to be that only a so-called affinity group could book a charter flight. An affinity group is a club, union, or business or other organization that exists for some definite reason other than obtaining cheap air fares. Naturally, when the law required affinity groups for charter flights, some quick-forming and quick-dissolving affinity groups sprang up. The "affinity" of some of them was rather difficult to see.

Now, affinity group charter flights are still permitted, but affinity is not required. Instead, there's a new classification, called a Travel Group Charter. It means just what it sounds like: The group is formed for the sole purpose of travel. Any travel agent or qualified broker can reserve forty or more plane seats. Anyone can fly on the charter who signs up ninety days before the flight and pays a 25 per cent deposit. You don't have to belong to any special group or sign up for any special tour after you land. But you must agree to stay at your destination for at least seven days before returning. If your destination's outside North America, you must stay there for at least ten days.

You may wonder what happens if you book space on a charter flight and then change your mind. Well, if what changes your mind is illness, you can get your deposit back—provided it's still forty-five days before the plane is scheduled to leave, and provided you get a statement from your doctor that you're too ill to travel. Otherwise, you must find someone else to take the seat or forfeit your deposit.

One curse of charter flight operations in years past was the (forgive the pun) fly-by-night operator. Some of these fast-buck artists would take people's money for a nonexistent charter flight, then disappear. Or they would arrange transportation out of the country for their victims, but not back. Thousands of American students were stranded in Europe one recent summer as the result of such a scheme. One thing you should know about charter operations is that reputable charter organizers book plane space first and then look for people to fill it. Merchants who do it the other way around are undependable at best, according to the CAB. So be suspicious if your charter organizer can't tell you what airline you'll be flying, for both the outgoing and the return legs of the trip. You can protect yourself against illegal charter schemes by checking with a reputable travel agent or with the Civil Aeronautics Board to make sure the charter flight broker you're dealing with is not about to vanish. In addition, travel group operators must now post a bond. So, assuming the broker was legitimate you always get your money back if the trip doesn't happen.

Travel group charters are usually the cheapest way to fly. You can find out about them through a travel agent or by looking at ads in newspapers and magazines. Of course, they're suitable only for trips planned long in advance, which usually means vacation trips. But then, vacation flights are a good place to save money, since the savings on the plane tickets might enable you to vacation in a more exotic locale than you otherwise would. Perhaps the suggestions elsewhere in this chapter will have saved you a little extra cash you can use to enjoy yourself.

Despite the tips you've encountered here, you might still fall prey to some of the less exhilarating aspects of air travel. If you do, there are ways of getting help after the fact. If you've returned from a complicated trip and you think you may have been overcharged, write to the airline involved, enclosing a photocopy of your ticket. They'll research it carefully—probably a lot more carefully than the agent who sold you the ticket. If you have it coming, they'll return the overcharge.

In general, any complaint you have should be filed with the airline and—if you don't get satisfaction within a reasonable time—the Civil Aeronautics Board. The CAB makes a public record of complaints and can put pressure on the airlines to correct questionable practices. Write the CAB at this address:

> Office of Consumer Affairs
> Civil Aeronautics Board
> Washington, D.C. 20428

Checklist for Air Travelers

1. How to Get the Best Fare
   A. Ask about special fares to which you may be entitled.
   B. Make sure fare is CAB-approved, if the fare is recently posted.
   C. For connecting flights, be sure ticket agent uses the nearest-farther-point principle.

D. Look for joint fares on connecting flights.
E. When flying complicated routes, see if fare can be cut by using a "hidden city."
F. Check the airline's tariff book to be sure you're being charged the correct fare.
G. Consider charter flights for vacations.

2. What to Do if Things Go Wrong
   A. If you're bumped from a flight, you're entitled to up to $200, plus your ticket back (to be used later or cashed in).
   B. If your flight's delayed more than four hours, you're entitled to meals and possibly lodging.
   C. If your luggage is lost, you're entitled to at least $500 compensation per bag.

3. How to Protect Your Luggage
   A. Use carry-on bags when possible.
   B. Check bags as close to gate as possible.
   C. Avoid split-second connections.
   D. Remove old tags and check new ones.
   E. Put your name and address on your bags.
   F. Don't pack bags too full.
   G. Report missing baggage immediately.

9

Buying a New Car

Putting Yourself in the Driver's Seat

Americans, it is often said, are wedded to their cars. That marriage, it seems, is truly a "for better or for worse" situation. Often one party or the other gets grumpy or acts up. Signs of strain can be seen in the fact that complaints about automobiles consistently rank number one among those received by state and local consumer protection offices. Yet Americans and their cars go on living together.

Perhaps the marriages would be happier, if buyers took more care in selecting their mates to begin with. This chapter is devoted to helping you pick out a new car. Chapter 10 is devoted to helping you pick a used car. If you feel extra-conscientious, you may want to read both chapters. Some used-car tips may help you in buying a new car, and vice versa.

As you approach the purchase of a new car, there are three considerations of great importance to you. First, and paramount, is *safety*. Without that, all other considerations are irrelevant. Second is getting the best possible *price* on the car. A smart car buyer can pay hundreds of dollars less for the same vehicle than an uninformed shopper would pay. Third is the area of *warranties*. You want a warranty that will really back up the car's performance, and a dealer who will really back up the warranty.

Let's consider safety first. To begin our discussion, let's assess how much you already know about safety considerations in new-car buying.

CSK Quiz

1. True or false: It's a good idea to order tinted windshields because they improve visibility.
2. True or false: A light-colored car is safer than a dark-colored one.
3. True or False: The more powerful the engine, the safer a car will be in emergency situations.

Number 1 is false. Far from improving visibility, tinted windshields dramatically decrease it. The combination of tinting and the usual 60-degree tilt of the windshield reduces incoming light by 35 per cent. At dusk or after dark, this reduction could make a big difference in how much you actually see.

Number 2 is true. Light-colored cars are considered safer than dark ones because they're easier to see. If you're safety-conscious, you'll avoid red and black models. The easiest colors to see are cream, yellow, and white. Of course, if you want your car to look clean, those very light colors will require frequent washings. But that might be deemed a small price to pay for safety. As a compromise, if the prospect of constant pail and suds seems too forbidding, you can always consider an intermediate-colored car.

Number 3 is false. A more powerful engine will not necessarily give you a margin of safety in an emergency. In fact, the opposite is often true. According to the Center for Auto Safety (a branch of the Ralph Nader organization), a car with too much extra power tends to be unstable and hard to control in emergency situations. The Center suggests this rule of thumb: Your car should have 70 horsepower for every 1,000 pounds of body weight. (If you're in doubt, the dealer can tell you both the weight and the horsepower.) Following this rule is likely to give you an extra bonus, since smaller engines guzzle less gasoline.

If you answered all three questions correctly, you've got a good start. Here are some additional safety considerations to keep in mind when you're test-driving what may become your new car. Check the visibility from the driver's seat. Can you see a small child standing close to any part of the car? Is there any distortion in the windows? How is the visibility in strong sunlight? Watch out for any reflections or glare that could impair your ability to see. And check the mirrors. The outside mirror should be far enough forward so you don't have to turn your head very far to see it. The inside mirror shouldn't obstruct your forward vision.

While you're sitting in the driver's seat, with your seat belt fastened, check the operating controls. You should be able to reach them all comfortably and see them easily day or night.

When you test-drive the car, test the brakes hard. They should be able to bring the car to a controlled stop from high speeds. Technically, braking horsepower should be greater than engine horsepower, so that theoretically you should be able to stop the car with the accelerator stuck on the floor. But don't try it. Incidentally, experts say that disc brakes are frequently a valuable option.

If the car has power steering, here's a good test to use: In an empty parking lot, coast the car, then shut off the engine and try to maneuver. You should be able to make emergency maneuvers with the engine stalled.

According to some safety experts, the fastback design may not be a better idea. It creates two large blind spots at the panels flanking the rear window. Also, the back window of a fastback easily collects snow, dirt, and dust. On the other hand, a truly better idea is a rear window defroster to improve visibility. It's well worth the price, both for safety and for ease of driving.

Some experts think the suspension systems of most new cars are inadequate. You may want to consider asking for heavy duty shock absorbers and springs, and an anti-sway bar. These options are designed to give you better emergency handling.

Consumers today, thanks partly to the consciousness-raising done by people like Ralph Nader, have become more safety-conscious than they used to be. Many have come to realize that safety involves not only the choice they make at the dealer's, but the choices they make as citizens too. There are all kinds of innovations on the horizon that could help make cars safer. According to Lowell Dodge, who heads the Center for Auto Safety, these include air bags (to take the place of seat belts) and, farther in the future, radar-controlled brakes. A radar brake system would slow the car if an object was sited ahead, even if the driver had let his attention lapse or fallen asleep at the wheel. Such futuristic devices cost money, of course. So long as they are available only as options, they will cost so much money as to be prohibitive for most motorists. If safety features such as air bags are mass-produced as standard equipment, however, the cost goes down. Whether the auto-makers decide to opt for mass production, however, depends to a great extent on how strong is the public demand for safer cars.

One figure that's been tossed around is that making cars safer has already inflated the cost of the average vehicle by $500 in recent years. That figure is "a fiction," according to Lowell Dodge. The auto industry has encouraged use of the $500 figure, he says, in order to put the rising price tag of cars in a favorable light. But according to Dodge, $500 "is closer to the price of annual styling changes. If the manufacturers would cut down on that frivolous aspect and put that money instead into safety and emissions, they could deliver to us safe, nonpolluting cars for roughly the same cost we now pay."

After safety, the consideration probably uppermost in your mind as a buyer is getting the best possible price on your new car. Price bargaining on a car is an advanced exercise in psychological warfare. In terms of intrigue and negotiation tactics, it should bring out the Henry Kissinger in all of us.

A proper car-buying strategy begins with a few diplomatic feelers. Put them out as you shop around and get to know the market. Get prices for comparable models (all equipped with the same options, of course) from several different dealers. Like much intelligence work, this isn't glamorous. But it pays off in hard, useful information. You need no special training. Just walk into the dealerships and start asking questions.

Timing is also important. If you can arrange to do your shopping between November and March, you'll have an upper hand in the bargaining. Dealers often have trouble meeting sales quotas in those winter months, so you catch them at their weakest. Another vulnerable time is the end of the model year, in late summer. Many dealers are in a hurry to make room for the new models coming out in September. So you may be able to bargain down the price on the car you want.

When you get down to serious negotiation, it helps if you have an idea of what the car cost the dealer. A special formula devised by Consumers Union will give you a pretty good idea. Take the sticker price of the car. Let's say it's $5,000. Subtract the transportation charge, which is indicated on the sticker. It will be around $150. So that leaves $4,850. Now take a percentage of this number. For a full-sized car, the percentage is 78 per cent; for an intermediate car it's 81.5 per cent; and for a compact its 85 per cent. Let's say the car in our example is full-sized. You would multiply $4,850 by .78 and get $3,783. Now you add the transportation cost back, and you have roughly the dealer's cost for the car. Here it's $3,933. That means the dealer has marked up the car by $1,067. Out of that markup he must pay the rent on his building, the salaries of his salesmen and mechanics, and other expenses—plus make a profit. So you certainly aren't going to get $1,000 off the sticker price. But you can see that there's room for bargaining. Don't be afraid to bargain hard. And don't be in a big hurry to buy. If the salesman can see you're willing to walk out of the showroom if you don't get the right price, he'll be much more accommodating. Cars, like cameras, are normally sold at a discount from the list price. A recent study showed that only eighteen of every hundred car buyers pay anything approximating the sticker price. How much below that you can go depends on your bargaining skill.

Watch out for a tactic called "close and bump." With this tactic, you and the salesman agree on a price. Then the salesman leaves the room, and you talk to the manager to sign the necessary papers. The manager is astounded that the salesman let you off so easily. Why, he would go broke if he sold cars at that price! Just to be a good guy, though, he'll let you have the car for a mere $100 more than you and the salesman had agreed upon.

If you're confronted by a close and bump tactic, hold firm to the price the salesman had agreed to. Most salesmen have been carefully instructed as to the lowest price they can let a car go for. It's highly unlikely that your salesman will have made a genuine mistake. So, if the manager won't honor the agreement you and the salesman have struck, leave the showroom. Don't be too surprised, though, if the manager stops you as you're walking out the door and relents.

A variation of the close and bump scheme is the padding of the sales tab by the last-minute addition of extras. Undercoating and a "protective" paint job are extras commonly tacked on as an apparent afterthought. If you can obtain the dealer's preparation checklist, you may find that he has already performed these services.

Like any good negotiator, you should keep one ace up your sleeve. Don't tell the salesman if you're going to pay cash for the car. Better yet, let him think you're going to finance it through the dealer. In some cases he'll quote you a lower price if he thinks you plan to use his financing, because he knows the interest charges will more than make up for what he loses on the initial price. After you get the final price in writing, calmly inform him that you plan to pay cash.

If you *do* finance the car, don't do it through the dealer if you can avoid it. You can save hundreds of dollars by financing through a bank or a credit union, institutions that offer car loans at much lower interest rates than dealers do. A particularly good alternative is a passbook loan from the savings institution where you keep your personal savings account. Don't go to a small loan company unless you have to. You won't do any better there than at the dealer's, and you may well do worse.

One more way to keep down the price of your new car is to avoid unnecessary options. We've suggested that some options, such as a rear window defroster, an improved suspension system, and disc brakes, deserve consideration because of their safety value. But if you want to hold down the cost of your car, look at each suggested option with a skeptical eye. Options add considerably to a car's cost. They can also add to repair bills. According to *Consumer Reports,* power windows and power antennas have a high repair rate. Eyelid-type headlight covers often stick, and automatic speed controls are unreliable. The simpler the car, the fewer the things that can go wrong.

Talking about repairs brings us to the third major area of concern to you as a new car buyer—the warranty. Warranties are important because they determine who will pay for repairs during the car's break-in period, you or the dealer. It's not exactly an academic question. In fact, the average new 1973 car tested by Consumers Union had nineteen defects *after* delivery (believe it or not, that was an improvement on the average of thirty-six defects found in new 1971 cars).

You might think that the warranty would naturally cover any such defects. But it won't necessarily. A warranty covers whatever it *says* it covers. It's true that a car should perform normal automotive services, just as a toaster should toast bread. You don't even need a written warranty to tell you that. A common-law doctrine known as the "implied warranty of merchantability" says that any product you buy can be expected to be fit for its intended use. If it's not, you take it back and get another one. There's no reason why a new car shouldn't come under this doctrine, as well as any other product.

Unfortunately, car makers (like the makers of some other products) explicitly *disclaim* this implied warranty. If you look carefully at your car warranty, you'll probably find some wording like this: "To the extent allowed by law, this warranty is in place of all other warranties, express or implied, including any implied warranty of merchantability or fitness." And your warranty probably goes on to say, "Loss of use of the vehicle, loss of time, inconvenicence, commercial loss or consequential damages are not covered by this warranty." So your warranty takes from you as much as it gives to you.

There is a bit of good news, though. In at least two states, Maryland and Massachusetts, recent laws have held that sellers (including automobile dealers) *cannot* disclaim the implied warranty of merchantability. Consumers can hope that other states will enact similar enlightened legislation.

Despite the common disclaimers, car warranties do cover a large number of specified defects. Most warranties promise that the company will repair defects involving workmanship or materials for a set period of time. That period is usually twelve months or the time it takes you to drive 12,000 miles, whichever comes first. Recently there have been some improvements in warranties. The American Motors Buyer Protection Plan was a pioneering step in the right direction. It is more comprehensive than most warranties and offers to pay for the car owner's lodging if he's stranded more than 100 miles from home because of a breakdown in the car. The Ford Motor Company now guarantees that service performed by its dealers will keep the problem that was treated from recurring for at least 4,000 miles or ninety days. And Chrysler Corporation's warranty now covers twelve months, regardless of the mileage driven. Competition may well bring further improvements in warranties.

The problem for the consumer is to translate the warranty's promises from theory into reality. Somehow, it's a long distance to travel from some words written on a piece of paper to satisfactory repairs done in the dealer's garage. Sometimes dealers have so much warranty work that their repairmen tend to get fast and sloppy in their work. And, with few exceptions, dealers get less money from the auto maker for warranty work than they would get from you for making the same repairs on a nonwarranty basis. The result: Dealer-run repair shops have an economic incentive to give preference to lucrative repairs and to slack off on warranty-covered repairs.

Some dealers have been known to duck warranty work altogether. One way to do this is to give the car what's called the "sunshine treatment." That means the car is left out on the lot all day and returned to the owner untouched. Another technique is to claim that the malfunction is the result of abuse and is therefore not covered by the warranty. This tactic is often used against male drivers under twenty-five. All in all, it's not a pretty picture for the person who wants to use his rights under the warranty. But if you're persistent enough, you may well get the repairs done, and done right.

If you have a complaint about your car, whether it's under warranty, or not, and you're not getting satisfaction from the dealer, your next step, usually, is to turn to the district representative of the manufacturer. You can normally get the manufacturer's rep's name from the dealer. Sometimes the manufacturer will put a little bit of pressure on the dealer in the interest of keeping customers happy. Sometimes the manufacturer's rep will just tell you that the dispute is between you and the dealer, and leave the two of you to fight it out.

If that happens, you'll probably need help from your state or local consumer protection agency. Or you might be able to get help from one of the recently formed organizations known as AutoCAPs. The initials CAP stand for Consumer Action Panel. At least seven AutoCAPs now exist around the country. They've been set up by the National Automobile Dealers Association and work through informal panels of dealers and consumer representatives who hear and try to resolve consumer complaints. The panel may well ask you for documentation of your complaint, so save all letters, receipts and other documents that pertain to your case. A list of AutoCAPs, arranged alphabetically by location, appears below.

AutoCAPs

AutoCAPs are sponsored by car dealers associations in the following localities:

Cleveland area
  Cleveland Automobile Dealers Association
  310 Lakeside Ave., NW
  Cleveland, Ohio 44113
Denver area
  Metropolitan Denver Automobile Dealers Association
  Suite 101, 70 W. 6th Ave.
  Denver, Colorado 80204
Oregon
  Oregon Automobile Dealers Association
  Box 14460
  Portland, Oregon 97214

Orlando, Fla., area
  Orlando Automobiles & Truck Dealers
  Suite 221, 1350 Orange Ave.
  Winter Park, Florida 32789
Pennsylvania
  Pennsylvania Automotive Association
  Box 2955
  Harrisburg, Pennsylvania 17105
Utah
  Utah Automobile Dealers Association
  Box 1019
  Salt Lake City, Utah 84101
Washington, D.C., area
  Automotive Trade Association, National Capital Area
  Suite 505, 8401 Connecticut Ave.
  Chevy Chase, Maryland 20015

Of course, the best way to avoid the warranty hassle is to buy a car that's virtually defect-free. That takes some luck, as Consumers Union's experience indicates. But vigilance on your part will improve your chances. Do test-drive the car, and do use the checklist on page 146 as an aid in remembering features to notice.

In addition, the Center for Auto Safety recommends that you get a copy of the dealer preparation checklist. This checklist itemizes the things the dealer is supposed to do to make your car ready for use after it arrives at his showroom from the factory. (These are the things you pay for when you pay a "dealer prep" charge.) The list is supplied to the dealer by the manufacturer. Dealers vary as to how well they perform their preparation task. Some do it excellently, some do it halfheartedly; a few do it not at all, even though they charge you for it. Try to have the dealer sign the checklist, and carry it with you when you drive the car away. This tactic does two things for you. It gives you another list (besides ours) of features to check. And it puts you on stronger ground if something allegedly put in tip-top shape by the dealer should fall apart in the early months of the car's use.

Lowell Dodge also recommends that you check around the hood opening and door latches, looking for paint where you wouldn't normally expect to find it. That can be a sign that the car was delivered to the dealer in damaged condition and repaired or touched up by the dealer. There's nothing unethical about this on the dealer's part. But buying a previously damaged car is starting the game with one strike already against you.

If, despite your precautions, you do end up with a lemon, you would be wise to get a lawyer. You and the lawyer can check the law in your state and see if you can make use of the implied warranty of merchantability. Sometimes the very fact that you've retained a lawyer will make a dealer more cooperative. (If you're frightened by the high cost of hiring a lawyer, see page 77 for some tips on low-cost legal help.) For further thoughts on how to deal with a truly hopeless car, read *What to Do with Your Bad Car: An Action Manual for Lemon Owners*, by Ralph Nader, Lowell Dodge, and Ralf Hotchkiss. It's available in many libraries and bookstores.

The checklist below will remind you of some important points to consider when you're buying a new car. These include points of safety, drivability, and financing.

New-Car Checklist

1. The make, model, and year car I want would cost:
   $_____ at _____ (name of first dealership)
   $_____ at _____ (name of second dealership)
   $_____ at _____ (name of third dealership)
2. Visibility
   A. From the driver's seat, could you see a small child standing anywhere near the car?
   B. Is the windshield tinted?
   C. Is there any distortion in the windows?
   D. Is there a lot of glare in bright light?
   E. Are the inside and outside mirrors well-placed?
   F. Does car have rear window defroster?
3. Are all controls easy to reach from driver's seat, with safety belt fastened? Are controls clearly visible, day and night?
4. Do brakes bring car to controlled stop from high speeds?

5. Does power steering work with ignition off?
6. Does suspension system work well? (If not, consider heavy-duty shock absorbers and springs, and an anti-sway bar.)
7. Is the car adequately powered for its weight, but not excessively powered?
8. Will the dealer give you signed copy of his preparation checklist?
9. Is there paint in unusual places around hood opening or door latches, indicating car may have been damaged and repaired?
10. If you're financing the car, what is the Annual Percentage Rate for the loan quoted by:
    A. Your bank?____%.
    B. Another local bank? ____%.
    C. Your credit union, if you belong to one? ____%.
    D. The dealer? ____%.

10

Buying a Used Car

What to Watch for

The used-car dealer occupies a unique place in the American psyche. He is trusted less than the politician, revered less than the tax collector. "Would you buy a used car from this man?" has become a standard slang measurement of trust. And used-car dealers are said to be today's successors to the horse-traders of old. Why the used-car merchant occupies this particular niche in public esteem is hard to say. No doubt, our fear of being stuck with a lemon is part of the reason. But many people have been stuck with lemons through their other purchases: stocks, insurance policies, dishwashers, television sets . . . not to mention new cars. In no case is the vendor of these items tarred with such a broad brush as the used-car dealer. Perhaps the real key is that the workings of an automobile are a mystery to most people. They think there's a good chance that the used car they buy will turn out to have problems, but they have no earthly idea of how to check for these problems or prevent them. In this chapter we'll try to provide some ideas for doing just that.

It's worth bearing in mind, incidentally, that a used-car dealership is only one of three places where you can look for a used car. You can also buy from a private party or from a new-car dealer. A private seller could be a friend or relative or someone whose ad you see in the classified section of a newspaper. The chief advantage of buying from a private party is the likelihood of picking up a car for a low price. One disadvantage is that you have to fix up the car yourself or pay to have it done. If you're not too mechanically inclined, that can mean trouble. You also usually have to pay a private party in a lump sum, which is impractical for many buyers. And, of course, when you buy from a private party there's no warranty. If you *do* buy a car this way from someone you don't know well, be sure the car's not stolen or about to be repossessed by a finance company.

The other alternative to the used-car lot is the new-car dealer who sells the cars that have been traded in to him. His prices tend to be somewhat higher, but he usually sells only late model cars in good condition, so you have a good selection. And the key advantage is that he offers a warranty on the car that presumably will be backed up by his own service department. Especially if you're not mechanically inclined, this can be one of the best ways to buy.

But don't rule out the used-car dealer out of hand. His prices are reasonable. If you need financing and can't get it from a bank, he'll help you finance the purchase. At best he gives you a very limited warranty, though, so it's important that you check out the car's condition before you buy. For this reason, never buy a used car from a dealer (or a private party either) who won't let you take it for a test drive, have it examined by your own mechanic, and have it taken through a state inspection line if there is one in your area. These points can't be stressed too strongly. If anyone tells you that, because of "insurance factors" or some other reason, you can't drive the car you're going to buy, forget him, his car, and his deal immediately. The same goes for having the car looked at by an objective third party. Taking a car through a state inspection line can't always be done: In some states no inspection services are provided. But a seller who lets you do it should go up a notch in your book, and one who won't should be able to give a pretty good reason why not.

We'll talk in a minute about what to look for on a test drive. But first, why not test your knowledge of the used-car game with this quiz?

CSK Quiz

1. Multiple choice: The most expensive operating cost connected with a new car is:
   A. Insurance
   B. Gasoline
   C. Taxes
   D. Depreciation
2. True or false: A used-car dealer is legally required to furnish you with the name and address of the previous owner, if you ask for it.
3. True or false: The most important consideration in selecting a used car is mileage.
4. True or false: You should never pick out a used car in the rain.

Now let's look at the answers. The answer to the first question is D, depreciation. A new car loses about half its original value in two to three years. That's why a good used car can be such a bargain. And with today's swollen new-car price stickers, it's a bargain that might well be worth looking into.

Number 2 is false. A used-car dealer is not required to give you the name of the previous owner. However, some dealers will if you request it. And requesting it is usually a good idea. The former owner can tell you how the car was used and explain any problems he or she had with it. Since the former owner presumably has no financial interest in your transaction with the dealer, you'll probably get straight information. By the way, if a dealer tells you he doesn't have the former owner's name and address, he's almost certainly lying. Federal law requires him to have it. If the former owner does clue you in on certain problems the car had, that doesn't mean you should pass the car by. Most dealers do a good job of rehabilitating cars. So your chat with the former owner will just help you know what to look for.

Number 3 is false: Mileage is not the most important consideration in buying a car. A car with 100,000 miles on the odometer that was driven by a salesman mainly on the highway may be in better shape than a car with 70,000 miles on it that was driven by a messenger boy around town. What's most important about a car is its current condition, and that's determined not only by mileage but also by the nature of previous use and the quality of previous care.

Number 4 is true. You shouldn't pick a car in the rain. Rain has a way of hiding the worst paint job and the worst body bumps. Some engines even run better in the rain, and with the ground wet you're less likely to crawl around under the car to check it out.

Now, just how do you check a car out? To start with, give the exterior of the car a good looking over. Look down the sides of the car for ripples in the paint or for repainted spots. These symptoms are easier to spot in daylight, and they may indicate that the car has been in an accident. By the way, you can tell if a car has been repainted a different color from the original by looking at the inside frame or at the firewall—the metal divider between the engine and the passenger compartment. These parts are seldom repainted and will almost always show the original color.

Look for signs of rust, especially in the wheel wells and around the rocker panels under the doors. Rust is expensive to repair, and in unit construction cars it weakens the car's basic structure.

You can also give the shock absorbers a quick test. Give each corner of the car a good bouncing and then let go. The body should bounce once and stop. If it continues to bounce more than once, the shock absorber needs replacement.

Suspension joints and wheel bearings can be expensive to repair. You can check them by shaking each front wheel hard, in and out at the top. If it is loose or has a lot of free play, or if you hear clunking sounds, the car needs work. (Note that this test is performed with the car sitting on the ground. When a car is up on a hydraulic lift, there *should* be a lot of play in the front wheels. Taking advantage of people who don't know this is a favorite trick of certain auto-repair gyp artists, who stick consumers with unnecessary suspension repairs at hefty prices.)

While you're looking around outside the car, take a close look at the tires and check the tire tread. You should be able to sink a penny into the tread past the top of Lincoln's head. If any part of the tread is worn thinner than that, you'll have to spend money on replacement tires. Also, if one side of the tire is worn thinner than the other, the car probably needs a front-end alignment. If the tires pass the penny test, check to be sure they aren't recaps (that is, that they haven't had a new tread cut into them). Recaps are easy to spot, because the tread is new but the sidewalls look used.

When you're done giving the outside of the car its examination, climb inside. Check all of the operating controls, including the turn signals, four-way flashers, windshield wipers, radio, inside light, headlights, high beams, and back-up lights. Make sure the windows roll up and down easily. Press down steadily on the brake pedal. If it sinks quickly, there's probably a brake fluid leak.

Now it's ignition time. Race the engine and have a friend check the exhaust. Blue smoke means burning oil. With the hood up, listen for unusual sounds in the engine. Check the radiator hoses and connecting hoses for leaks.

You should also check to see if the wheels are in line. This marks the beginning of your test drive. On a straight, level spot, have a friend drive the car slowly away from you. If the car travels with its front wheels out of line with the back ones, it may have been badly damaged in an accident.

Pull out into the road. The car should accelerate smoothly from a slow speed. The engine should neither skip nor hesitate. When you find a road that's wide and straight with little traffic, you can check the brakes. Drive at 45 miles an hour and check to be sure there's no one behind you. Then step on the brake hard (but not hard enough to lock the wheels). Repeat this test three times. The brake pedal should stay solid and well above the floor. It should *not* feel soft or spongy. As the car slows down, it shouldn't pull to one side, and the brakes shouldn't grab or chatter. Brake repair can be expensive.

When you find a long hill, you can check the piston rings. On the downslope keep your foot off the accelerator. Just before you get to the bottom, step hard on the accelerator, and look in the rear view mirror. If you see a cloud of heavy blue smoke, the engine needs an overhaul. If you see black smoke, probably the fuel mixture is too rich.

These are just a few simple tests you can perform yourself to make sure a car is in good condition. But if it's at all possible you should go farther in your precautions. You should take the car to a mechanic or a diagnostic center. That will cost you something (perhaps $15 to $25). But it can save you from making a very costly mistake. A mechanic can check things like engine compression that you'd probably be hard put to evaluate yourself.

If you're in the market for a used car, you should first decide what type of car will fill your needs. Then shop around until you have a good feel for the market value of that type of car. Only then will you be in a position to spot a bargain when you see one. Your shopping should include the factors of warranties and financing, as well as the car's basic price and mechanical condition. Some dealers say they give a warranty; but, if you actually read the document in question, you find it guarantees practically nothing. A fairly standard used-car warranty provides that you and the dealer split the costs of any servicing fifty-fifty for the first thirty days or 2,000 miles. After that, for a period of two years you get a 15 per cent discount from the dealer on parts and labor. Compare warranties, just as you compare cars.

Unless you're going to pay a lump sum for the car, you must also concern yourself with the financing terms. Every day, people lose on the financing what they gained on a favorable price for the car. The best way to borrow money for a car purchase is to borrow from a credit union (if you belong to one) or your bank (if they'll give you a loan). Dealers generally charge more interest than banks or credit unions do. But dealers usually charge less than do small-loan companies. Now, finance charges and interest rates can be stated in a variety of ways. People who are lending money sometimes like to state them in a way that makes it look as if you're paying less than you are. You needn't be confused, however. Federal law (the truth in lending law) requires that the interest rate be stated as an annual percentage rate (APR). Make sure you get that rate quoted to you, and use it in comparing one financing deal against another. Generally speaking, the shorter the term of the loan, the better off you are. So if you can get a three-year (thirty-six-month) loan, prefer it to a four-year loan. If you can afford the monthly payments on a one-year loan, you're usually better off with that than with a thirty-six-month loan. And so on: The shorter the better. Paying cash is best of all, for most buyers who can afford to plunk down the cash. But don't feel so eager to pay cash that you drain your savings account of funds that you'd need if an emergency arose. Paying cash or shopping around for financing, using the APR, will save you some money. Knowing something about the psychology and tactics of used-car buying will save you some more. First, don't be in a hurry. Salesmen seem to have antennae that help them spot the customer who can't wait to buy a car. They'll strike a much tougher bargain with an eager customer than with one who seems to be taking his time and waiting to be convinced of a car's merits. The dealer holds most of the cards. He knows how much the car cost him and how much he spent to fix it up. He knows what's wrong with it, and he knows how much he really expects to make by selling it. You can nullify much of this advantage, though. You can get a good idea of the car's market value by shopping around. And if you have it checked out by a mechanic, you'll know as much about the car's condition as the dealer does. The crucial thing to remember is that the dealer doesn't really expect to get the sticker price. Most times he'll settle for a hundred or two hundred dollars less. Sometimes you can bargain even more off the price.

Before you start to talk with the dealer you should have an idea of what a fair price might be for the type of car you're seeking. In this regard a useful publication is one called the *Red Book*. (Some people call it the *Blue Book*, which was its name in former years.) The *Red Book* is published by National Market Reports, Incorporated, 900 S. Wabash Avenue, Chicago, Illinois 60605. You can get it from the publisher if you can't find it at a bank or library near you. It lists "official used car valuations" for all makes and models. There's really nothing "official" about them; they're simply average prices prevailing around the country at the time that edition is published. (The *Red Book* is updated every few months.) If the car you're looking at is in very good condition, it may cost more than the *Red Book* figure. If the car's in lousy condition, it should cost less. The editors of the *Red Book* calculate that figures should vary about 20 per cent to either side of the average, depending on the car's condition.

If you pick up a copy of the *Red Book*, you'll see a lot of tiny type that looks rather forbidding. But it's really not too hard to read. First, get out a magnifying glass if you want to save on eyestrain. A key figure to look at is the average retail value of the car you're interested in. This is a rough indication of what the seller might reasonably be expected to charge you. Note that below the average retail value there will be a list of options and features that can add to, or subtract from, the car's value. Take these into account in totting up the possible value of the car you're interested in. Don't, however, regard this figure as holy writ. If you try hard, you may very well be able to buy a used car at a much lower price.

To help you in bargaining, note also what's called the average wholesale price of the car you want. That figure gives you a very rough idea of what the person who traded the car in got for it. The difference between the wholesale and retail figure is the dealer's markup. Not all the markup is profit, of course. Some of it has to be there just to meet expenses. But knowing the rough size of the markup puts you in a better position to bargain than you would be if you started from scratch. Of course, if you talk to the previous owner of the car, you'll know the proposed markup exactly.

The wholesale price listed in the *Red Book* is also a guide to what you might expect to get for your old car if you're trading it in. Again, the figure is only an average, or a guideline. If your car's in excellent condition, you should get more. In any event, when trading in a car (whether to buy a new or a used car) beware of the "highball" and "lowball" games. With the highball, the dealer offers you what seems like a glitteringly favorable price for your car—more than you secretly expected to get. You are so pleased that you fail to question the price for your new car. That price has been jacked up so that the dealer more than makes up for his "generosity" on the trade-in. So, don't forget to research the price on *both* cars, and then bargain on both. What matters to your pocketbook is the difference between the price you pay for the car you're buying and what you get for the one you're trading in. (It might not hurt to offer your old car for sale privately before you go to see the dealer. But hold off on accepting any bids. Then the dealer and private bidders are competing for your car, and you can take the best bid.)

With the "lowball," the dealer offers you a ridiculously low price at first for your old car. This is to soften you up psychologically. After you argue vigorously, he will grudgingly yield, a little bit at a time, as if he's doing you a big favor. You end up accepting something less than you first intended, while the dealer ends up with a figure that he intended to reach all along. Incidentally, we've been talking about "the dealer" here as if there were only one person involved on the other side of the transaction. But very often there are layers of personnel, from the salesman to the higher official who actually signs the papers. This arrangement allows the dealership to pull the old "friend-and-enemy" trick on you. The salesman becomes your "buddy." He will "try his best" to "talk his boss into" the deal you and he have settled on. Then word comes back that the boss won't accept it. The salesman talks with you some more, strikes a compromise proposal, and—with great difficulty—gets his boss to swallow it. The salesman has "done you a big favor" and the dealership has pulled the wool over another customer's eyes. But of course *you'll* be too smart to let such shenanigans cloud your bargaining judgment.

One good way to get a bargain is to do your shopping near the end of a month. Salesmen are usually trying to make their sales quota for the month at that time, to earn a bonus. So they become a little more forthcoming, a little less tough in bargaining.

Another bargain-spotting technique is to keep your eye on one or two dealerships for a month. If you see a car that's been sitting on the lot for thirty days or more, you may be able to pick it up for a song—almost. This technique works especially well at a new-car dealership, which has to make room for trades coming in. Turnover is important to a dealer; he'll do a lot to get rid of a model that's been hanging around the lot.

Yet another way to save yourself some money is to get a car whose color approaches the weird. You may not like wild purple or antique flamingo. But neither do most other people, and many times a dealer will be glad to move a strange-colored vehicle off the lot. So you may be able to strike a bargain and then repaint the car at your own expense. Of course, in no case should you let your bargain fever cause you to forget to have the mechanical condition of the car carefully checked out.

One aspect of a used car's condition that's attracted an awful lot of attention is the condition of the odometer. That's the instrument that shows how many miles a vehicle's been driven. For obvious reasons, tampering with the odometer can be a temptation for someone selling a used car. As the odometer is pushed back, the apparent resale value of the car is pushed up. Odometer tampering is illegal under federal law and under the laws of just about every state as well. But it still goes on. If you're alert, you may be able to spot it. The first check you can make is to call the former owner. He can tell you what the mileage was when he left the car at the lot—unless, of course, he was in on the tampering.

The next thing to check is the way the digits on the odometer line up. If two or more of the digits don't line up straight, someone has probably been tampering. As a rule, the irregular alignment will show up most clearly on the one-tenth dial, the mile dial, and the ten-mile dial. Also, if the one-tenth dial (at the extreme right of the odometer) vibrates while the car is moving, you can be pretty sure someone has tampered.

A final way to spot a fixed odometer is to look for an unusual pattern in the mileage number. This has to be done before your test drive, of course. It seems some tamperers just can't resist setting the numbers in a pattern, like 27777.7, or 26262.6. Of course, a pattern could show up by pure chance. But if you see one, be extra alert for other signs of tampering.

While we're on the subject of tampering, here's a related point worth mentioning: Once you pay for a car, drive it away. Don't leave it with the dealer on the understanding you'll come back and pick it up later. As a former used-car dealer told *Changing Times* magazine, "The new tires you saw may be replaced with worn ones and the good battery may be switched for an old one."

One way you can get a car that probably hasn't been tampered with is to buy a used police car. To keep up with the crooks, the police have to trade in their cars frequently, so a lot of these cars come on the market. Cars from other government agencies may also be good buys—and they certainly ought to be able to pass inspection requirements in your state! All of these cars tend to be sold at special auctions. You can watch your newspapers for news of these auctions. Or you can speed things along by calling the state police, the police department of a city near you, or the public relations department of various government agencies.

Naturally, the same rules apply to buying used police, taxi, or rental fleet cars as any other used cars. But some of these cars offer unique advantages. It's true that a former police cruiser will probably have seen some hard wear over a couple of years. But on the other hand it probably has an unusually powerful engine, heavy duty brakes, a heavy duty battery, and other extras that you don't get on cars sold to the average consumer.

Whenever you buy a used car, you should check with the federal Department of Transportation to see if the make and model you've bought has ever been recalled for a safety defect. It's best, of course, to perform this check before you buy the car. In the real world, though, that's not always possible. Whether you do it before or after the purchase, do check about recalls. Simply write a short note mentioning your car's make, model, and year, and mail it to this address:

> Administrator
> National Highway Traffic Safety Administration
> Department of Transportation
> 400 Seventh Street, S.W.
> Washington, D.C. 20590

If you haven't actually purchased the car yet, you can make

repair of the defect at the dealer's expense a condition of your purchase. If you've already paid for the car, fixing the defect may or may not require you to pay out your own money, depending on the terms of the recall. In any event, even if you have to pay, it's nice to know you're riding in a car that's likely to get you to your destination alive.

Even if you follow all the good advice in this chapter (a summary of which appears below), it would be foolhardy to predict you'll never run into a problem with your used car. If you do have a complaint, the place to start is with the outfit that sold you the car. If they're reputable they'll try to make you happy. If not, they'll just try to make you leave.

If the salesman misrepresented any information about the car or if he won't honor his own warranty, your state motor vehicle administration may be able to help you. You can usually find a local number for the motor vehicle administration in the phone book. People at the local office can probably give you the address to write to at state headquarters. The motor vehicle administration will probably also be interested if you have any solid indication that the odometer on any car has been tampered with.

If you don't get redress from the seller or the motor vehicle department, try the consumer protection agency for your state listed in the Appendix to this book. It should be able to help you or direct you to an agency that can.

Used-Car Checklist

1. Will the seller let me:
   A. test-drive the car?
   B. have the car checked by my own mechanic?
   C. take the car through a state inspection line?
2. Is the seller's asking price reasonable:
   A. compared to what I've seen similar cars selling for?
   B. according to the *Red Book*?
3. How about the old car's mileage?
   A. Mileage shown on odometer is _____.
   B. Any signs of odometer tampering? (See page 157.)

    C. Is this mileage unusually heavy (i.e., significantly more than 15,000 miles a year)?

    D. How was the car driven? (Talk with previous owner, if possible.)

4. How does the outside of the car check out? (See pages 151-152.)

    A. Paint

    B. Rust

    C. Shock absorbers

    D. Wheels

    E. Tires

5. How does the inside of the car check out? (See page 152.)

    A. Turn signals, flashers

    B. Headlight (including high beam), back-up lights, inside lights

    C. Windshield wipers

    D. Radio

    E. Windows

    F. Brake pedal

6. How does the car perform on a test drive? (See pages 152-153.)

    A. Color of exhaust when engine is raced: _____.

    B. Any unusual noises in engine? Rattles or squeaks in car?

    C. Any leaks apparent in hoses with hood up, engine running?

    D. Are front and back wheels in line?

    E. Is acceleration smooth?

    F. How do brakes react in test?

    G. Do piston rings pass simple test?

7. What does my mechanic say about the car?

8. What warranty is offered with the car?

9. If the car will be financed, exactly what are the financing terms?

    A. Down payment is _____.

    B. Each installment payment will be _____.

    C. Installment payments are due every _____.

D. The total number of installment payments will be ___.

E. Is there a final balloon payment? If so, it will be _____.

F. Most important, the annual percentage rate is _____, and the total finance charge is _____.

G. Are this annual percentage rate and this finance charge better than those offered by other possible sources of financing (such as local banks and credit unions)?

10. Have cars of this make, model, and year ever been recalled? (See page 158.)

11

Surviving
the Service Station

Repairs, Gas, and Tires

When you bought your car, you probably drove it home with pride in your heart and an empty feeling in your wallet. The last thing you wanted, and probably the last thing you expected, was to pour money into the car to keep it running. Yet between the costs of repairs, fuel, and tires, some people swear that cars don't really run on gasoline—they run on money.

In the old days, perhaps, keeping the family wheels moving was no big problem. But now that horses have been replaced by horsepower, things are a little more complicated. The village blacksmith who used to hold forth under the spreading chestnut tree has been replaced by the neighborhood auto mechanic, who works in less poetic surroundings. When a horse threw a shoe, people knew their reliable blacksmith could fix it. But how many people would you trust with your brake shoes? "No one," is the all-too-common answer. As a result, when your car runs a little rough, loses some pep, or pulls to one side when you hit the brake, you may be reluctant to take it in to be fixed. You're afraid you might be gypped. But you should take it in for safety's sake. This chapter is devoted to telling you how you can protect yourself and how you can avoid pouring too much money down the hungry throat of your mechanical steed.

Let's start by focusing on a scene that might occur, involving you and a mechanic at a repair shop or gas station.

MECHANIC: Now what exactly seems to be the trouble?

YOU: Well, at high speeds, like over 45 or 50, there's a shimmy in the steering wheel. Feels kind of loose.

MECHANIC: (Pushes button, raising your car on the shop's lift.) We'll take a quick look at her and see if we can find the problem. (Turns wheel, shakes it.) Holy smokes! Look at this. Hey, Charlie, take a look at this. Did you ever see anything like this? (Turns to you.) Did you hit something with this?

YOU: No.

MECHANIC: You drove this thing in here like this?

YOU: Yeah.

(Mechanic shakes head in disbelief.)

YOU: Why? What's the matter with it?

MECHANIC: Well, you see the play you have in your wheel here?

YOU: Yes. Is that bad?

MECHANIC: Bad? It's dangerous! You could lose control of this car like nothin'.

YOU: Well, what is it, the alignment?

MECHANIC: (Starts looking under the car.) Could be. Could be. Let's see here. Well, first off, you got a bad idler arm. You see this piece here? It's an idler arm. It holds the wheel steady, but you can see how loose it is. You need a new one. Now over here (shakes wheel) you have a bad ball joint. See the way the wheel moves here? The ball joint is shot. Probably the same on the other side. How many miles you got on the car?

YOU: About 45,000 I think. And I already had ball joints put in.

MECHANIC: Well, it's a strange thing. In some cars the darn things last forever. But in these heavier cars, they're always falling apart. Yeah, you've got real front end problems here. (Pause.) Well, you want us to go ahead with the work?

YOU: What's it going to cost?

MECHANIC: Oh, I'd guess somewhere between $80 and $100.

You: (Taking deep breath.) Between $80 and $100? Well, I have to have the car as soon as possible. I can't afford to be without it.

Mechanic: (Figuring.) Well, I can put a man on it right away, have 'im work late tonight, and probably have it for you first thing in the morning.

We're going to review the hidden meaning of that little drama in a minute. First, here are three questions to test your knowledge of the auto repair business.

CSK Quiz

1. True or false: When a car is up on a lift and the wheel is turned all the way to one side, any extra play in its movement is a definite danger signal.
2. True or false: Any looseness in the idler arm is a sign it needs to be replaced.
3. True or false: You've had no trouble with your car lately, but suddenly it won't start. You probably need a new battery.

If you're like most of us you probably don't know the difference between a ball joint and a bumper bolt. So forgive us for asking such technical questions. We went to an expert ourselves to find the answers. He's Pat Goss, an experienced mechanic who knows the repair business from the inside. He has testified about fraudulent repair practices at federal hearings in Washington, D.C., and at state hearings in Annapolis, Maryland. In Prince Georges County, Maryland, he has helped draft legislation requiring the licensing of mechanics. For the past five years he has been teaching courses on auto repair, and he's now writing a book on the subject.

According to Goss, number 1 could not be more false: "Whenever a mechanic or a salesman goes to the front wheel, turns it in, and shakes it, he's trying to take you—no two ways about it. There can't be any mistake involved; it's just an out-and-out fraud. What you have to remember is that, whenever they're checking the parts under the front end of the car, the wheels must be in a straight-ahead position." Number 2 is false, in a similar vein. Just because an idler arm can be jiggled doesn't mean it needs to be replaced. Any mechanic who gives you that sort of pitch deserves to be pitched out of the list of reputable repairmen.

Number 3, as you've probably guessed by now, is also false. If your car won't start, it usually *doesn't* mean you need a new battery. According to Goss, "one of the most common problems you find with the battery is simply dirty battery cable connections. What usually happens in this situation is that you assume you have a dead battery. You call some type of garage or service station to have a serviceman come and give you a jump start or boost start. Now, if you run into a mechanic who's dishonest, what he's going to do is connect his booster cables back on the rubber-coated part of your battery cables, the insulated part, where they couldn't possibly have any effect on starting your car. At that point you're towed into the garage, where you may be sold any number of different parts, from a battery to a starter motor."

When you go into a repair shop, you can protect yourself in a variety of ways. First, you should know and understand what's called the "repair order." That's *your* authorization for the shop to do repairs on your car. In the fine print of most repair orders, three things are stated: (1) that you give your permission for the mechanic to operate your car; (2) that you authorize the repairs as outlined on the form in writing; and (3) that the mechanic can keep the car until you pay for the repairs. That gives the shop three trump cards to begin with. So you've got to be careful how you play your hand.

First of all, avoid busy days at the garage (which are usually at the beginning of the week). If you go when things aren't too hectic, the service writer (the person who writes up the repair order) may have the time to road-test the car and figure out exactly what's wrong. *Don't*—we repeat, do *not*—tell him what you think is wrong, mechanically. Customers who do leave themselves open for a trick of the repair trade, which amounts to double repairs. First, the mechanic will "fix" what *you* diagnosed as a possible cause of the trouble, then he'll make additional repairs to fix the actual symptoms that the car displays. The moral: Describe the symptoms, and only the symptoms, in the first place. What happens? Does it happen at high speed or low, when the engine is hot or cold? The more details you can give, the better the chances your car will be fixed properly.

Hand the service writer a written list you've made up of the symptoms. Keep a copy for yourself, and have him initial it. This will protect you from paying for unwanted repairs. When he writes up the repair order, make sure he hasn't added anything. And watch out for vague descriptions like "check valves." Some mechanics take the word "check" to mean "check", and repair if you think it's necessary." So a "check valves" job can end up costing a couple of hundred bucks. If the repair order says "check" anything, add a notation that you are to be notified before any work is done. Try to take a copy of the repair order with you. That gives you further protection against unwanted repairs.

If possible, talk to the mechanic who's going to do the work. Make sure he understands what you want done. Above all, unless you know the shop's personnel and trust them, don't let them talk you into other repairs that you didn't plan on. The rationalization, "Well, as long as I have it in the shop, I might as well have it done," can cost you a lot of money. If the people at the shop say you need extra repairs, thank them for the information and tell them you'll take the car elsewhere to have their diagnosis confirmed. Then do it. If a second (or perhaps a third) mechanic confirms that other repairs need to be made, you can then take your pick as to where they'll be done. Just remember that the service writer and mechanic have a built-in incentive to run up your repair bill. The higher the tab, the more money is probably in it for them, because most repair personnel operate on a commission or bonus system, not strictly on salary.

After the repair order, the next piece of paper you should get to know is the estimate. If you have a major repair to do, it pays to take the car to several mechanics and get written estimates of costs. This makes it easy to compare costs, and most mechanics will stick pretty close to their estimate, especially if it's written down. A written estimate will cost you about $5 at some shops. Sometimes that money will be refunded to you if you actually have the repairs done at that shop. In any case, the expense can be worth it if it saves you money on the ultimate tab. For some repairs, you can compare costs just by making a few phone calls. If you need new shock absorbers, for instance, call several places for prices.

One last piece of paper can save you loads of trouble. It's something you probably carry all the time in your car's glove compartment: the owner's manual. You should read it and be familiar with it. If you take care of your car as the manual suggests, you'll have fewer problems in the first place.

A good way to save money on auto repair is to do the routine maintenance yourself. Quite a few auto repair courses, as well as books on the subject, are available. If you want to take a course, you can watch for ads or contact local night schools, adult education organizations, or perhaps the local chamber of commerce.

When you have left your car with a mechanic, always test drive it when you come back to pick it up. Make sure it's working right. If it's not, give it right back and insist that the work be done properly, at no additional cost to you. If the mechanic is reliable, he'll comply.

There are, of course, quite a few honest, competent mechanics around. But suppose you run into one who does fraudulent repair work, or maybe one who's just plain incompetent. What can you do about it? The first thing you should do is make some noise. Complain like mad. Ask for the phone number of the company president. Threaten to call a lawyer. You'd be surprised how many mechanics change their attitudes when they see you're not fooling around. If that doesn't work, you can contact your state consumer protection agency, listed in the appendix to this book. They should be able either to help you or to refer you to a specialized agency that can. Another possible source of help is the state motor vehicle bureau, though its areas of responsibility vary from state to state.

If you find a good mechanic whom you can trust, stick with him. He's worth his weight in gold. If you're looking for this paragon and haven't found him yet, there are a couple of ways you might get a clue. Pay attention to word-of-mouth advertising and not much attention to other advertising. As a rule, look for a local mechanic who depends on repeat business for his income, rather than a high-volume place near a big highway, where most of the customers are seen only once.

Some states are beginning to require the licensing of mechanics. If your state does, never waste your time on an unlicensed one, even if he claims to offer lower prices. Then there's an organization called the National Institute of Automotive Service Excellence (NIASE). It certifies mechanics who meet its standards. Such mechanics are given a blue, orange, and white shoulder patch to wear and are listed in a directory printed by the institute. The certification program began in 1973, and the institute expected to have some 20,000 mechanics certified by mid-1975. That's not many, considering there are some 800,000 mechanics in the country. But if there's a certified mechanic near you, he might be a logical candidate for your business. If you do find the man you're looking for (whether certified by the NIASE or not), take all your repair business to him. If he's associated with a gas station, consider buying your gas there too. The better you know him, the better off you'll be. Of course, if the gas there is very expensive, you have to think twice. Gasoline costs are quite a significant budget item in themselves.

In fact what you save by being savvy about repairs can go right down the drain if you're careless about gas. While many people frankly confess their ignorance about automotive repairs, few of us regard ourselves as ignorant about gasoline. Yet we are; perhaps we don't even realize that there's anything important to know about the subject. Saving money on gas involves a lot more than just buying a cheap brand—although that's a step in the right direction. To open up the subject, here are a few questions.

CSK Quiz

1. True or false: Because of emission control devices, most new cars require low-lead or unleaded gasoline.

2. True or false: The major reason new cars get fewer miles per gallon than their predecessors did is the pollution control system.
3. Of the following twelve cars, how many require high-test or premium gas? The cars are the Catalina 400, Charger 318, Javelin 360, Thunderbird 460, Ambassador 401, Datsun 510, Superbeetle Volkswagen, Firebird 350, Monaco 400, Maverick Grabber, LTD Brougham 400, and the Mazda.

Here are the answers. Number 1 is false. Most new cars do *not* require unleaded gasolines. Of the big four carmakers, only General Motors recommends low-lead or unleaded gas. Ford, American Motors, and Chrysler state that leaded, low-lead, or unleaded gasoline may be used in their cars. You should check the owner's manual to be sure. For cars built before 1971, you're probably better off using leaded gasolines.

Number 2 is also false. There are three reasons why new cars tend to get poorer mileage than their forerunners, and emission controls are the least important of the three. Emission controls, on the average, have decreased gas mileage by about 8 per cent. Air conditioning decreases it by an average of 9 per cent, and sometimes as much as 20 per cent. And the biggest culprit of all is increased vehicle weight. Added weight can cut gas mileage by up to 50 per cent. And, up until the great gas shortage of 1973, American cars had been getting steadily longer, wider, and heavier. For example, the 1973 Impala weighed 1,500 pounds more than the 1958 model. In general, the smaller the car, the better the gas mileage. A Honda sedan weighs about 1,600 pounds and gets about 25.8 miles per gallon. A Ford station wagon weighs about 4,600 pounds and gets about 7.6 miles to the gallon.

The answer to number 3 may surprise you. None of the cars listed requires high-test or premium gas. They all run just fine on regular. Even a Cadillac Coupe de Ville runs on regular. Very few cars require premium. So if you're buying premium, you may very well be paying for more octane than you need.

"Octane" is a word we've all heard but very few of us really understand. Perhaps a really comprehensive understanding would require a degree in chemistry. But all the consumer really needs to know is that the octane number is an index—an index telling you what the antiknocking quality of the gasoline is. The higher the octane number, the more the fuel prevents knocking. But the important point is this: Once you get a high enough number to stop the knocking, any higher octane does absolutely no good. So experiment a little. Start with a low octane gas, between 87 and 91. If your engine knocks, work your way up until it stops knocking. When it does, you've found the right octane for your car. Look for the octane sticker that should be on every gas pump. If you see any number from 87 to 91, its regular gasoline. If the octane index is between 92 and 97, the gasoline is premium.

Let's explore for a minute the implications of the answers to the quiz questions. Most cars need neither unleaded gas nor premium gas, and the biggest determinant of mileage is car weight. Now, gas prices are constantly changing, but let's suppose that you've been paying 55 cents a gallon for a big name brand of premium or unleaded gas. You now switch to a lower octane, perhaps, or a cheaper variety of gas. And you buy your gas at a discount gas station of some type. (Such stations get their gasoline from the same refineries as the highly advertised brands.) As a result, you might be able to cut your cost down to, say, 45 cents a gallon. The average person drives 12,000 miles a year, and the average car gets about 12 miles to the gallon. So, if you're typical, you buy about 1,000 gallons of gas a year, and a 10-cent saving on each gallon is a saving of $100.

Incidentally, one good way to cut down on gas costs per gallon is to go to a self-service gas station. These are springing up in an increasing number of locations around the country. If you've never pumped gas, you may think it's a lot harder than it really is. It's simple. And it's not dirty either. Most gas pumps are relatively clean—probably at least as clean as your car. There will be written instructions for you to follow, but basically the procedure is predictable. You pick up the nozzle from the niche where it rests. You flick up a clearly visible switch on the pump. Then you put the nozzle in your gas tank and pull the trigger. You're not likely to overfill the tank, because the trigger will suddenly feel loose in your hands when the tank's almost full. Now all you do is put the switch back, put the nozzle back in its niche, and put the cap back on your tank. Oh, yes, and pay the attendant. But what you pay him will probably be at least 2 cents a gallon less than you would have had he been pumping the gas.

The $100 you save by buying cheaper gas (more if you drive a lot) is only the beginning of the gas economy story. You can achieve much greater savings if you can increase the mileage you get per gallon. Obviously one way of doing this would be to switch to a smaller car, if you own a big one. If you have a station wagon that gets 8 miles to the gallon and you drive the typical 12,000 miles a year, you use 1,500 gallons of gas. Supposing, for simplicity's sake, that you pay 50 cents a gallon. That works out to $750 a year for gas—quite a huge chunk of your budget! Now, if you had a little subcompact that got 24 miles to the gallon, you'd use only 500 gallons a year and pay only $250. However, it's pretty unlikely that you'd switch from a station wagon to a subcompact, since you probably bought the station wagon in the first place because you needed a lot of room. More likely, you'll do what many people are doing—buy a somewhat smaller car next time you're in the market for a car.

There's another way, though, that you can get better mileage: Sharpen up your driving and car-maintenance habits. If your car has a manual transmission (i.e., if it's a "shift" car), don't stay in each gear too long. You use up to 45 per cent more gas by staying in second than by shifting into high. When you're approaching a traffic light, try merely to slow down rather than come to a complete stop. It uses extra gas to stop and start again. Since many city lights are synchronized, this isn't as hard to do as it sounds. But it requires alert driving.

When going up a hill, don't maintain the speed you were going before. Let the car slow down, as it naturally wants to do. If you maintain full speed going up a hill, you use five or six times as much gas as you would on a level stretch. So slow down five or ten miles per hour as you go uphill. You lose a little time, but you save a lot of money. One thing: Don't try to save by coasting downhill in neutral. It wears on the engine, and besides that it's illegal.

Don't race your engine when you start up. It pours gas through the carburetor and doesn't give you a thing in return. It's not particularly good for the engine either. When you're waiting at a light, keep your foot on the brake—not on the gas pedal, even if you're on an upgrade. Using the gas pedal as a substitute brake only wastes gas. When you accelerate, do it smoothly and slowly. And finally—a well-publicized tip since the 1973 gas crisis—go 50, or at most 55 miles per hour on the highway. You'll save a good deal of gas that way compared to doing 60 or 65.

So much for driving habits. Now let's consider car maintenance that will help you get better mileage. First of all, check your air filter regularly. If it's dirty, clean it with a vacuum cleaner at least every six months. Or better yet, replace it. If you let an air filter get dirty enough, it can cost you two gallons out of every ten. Have your spark plugs checked from time to time to make sure they're clean and properly gapped. A single misfiring plug can easily cost you one gallon of gasoline in eight.

If your car has an automatic choke, make sure it doesn't stick. If it does, it will waste gas by making your fuel mixture too rich. You can buy fluids that will unstick it. Then there's the carburetor. Unless you're really an expert, don't touch it yourself. Go to a mechanic to make sure it's properly adjusted. If your carburetor is out of kilter—and a great many of them are—you'll be using up to 30 per cent more gas than you should.

Keeping the car engine well oiled is something you can do yourself or have your gas station attendant take care of. If you're going to do it yourself, you can buy oil by the case at an auto supply store and save yourself some money. In any event, make sure the car is well oiled and well lubricated. This cuts down on friction that robs you of gas mileage.

Another place where you can save on gas is in your tires. That may sound strange, but low tire pressure can cost you a mile a gallon. So get yourself a cheap little pressure gauge (they cost about a dollar and keep the tires properly inflated). The owner's manual will tell you how many pounds of pressure there should be in each tire. Don't depend on the built-in pressure gauges in gas-station air pumps. They're often wildly inaccurate.

Speaking of tires, they're an important element in their own right. Inflating your tries properly is not only helpful to gas economy but also helpful in making your tires last longer and your car run safely. An underinflated tire is dangerous. It builds up heat and has a tendency to blow out easily. Underinflation also makes the tread wear unevenly. In spite of these facts, the Kelley Springfield Tire Company estimates (based on a survey in Cumberland, Maryland) that more than half the tires on the road are underinflated. Even by a conservative estimate, a third of all tires need more air in them. So don't forget to check yours.

A set of four tires typically costs from $100 to $300. So spend a little time and effort (and even a little money) to keep them running longer. Proper inflation is the first step to good tire health. The second is to make sure all the tires point in the same direction. That's called alignment, and it's something your mechanic can help you with. It's also important that your tires be balanced. If they're not, they may wear unevenly, with the result that you'll have to scrap a whole set before you should. To prevent uneven wear, you should also rotate your tires every five thousand or ten thousand miles.

There are three basic types of tires: bias ply, belted bias, and radial. We'll discuss the pros and cons of each in a moment. But no matter which you buy, *never* mix two different types on the same car. It's not only bad for the tires, it's unsafe.

For safety's sake, you should check your tire tread every once in a while. It should be at least a sixteenth of an inch deep. But you don't have to delay checking until you have a ruler handy. Use a penny. The distance between the edge of the penny and the top of Lincoln's head is one-sixteenth of an inch. So part of Lincoln's head should be obscured. Incidentally, check your spare tire once in a while too. A flat spare, or one with bald tread, won't do you much good.

Before we delve further into the mysteries of tires, perhaps you'd like to test yourself on how much you already know. Here, in our standard quiz format, are three questions.

CSK Quiz

1. True or false: Radial tires give better mileage than other types.

2. True or false: Load range is a designation of how much weight a tire is designed to carry.

3. True or false: Tire pressure should be checked only after the car has been driven a few miles, so the tires have a chance to warm up.

Now let's look at the answers. Number 1 is true. Radial tires do give better mileage than other types. They are also outstanding in cornering ability and in rupture resistance. And, as you might have guessed, they're the most expensive tires you can buy.

Number 2 is also true. Load range is a designation of how much weight the tire is designed to carry. That's a very important consideration in buying tires. If your car is often used to haul lots of people or luggage, you need a tire with a high load range. Ask your salesman about it.

Number 3 is false. Tire pressure should always be checked when the tire is cold, not warm. When a tire's been driven for a little while, the air inside heats up, and you can't get a dependable reading on the pressure. So check your tire pressure *before* you drive the car.

A new wrinkle, provided by the federal government, is about to enter the tire game. It's called the Uniform Tire Grading System, and it's scheduled to take effect around May of 1975. Starting then, all tire manufacturers will have to mark their tires in a uniform code. There are three parts to the code: tread life, traction, and high-speed performance. These characteristics will be represented by a series of numbers, stars, and letters stamped into the side of each tire.

The numbers will represent the anticipated tread life. A 25, for example, would mean you could expect the tire to last about 25,-000 miles. A 45 would mean you could expect it to last about 45,000. The government will test the accuracy of the figures being used by manufacturers by measuring the tread life achieved by sample tires on a government track.

The stars measure traction. A three-star tire holds the road the best. A one-star tire holds it least well. But to qualify for even one star, a tire is supposed to be designed to certain minimum safety standards.

The letters grade high-speed performance. The three letters used are A, B, and C. A tire rated "A" is supposed to take speeds up to 105 miles per hour without disintegrating as a result of the heat. B-rated tires will go up to 95 miles per hour without damage, and C-rated ones up to 85. A question here is whether you really need an extra margin of high-speed performance. How often do you drive 105 miles per hour? Perhaps the cheaper C-rated tires will serve you just as well. For that matter, how often do you do 85?

The new uniform system should be a big help to consumers in comparing tires and judging whether price differences among them are justified. Eventually the National Highway Safety Administration hopes to include additional factors in the grading system. But you probably shouldn't hold your breath, since it took about seven years for the current grading system to evolve and to clear industry resistance.

When you shop for tires, by all means make use of the Uniform Grading System. To make an informed decision, though, you'll need to know some other basic information about tires and how they're built. Tire salesmen often talk of three elements in a tire. The "bead" is the part where the tire meets the wheel rim. The tread, of course, is the grooved section that touches the road. Everything else is called the carcass of the tire.

As we mentioned before, there are three basic tire types. The least expensive is the conventional bias ply tire. 'A "ply" is a layer of cord inside the tire; it's what gives the tire much of its strength. Tires are called "bias" ply when the ply runs at a diagonal angle to the direction the tires roll. A two-ply tire has two layers of this ply, and (strangely enough) a four-ply tire has four.

Somewhat higher in price than a plain bias ply tire is the belted bias tire. It's similar to the basic bias ply, except that it has something added: a belt (usually of fiberglass) between the plies and the tread. Tests conducted by Consumers Union suggest that the main advantage of this type of tire is its outstanding stopping ability. It does not perform well under extreme conditions, such as high speeds, overload, or underinflation. And its tread life does not seem to be noticeably better than that of the plain bias ply.

The most expensive, but in many ways the best, type of tire is the radial. In a radial tire, the plies go not on a diagonal but perpendicular to the tire's direction of movement. These "radial plies" go all the way from one bead to the other. This gives great rigidity to the tread and flexibility to the sidewall. The radial also has a belt under the tread, like the belted bias. The result of this construction is a tire that has very long tread life but often has a comparatively harsh ride. It is outstanding in cornering and in performance at high speeds. Some older cars are not equipped to take radials, so check your owner's manual for guidance.

Which type of tire should you get? There's no simple answer. You'll probably choose bias ply if you want to lay out the smallest possible amount of money, belted bias if you consider stopping ability the primary criterion, and radials if mileage or performance is the main thing you're looking for. Whatever kind of tires you buy, they'll last longer if you follow the tire-care suggestions given in this chapter. It also helps to drive moderately. Avoid hard cornering, fast stops and starts, and unnecessary high speeds. If you "drive lovingly," as the saying goes, you'll probably save money on tires, gas, *and* repairs. And you'll be around longer, too, to enjoy the money you've saved.

MONEY

12

Making Your Budget Work for You

Today, consumers face a baffling contradiction. They're making more money than ever before. Yet they seem to have less and less to spend. If our dollars aren't being "laundered," how come they are shrinking? This chapter will try to answer that question and provide you with ways to stretch your dollars out again. As consumer writer Sidney Margolius points out, a budget shouldn't be thought of as an unglamorous, belt-tightening set of restrictions. Rather it's a "spending plan" designed to help you get maximum use out of your money.

In the shrinking dollar caper, there are really three villains at work. The first and largest is inflation. Rising prices have simply eaten up a sizable chunk of the rise in people's incomes. If your salary goes up 10 per cent, but prices go up 10 per cent, you're exactly where you started. You still have to work the same number of hours to buy any given commodity. Real gains for the wage earner occur only when salaries rise faster than prices. That *has* happened over the past couple of decades. But in the mid-1970s it was the lucky wage earner whose salary increases were outrunning the raging double-digit inflation.

The median family income in 1949 was about $3,000. In 1972, half of all the families in the country were making more than $10,000. That's a hefty wage increase. But it's not as great as it seems. If you made $10,000 in 1973, it would buy you only about as much as $5,000 would have bought you in 1949. So, after you take inflation into account, family income went up about 66 per cent, not 233 per cent, as it first appears.

But the average family didn't get to keep that 66 per cent increase either. Taxes have been soaring to new highs almost every year. In 1972 personal taxes were eight times as high as they were in 1949. If you work a forty-hour week, you probably spend about thirteen hours laboring to pay your federal, state, and local taxes. That means that if your gross income (before taxes) is $10,000, your after-tax income is only about $6,750. Taxes, then, are the second-worst villain in the shrinking dollar caper.

The third villain is indebtedness. We'll talk in detail about credit and debt in Chapter 13. For now, suffice it to say that many of us buy many of our belongings on credit. And, therefore, an ever larger percentage of our income belongs to somebody else before we ever get our hands on it. It also means that many of us may be living on the brink of disaster. One long illness in the family, one medium-sized car crash, one purse or wallet snatching, or just one missed paycheck could mean big trouble. It's startling, but true, that there are more personal bankruptcies now (about 120,000 a year) than there were during the Great Depression of the 1930s.

A good budget can help you avoid that kind of bleak fate and achieve positive goals. If you already have a family budget, perhaps this chapter can help you sharpen it into an even more useful tool. If you don't have one, we'll give you suggestions for how to set one up. To start with, let's look at some questions underlying the budget picture.

CSK Quiz

1. True or false: During the course of your working lifetime you'll probably earn between a quarter and a half million dollars.

2. True or false: If you are deep in debt, you should put everything you can into paying off creditors and defer savings until later.
3. True or false: Fortunately, your income will probably reach its peak during the time of your life when your financial needs are greatest.

Now for the answers. Number 1 is true. During your working lifetime between $250,000 and $500,000 will probably pass through your hands, as the case may be. If you can retain a significant portion of that money to save or invest, your chances of meeting long-range goals (such as a house or a college education for your children) are greatly increased. Let's suppose, for example, that you manage to put away $1,000 a year, starting now. We'll say the money goes into a savings account (or other investment) paying 5½ per cent interest annually. At the end of twenty years, you would have not $20,000 but $34,868. Making compound interest work for you this way is one of the aims of a budget plan.

Number 2 is false. Many financial counselors say that if your budget is strained, you need a nestegg more than anybody else. Sure, they say, pay off those creditors, even if it means going on a crash economy program, cutting food costs to essentials, and postponing clothing purchases and vacations. But every payday sock something away, even five or ten dollars. You need some cushion against emergencies that could tumble you into bankruptcy. And the saving habit will stand you in good stead when you pull out of debt. Besides, suppose you got a flat tire and couldn't make it to work! Then your creditors wouldn't get paid anyway. In short, it's not immoral to save when you owe.

Number 3 is unfortunately false. Some people's incomes peak at the time when their financial needs are greatest. But for many others it doesn't work out that way. For example, many breadwinners find their earning power peaks when they're in their fifties or sixties. By that time, their heaviest financial responsibilties may already be past.

Because they need things *now* and anticipate higher income later, some people in effect mortgage their futures by going heavily into debt. That's not wise. Career reverses can happen even to the most capable people. So use your budget to help yourself live within your means. One guideline: You shouldn't be spending more than 20 per cent of your income, at most, to meet installment payments. (Monthly mortgage payments for purchase of a house are not included in that figure.)

The first step to good budgeting is spelling out your long-term goals. Of course, getting through next week or next month is important. But you should be equally concerned with your financial picture five, ten, or more years from now. That's the only way to prepare for your children's education or for your own retirement. Social security and company pensions are almost never enough to live on in any degree of comfort. You simply *have* to save. So, discuss your goals with your family and try to decide what you want most, what your order of priorities is. Figure out which items you can aim for this year and which ones will take longer. To help you work out a schedule, you can use the goals worksheet that appears below.

Goals Worksheet

What Do We Want?	Estimated Cost of Each Item	Monthly Amount to be Set Aside
NOW		
THIS YEAR		
NEXT YEAR		

LONG-RANGE GOALS

Just as an example, your goals for this year might include paying off all the money owed on, say, your dryer and your dentist's bill. Goals for next year might include taking a vacation or buying a new car. And in the long run, your chief goal might be to set up a college fund. Rational planning will help you achieve these goals.

The second step to take in putting your finances on a rational basis is to analyze your income. A table to help you do this appears below.

What's Coming In

Gross annual salary	$_____
Other income	$_____
Gross annual income	$_____
Left at the Gate:	
Federal income tax	$_____
Social Security	$_____
State tax	$_____
Pension plan	$_____
Company health insurance	$_____
Union dues	$_____
Total left at the gate:	$_____
Gross annual income	$_____
Minus total left at the gate	$_____
Net annual income:	$_____

If you're salaried, you may get a statement every payday that will help you fill in the chart. On the top line, you put your gross annual salary. ("Gross" means what you make before taxes and other deductions from your salary; "net" is what you make after these deductions. Of course, by the time they finish taking things out, the net is pretty gross. But that's another story.)

By "salary" we mean your main source of income. In most cases, it will be a regular salary. But it could also be what you expect to make from your own business if you're self-employed.

On the second line of the "What's Coming In" chart, enter your other income. This could include a lot of things: pinochle winnings . . . royalties on your best-seller . . . capital gains on the sale of your yacht. Perhaps the most common entry under "other income" would be interest from a savings account or a bond, or dividends from some stock you own.

The third line is the total of the first two lines, and presto! There's your gross annual income. Now you have to figure out how much goes to Uncle Sam and all the little uncles in state and local government. There may also be deductions for a company health insurance plan or pension plan, and perhaps union dues. All of these things take money out of your pocket and leave you to hope they'll give you back fair value in return. In any event, you can't possibly manage your money rationally unless you take these items into account. So enter them all in the section marked "Left at the Gate." Now subtract the left-at-the-gate total from your gross annual income. You've got your net annual income. This is the crucial figure for budget purposes.

The third step in budgeting involves some family cooperation, and requires that everyone in the family keep a grip on his or her temper. Think of it as a game, albeit a serious one. The name of the game is "Where Have All the Dollars Gone?" And the playing board appears opposite.

In this game, every member of the family has to keep track, for a month or two, of every penny he or she spends. So much for the popsicle man. So much for shoelaces. So much for two beers at Joe's Bar. Every penny. It's the only way you can really get a fix on your family's outflow. And, as we said, this is no time for fights.

Where Have All the Dollars Gone?

	Jan.	Feb.	March	April	May	June	July	Aug.	Sept.	Oct.	Nov.	Dec.	Year
Savings													
Food													
Clothing													
Shelter													
rent/mortgage													
property tax													
home insurance													
maintenance													
Utilities													
heat													
gas, electric													
water													
telephone													
Transportation													
bus, train, etc.													
car payments													
car insurance													
gas, oil													
license, fees													
maintenance													
Insurance													
life													
health													
Medical													
doctors, dentist													
drugs													
other													
Furniture													
Appliances													
Household items													
School costs													
Recreation													
Vacation													
Gifts													
Installment Debt													
Miscellaneous													
TOTAL													

Like Sergeant Friday, you should want only the facts. After a month or two of this exercise, you can look at the total that's being spent in relation to how much you should be spending. And this may inspire you to start making some thoughtful choices. Like, "Hey, do we really want to spend twenty bucks a month at the hamburger joint, or do we want a night on the town instead?" This is the place for give-and-take.

At the bottom of the "Where Have All The Dollars Gone?" sheet, you total up all the money spent and saved for the month. (The total, logically, should equal one month's net income, or about one-twelfth of the net income total on page 183.) The obvious questions to ask are "Have we saved anything this month?" and "Have we saved enough?" What, you may ask, is "enough?" Well, that's an eternal question. There's no easy answer. But one thing's for sure: If you've saved nothing, that's not enough. One common guideline, advocated by the Boston Better Business Bureau among others, is that you should save at least 10 per cent of your net income. According to the BBB, if you're single or married but childless, you should be able to save much more than that.

Once you have a firm grip on the question of where your dollars have been going, it's time to take the fourth and final step—deciding where all the dollars *should* go. In other words, write down a formal budget. You'll find Consumer Survival Kit's Budget worksheet opposite. If you think it looks like the "Where Have All the Dollars Gone?" game board, you're right. But the numbers you enter should make it different.

One thing that makes it difficult for some people to use a budget is that some expenses are paid yearly, some quarterly, and some every month (or even every day). Don't let that throw you. If you pay for something once a year (like automobile license plates and registration), just enter the yearly total in the last column. Then divide it by 12, and enter one twelfth of the yearly expense under each month. With quarterly expenses, the procedure is similar. Divide by three to get the monthly allotment. If you buy a certain item five days a week, multiply by 22 to get its cost per month. If you buy something every day, multiply by 30.

Consumer Survival Kit Budget

	Jan.	Feb.	March	April	May	June	July	Aug.	Sept.	Oct.	Nov.	Dec.	Year
Savings													
Food													
Clothing													
Shelter													
rent/mortgage													
property tax													
home insurance													
maintenance													
Utilities													
heat													
gas, electric													
water													
telephone													
Transportation													
bus, train, etc.													
car payments													
car insurance													
gas, oil													
license, fees													
maintenance													
Insurance													
life													
health													
Medical													
doctors, dentist													
drugs													
other													
Furniture													
Appliances													
Household items													
School costs													
Recreation													
Vacation													
Gifts													
Installment Debt													
Miscellaneous													
TOTAL													

187

When you fill out the budget sheet, first enter the things you are locked into: rent or house payment, utilities, insurance, *and* your savings goals. Then enter other items, using your experience from the "Where Have All The Dollars Gone?" game to guide you.

The budget total at the bottom right-hand corner of the budget should exactly equal your net annual income. If the budget total is less than your net income, there's no big problem. You can afford to save some more. But if the budget total exceeds your net annual income, consider that an alarm has rung and a red light is flashing. Although the U.S. government has often engaged in deficit spending year after year, you as a family do not have that option. So you have to either trim back on your goals or (better) find a way of cutting down on your expenses. Most of this book is devoted to giving you hints for keeping your expenses down.

In addition to using our suggestions, you can trim some expenditures by delaying purchases until there's a sale. Since some sales are seasonal, it's possible to plan ahead. Below is a list of some items you can pretty well count on picking up at a discount if you wait until the months indicated.

Seasonal Sales List

Item	Best Month to Buy
Air conditioner	February, August
Appliances	February, October, November
Bicycles	January, February, fall
Car (new)	August, winter
Car (used)	end of any month
Children's clothes	July, September, November
China, glassware	January, February, September
Cosmetics	January
Drapes, curtains	February, August
Fabrics, notions	February
Fishing equipment	October
Furniture	January, February, summer

Gardening equipment	August, September
Jewelry	January
Linens	January, May, August
Lingerie	January
Luggage	May
Radios, phonographs, stereos	January, February
Refrigerators, freezers	January, July
Rugs, carpets, floor tile	January, February, summer
School supplies	August, October
Ski equipment, skates	March
Tires	May, end of August
Toys	January, February, November
Washing machines	February
Women's clothes	January, May

You'll note that, with many of the items on the list, sales occur just *after* the season in which the item is normally used (for gift-type items, this means immediately after Christmas). Merchants want to get rid of the left-over items, so sales are common. The trick for you, then, is to nurse your old whatever-it-is through one more season and to replace it as soon as the season ends.

In years past, financial advisers were quick to quote figures telling you what percentage of your income should be spent on what. It was commonly said, for example, that housing should take no more than 25 per cent of your net income, and that food should take no more than 25 per cent. These figures are heard less often nowadays. People who used to quote them have come to realize that, for some families, there will be no choice but to spend more than 25 per cent of the budget on shelter or on food. Nonetheless, these percentages can be a useful tool for you if you keep in mind that they're not sacred numbers, only rough guidelines.

Once you succeed in setting up a budget that fits your family, you'll need two things: will power and flexibility. You'll need will power, of course, to stick to the budget. And you'll need flexibility to review the budget and modify it every year or so, as your circumstances change. You might want to make photocopies of our sample budget sheet to use in your future reviews.

When you've set a savings goal, whether it be $5 a month or $500 a month, you confront the question of where to put those savings. The most obvious place would be a bank. But there are three kinds of "banks." First, there are commercial banks, which often have the word "bank" or the words "bank and trust" in their names. At a commercial bank you can get a checking account, so you might find it convenient to have your savings account there also. But you can get a somewhat higher interest rate on your savings if you keep them in a mutual savings bank (they exist in eighteen states) or a savings and loan association (also called a building and loan association in some places).

Then again, there's a chance you might want to put your savings somewhere other than a bank. Mattresses aren't recommended: They are rather flammable and pay no interest. But if there's a credit union where you work, you may be able to get a very favorable rate of interest on your savings there.

Or perhaps you're thinking of stocks or bonds. Here a word of caution is in order. No one should buy securities until he has enough savings stashed away to meet a medium-sized emergency. Six months' salary is an amount commonly cited. But in view of the sharp fluctuations of the securities markets in the 1970s, the equivalent of a full year's salary might be more prudent. In addition, if you have children you should have life insurance. This purchase should be taken care of before any money is put into stocks or bonds. (For suggestions on what type of life insurance to buy, and how to shop for it, see Chapter 15.)

If you've got a sufficient nest egg, you can start thinking about stocks and bonds. The two, of course, are quite distinct animals. Bonds are really IOUs, issued either by a government or a company. They are guaranteed to pay a certain rate of interest, unless the issuing organization goes bankrupt. The actual rate of interest paid will vary among bond offerings, depending on market conditions. But there will always be a range, with the safest investments paying a lower rate of interest than the riskiest. (A venture that isn't firmly established has to pay a higher rate to attract capital.) Unless you're both well-to-do and well-informed, don't go running off after unusually high bond returns. Play it safe and stick with the bonds of the U.S. government, well-established corporations, or well-run local governments.

Stocks (and related vehicles like commodities and precious metals) are a much riskier investment than bonds. When you buy stock in a company, you are actually buying a piece of the ownership of that company. If the company doesn't make a profit, you don't get any income, and the price of the stock will probably go down. If there is a profit, it's up to company management how much of it will be parceled out in the form of dividends. Of course, the price of your stock could go up. Some people have doubled or tripled their money in the stock market. Others have lost their shirts. It may pay to put some money into stocks, in the hope of making big gains. But if you do this, be sure it's money you can afford to lose.

For some people, resisting that plunge into the stock market takes a lot of self-restraint. There's always someone around who claims he has the system to help you double your money in a year or two. It's worth exercising that self-restraint, however, until you have money you can really afford to risk.

The fact is you'll also need self-discipline to stick to a regular savings plan and to the budget you've made up. But think of the satisfaction you'll get enjoying that vacation or driving that new car or watching your kids go to college. Those rewards make the budget game worthwhile. A budget, after all, is simply a tool for deciding what's most important to you—and then getting it.

13

Playing with Credit and Flirting with Debt

In 1856 Isaac Singer came up with an ingenious solution to a merchandising problem. His company's cheapest sewing machine sold for $125, but the average American family's income was only $500 a year. Hardly anybody could afford to buy the machines. Singer's solution was startling in its simplicity: five dollars down and five dollars a month. "Buy now, pay later" became a basic part of the American way of life.

At the end of 1973 consumers in this country owed $175 billion. That figure refers to individuals, not businesses, and it does not include mortgages—just personal loans, credit card bills, auto financing, appliances, and department store accounts. That works out to an average $875 debt for every man, woman, and child in the country. Businessmen contend that this debt load is good for the economy. It keeps the factories humming. It enables us to enjoy what we want while we're still earning the cash to pay for it. And it relieves us of the need to tempt thieves by carrying a lot of cash around.

But there's another side to the credit question. Buying on credit can tempt you to spend more than you otherwise would. Some studies show that people who charge their purchases spend 25 to 35 per cent more than those who pay cash. As for the theft problem, some consumer advocates contend that the usual 18-percent-a-year interest charge on so-called revolving consumer loans itself amounts to highway robbery. At those rates, buying "on time" can be a costly practice. And if you get very far into debt, it can cripple any savings goals you set for yourself, such as a future vacation or money for the kids' college education.

Despite these objections, credit is here to stay. So, unfortunately, are delinquent accounts, repossessions, and personal bankruptcies. All of those messy situations have become increasingly frequent in the inflation-plagued economy of the mid-1970s. Bankers say that inflation naturally leads to some default on consumer debt. When food, gas, and heating oil go up in price, it's common for some folks to have trouble meeting car payments, for example. Here are a few questions that would become vital to you if you couldn't meet your obligations.

CSK Quiz

1. True or false: An overdue bill can permanently damage your credit rating.
2. True or false: A creditor can get a court order and take up to 90 per cent of your paycheck.
3. True or false: A creditor can legally repossess merchandise without warning.

Now let's have a look at the answers. Number 1 is false, at least in theory. Federal law requires the agencies that keep tabs on consumers' credit ratings to discard adverse information after seven years—or fourteen years in the case of bankruptcy. There are two problems with this. One is that seven years, while not "permanent," is still a pretty long time. The other is that the law contains loopholes. If you apply for a job paying more than $20,-000 or if you apply for life insurance in an amount more than $50,000, a credit-reporting agency is allowed to drag out any dirt it has on you—no matter how far back it goes.

Number 2 is also false. The practice of a creditor's taking a slice of your paycheck before you do (called garnishment) is regulated by both state and federal laws. Federal laws says creditors can't take more than 25 per cent of your after-tax earnings. It also says that they can't leave you with less than thirty times the federal minimum hourly wage for your weekly take-home pay. Some states have additional restrictions on the practice of garnishment. Maryland, for example, requires that the debtor be left with at least $120 a week to live on. So if someone starts withholding money from your paycheck, don't accept it meekly without checking to see what your rights are.

Number 3 is true, at least in most states. A creditor can repossess merchandise without warning if you're delinquent in your payments. As a matter of practice, most creditors do give written notice of their intention to repossess, but they're under no legal obligation to do so. They *are* obligated to tell you when and how they're going to sell the merchandise they've repossessed. If it's going to be sold at an auction, you must be given a chance to bid.

More likely, your creditor would sell the merchandise privately. In some eight or ten states, he must give you a chance to buy it back before he does so. In most places he's under no such obligation.

When your repossessed goods are sold, the proceeds are applied to your debt. But in most states you must make up the difference if the sale brings your creditor less than you owed him. For example, if you owe $3,000 on a car and it's sold at auction for $2,000, you still owe $1,000 unless you live in a state with laws to the contrary. Check with your Consumer Protection Agency (listed in the Appendix to this book) if you find yourself in this situation. By the way, if your goods are repossessed and then sold for *more* than you owed, the creditor who repossessed your goods legally owes you the excess money.

Most people don't realize how pervasive is the use of credit in our everyday lives, how easy it is to slide into debt. The dialogue that follows is a perfect example of how it's done. We'll interrupt it every so often with some pointers.

Salesman: You've got yourself a real buy there, a real bargain, I'll tell you. You're gonna love that freezer. Believe me, I've got one just like it myself. The wife says it saves her a fortune on food bills. (Shuffles some papers on his desk.) Now I just need this credit application—oh, I see you've got it all filled out.

CUSTOMER: Well, I put down all the stuff about my job and everything, but there are only three lines here for my other accounts.

SALESMAN: Doesn't make a bit of difference. Just put down a couple. It's only a formality anyway. Then you write down on this line, "I have no other debts." And you sign your name right here.

That little gambit is called the "best-foot-forward" trick. Watch out when a salesman tells you to misstate or leave out information. If anything goes wrong later, the creditor can charge fraud. And your friendly salesman could have moved to Tahiti or (more likely) forgotten that he ever told you to fudge on the form. Be honest! Tell the whole truth, even if you need to attach another page.

SALESMAN: Now we have here (takes out a pen and points to the contract, talking rapidly) the cash sales price, $755 including taxes. Down payment zero, thanks to our special homemaker's credit plan. Unpaid balance here. (He is talking very fast, but casually, as if this is all unimportant.) Here's the group life insurance, which incidentally includes at really low rates, terrific bargain, disability insurance, at a cost of only eleven cents per month per $100 of the unpaid balance. And we throw in property insurance covering all merchandise specified in this contract at a monthly rate of only ten cents per hundred.

It's not unusual, on large debts, for the consumer to insure himself in the amount of the loan. That way, if anything happens to him, the loan would still be paid off. What it amounts to is peace of mind. But it's mainly the creditor who will rest easier because of it. Now, the seller can make you take out insurance to cover the debt if he wants to. But he cannot force you to take it from him. If the seller insists that you have insurance to cover the debt, you might tell him you'll buy the insurance independently.

It's usually cheaper that way. And most times, once the seller learns you're not going to buy the insurance through him, he'll just let you skip it.

SALESMAN: (Going even faster, as if to wrap this all up) Finance charge is $268.12 for a total of $1,023.12, which gives us an annual percentage rate of 21.18 per cent, with thirty-six payments of $28.42 due on the fifteenth of each month, and now I need your signature again on all three copies.

Did you catch that? The APR was more than 21 per cent! Remember, the customer here is borrowing money from the seller to buy this freezer; but he could just as well borrow the money somewhere else. And he could get a lot lower interest rate from a bank or a credit union. Over a three-year period the customer will pay a dollar in interest for every three dollars that actually went toward the purchase of the freezer. Most people shop around for the freezer, comparing styles, features, and prices. But not enough people shop around for the money, comparing annual percentage rates. When you're in the market for money, do your comparison shopping on the basis of the annual percentage rate and ignore all other interest rates that may be quoted to you. These may include simple interest, discount interest, add-on interest, or some other kind of interest. Look for the lowest APR and you can't go wrong.

CUSTOMER: (Signing documents) Well, that should do it. Thanks a lot for your help.

The customer just made a big mistake. He never even looked at the fine print. He has no idea what he signed—especially what's on the back. If he had taken his time and done some squinting, he would have seen this notice: "Buyer has read and understands all of the Additional Terms on the reverse side hereof and agrees that they are part of this contract as though set forth at this point."

And what do you suppose is "on the reverse side hereof"? Well, for one thing, there's a clause saying, "Any default hereunder by the Buyer, including failure to make any payment when due, may at Seller's option accelerate all remaining payments and Seller may repossess the property." The meaning of "accelerating" all the remaining payments is that the whole outstanding balance becomes due at once. Then there may be another clause that says if you miss a payment and the creditor has to go to court, you will pay his court costs and attorney's fee, plus 15 per cent of what you owe, as a penalty—plus what you owed in the first place.

Here's another provision that appears in the fine print of many contracts. It says that the merchandise remains the property of the seller and can't be moved from the buyer's address without written permission from the seller. The merchandise cannot be fastened down or built into any house or property. The buyer must keep the property insured against fire and other peril. And —last, but certainly not least—get this: "No transfer, renewal, extension, or assignment of this contract, nor any loss, damage to, or destruction of said property shall release Buyer from his obligation hereunder." That clause is a real beauty. It means that the seller can turn the contract over to a third party, such as a finance company. Then, even if the merchandise doesn't work right, the customer must still keep making installment payments to that third party. The customer has to take up his dispute with the original seller. And the seller isn't really worried about the whole thing, because he's already got his money—from the third party. It adds up to a bag of worms legally known as the "holder-in-due-course" doctrine. There are a few states (New York, California, Vermont, and Massachusetts, for example) where the consumer is fairly well protected against this kind of shuffling. But in most cases the consumer can be left holding the bag—or the defective product that still has to be paid for. (In late 1974, as this book went to press, the FTC had held hearings on the holder-in-due-course problem and was considering issuing a nationwide regulation. Such a regulation might help curb the abuses that have gone on in this area.)

The examples given here should be enough to convince you of

two propositions. First, never sign anything you haven't read *both* sides of. Second, don't sign a contract that makes you uneasy once you've read it. You can, if you wish, ask that certain clauses be stricken. If you do this, make sure the undesirable clauses are crossed out on *all* copies of the contract and that both you and the seller put your initials next to the deletions. Somewhere on the contract both of you should sign your names, with initials next to them, so it will be clear later what the initials meant.

Once you've learned to protect yourself in the fine-print jungle, the next important step in using credit is to know how much credit you can afford. Here's a good rule of thumb: If you're spending more than 20 per cent of your take-home pay to meet installment payments (not including a mortgage), you're probably overextended. Some further questions to ask yourself are these: Do I ever have to skip payments in order to leave enough money for living expenses? Do I find myself taking out new loans to pay off the old? If the answer to either is yes, watch out. You've got some belt-tightening to do. Or you might find yourself in *this* situation:

(Telephone rings. A worried-looking woman answers it. She sounds tentative and frightened. The voice of the man at the other end of the phone line is loud and scornful.)

Voice: Mrs. Mary Wilson, please.

Woman: This is Mrs Wilson.

Voice: This is the city office of the National Federal Collection Bureau. Did you receive a Court Action Notification form?

Woman: Yes, but I—

Voice: Mrs. Wilson, just what's going on with this unpaid MAGIC-KARD account?

(A young girl enters and clings to the woman's skirt. The woman waves the child away and signals her to leave the room. She drops her voice as she speaks into the phone.)

Woman: Look it's late and—

Voice: So is your payment. Now what are you going to do about it?

Woman: Look, give me your number. I'll call you from work tomorrow.

VOICE: Don't give me that. I've called you repeatedly at work and you refuse to talk to me.

WOMAN: We're not allowed to take personal calls on the job.

VOICE: All right, let's wrap this up. Just answer me—are you going to pay this bill or not?

WOMAN: Yes, I am, but I'm having some problems right now—

VOICE: Then you refuse to pay. I see. Well, I'm sure your supervisor will be very interested to know just what kind of an employee he has. What is his name?

WOMAN: (her voice rising in panic.) Look, if you get me fired, you'll never get the money.

VOICE: Oh yes we will. We'll get our money one way or another. We'll take your car and your furniture and anything else you have.

WOMAN: You can't do that!

VOICE: Lady, we can do anything necessary to protect our interests, including the use of force. And let me tell you something else. When we get through with you, you'll never get credit again as long as you live.

WOMAN: Look, I can send you $20. I'll mail it tomorrow.

VOICE: Did you say $20? You've got to be kidding. I want a check for the full amount on my desk first thing Monday morning. Otherwise (rustling is heard as he flips pages) your next-door neighbors the Millers might be very interested in the way you honor your obligations. And on the other side, the Lawsons—

WOMAN: You wouldn't.

VOICE: Why don't you just pay this bill?

WOMAN: I told you, I haven't got the money! If I did, do you think I'd go through this?

VOICE: Mrs. Wilson, where is Mr. Wilson?

WOMAN: We're separated.

VOICE: I'm not surprised. He probably found out what a deadbeat you are.

WOMAN: I don't have to listen to this. I have rights—

VOICE: Listen, lady, don't talk to me about your rights. We have a right to be paid. Do you realize I could charge you with a federal offense? When you accepted a credit card you couldn't afford, you used the U.S. mails to defraud. Now this is your last chance, lady. You mail me a check for the full amount immediately or we're going to take other action. (A bang is heard as he slams down the receiver.)

Being dunned for money owed is unpleasant. The scene you were following was only a stimulation, and the characters in it are imaginary. But real dunnings can be every bit as nasty.

You don't, however, have to put up with the abuse Mrs. Wilson went through in that conversation. Laws in many states give the debtor some rights. Those laws were broken time after time by the bill collector in the simulated dialogue.

First, you'll notice that the collector identified himself as being from "city office of the National Federal Collection Bureau." That's illegal. The Federal Trade Commission has a regulation that says a bill collector cannot use a name that implies he's part of a federal agency. Some thirty-one states also have laws prohibiting names that sound like state agencies.

The caller asked the woman if she had received a "court action notification form." Such forms are often made up to look like court documents. But if a form isn't really issued by a court, it's against the law in most states to try to make the form resemble an official document.

You may have noticed that Mrs. Wilson said it was late when the collector called. And the collector said he had called her "repeatedly" at work. Both late calls and frequently repeated calls are often viewed by courts as a form of harassment. Such harassment is illegal in most states. And if it's done over the phone, it's illegal under the regulations of the Federal Communications Commission (FCC). The job of stopping such calls has been delegated by the FCC to the telephone company. So complain to the phone company if a creditor is calling you so late, or so often, as to make you feel you're being unreasonably harassed.

After Mrs. Wilson said she was having some problems scraping up the money to pay her debt, the collector threatened to call her employer to let him know "just what kind of an employee he has." This tactic, unfortunately, is allowable under current laws in most states. It would be banned, however, under reforms proposed by the National Consumer Law Center. At the moment only a few jurisdictions (such as Maryland and New York City) prohibit a creditor from notifying an employer without going to court first. A few other jurisdictions (Illinois, for example) say that a creditor can get in touch with a debtor's employer only for the purpose of verifying that the debtor really works there.

The tactic of threatening to inform the neighbors about the debt may have struck you as particularly dirty. However, it is legal in most places. It is banned in a handful of progressive states. Similarly, only a few jurisdictions (Maryland and Florida among them) have statutes prohibiting creditors from inflicting emotional distress or mental anguish.

Most states do, however, prohibit creditors from threatening debtors with actions that the creditors cannot legally take. An example in this category was the caller's ridiculous assertion that he would prosecute Mrs. Wilson for "using the U.S. mails to defraud." If someone uses such a line on you, don't fall for it. And if it involves the mail-fraud gambit, report what's happening to the U.S. Post Office.

The use of abusive language (eg. "he probably found out what a deadbeat you are") is prohibited in quite a few states. And threats to use force are illegal everywhere. If you encounter these or similar abuses from creditors, contact your state attorney general's office or the consumer protection agency listed in the Appendix to this book. In some cases you might also get help from a regional office of the Federal Trade Commission.

If you're having trouble paying a bill, the most important thing you should do is face up to the situation and advise your creditor. Explain that you're having difficulty and ask if something can be worked out. Some creditors, especially local companies that want your continued patronage, will accept partial payments. Others will go so far as to allow you to pay only the interest. They add the unpaid amount on the far end of the contract. The main thing is to let them know you are concerned.

There are some creditors, often including the national and international credit card companies that handle travel and entertainment expense items, that will not let you off the hook. They insist upon the full amount as soon as it is due. Some will send more and more strongly worded notices. Then come phone calls from company headquarters, no matter how far away. And ultimately the account will be turned over to a separate bill-collecting company. The professional collector works on a commission— from 15 to 50 per cent of whatever he can get the debtor to part with. He often specializes in the kind of tough methods portrayed in the simulated dialogue presented above. And since he is likely to be calling from out of town, he may not know (or care) whether he is violating local laws in the way he pursues the collection of the debt.

When you have a creditor who won't accept a compromise and you simply can't pay his bill in full, the best thing to do is pay him as much as you can every month, regularly and without fail. Chances are you won't be taken to court, though you'll probably be threatened with that possibility. If you do find yourself in court, a record of faithful (though small) payments will probably make the judge treat you more favorably than he otherwise would.

Once you get all your bills paid up, you can and should get your credit rating updated. That fancy term "credit rating" is just a name for the record that's kept of how well you pay your bills. The keepers of the record are known as credit bureaus, or credit reporting agencies. Some of these, like Retail Credit Company, are national firms. (Retail Credit, based in Atlanta, maintains files on some 48 million individuals.) Others are local outfits. All of them are regulated by the Fair Credit Reporting Act, a federal statute passed in 1971. If you apply for credit and are turned down because of a bad credit rating, you must be so informed in writing by the credit reporting agency that gave you the bad report. Notify the agency immediately, in person or in writing, and request that your file be updated to show that the bills have been paid. Under the law, they must reinvestigate upon your request. If their new investigation shows you're correct, they'll change their records. If they still think they're right, you are entitled to enter a one-hundred-word statement giving your side of the story. Your statement then must be included in all future reports they send out involving the disputed information.

It has been known to happen that a person was denied credit (or insurance or a job) because a credit-reporting agency made an error in his file. If this seems to be happening to you, by all means notify the credit bureau that issued the adverse report and try to correct your record. Most mistakes involve a mixup of identities and can be straightened out fairly readily.

Unfortunately, most consumers who have bad credit ratings are not the victims of human or mechanical error. They are the victims of their own inability to use credit wisely. If you find yourself running deep into debt (if, for example, your debt exceeds the limits described on page 198), you should step back and try to evaluate your temperament. It could be that credit is simply a weakness of yours. You may be a "credit-holic" who needs to swear off the plastic as surely as someone else may need to swear off alcohol.

If the debt pinch you feel is only a slight annoyance, however, you may be able to remedy things by cutting down on the amount of interest you pay. You can do this if you understand how creditors' billing procedures work. There are three basic kinds of billing procedures. If you understand them and know which of your accounts uses which procedure, you can cut down considerably on the interest charges that are emptying your wallet.

With most charge accounts and bank credit cards the APR you pay is 18 per cent. That means you pay 1.5 percent a month on your balance for the month. But what's the balance? That's the crucial question, and that's where the three different ways of calculating interest enter the picture.

The first and most common billing procedure uses the average daily balance. If you owe a merchant $100 for twenty days out of the month and then pay him $50, your balance for the remaining ten days is only $50. Your average daily balance for the month would be $83.33. The way you get that figure is simple. You add up the amounts owed on each day of the billing cycle, and divide by 30 (because there are thirty days in the cycle). So, in this example, from day one to day twenty you owed $100, so that's $100 per day for twenty days or $2,000. Then for the last ten days you owed $50, so that's another $500. The total is $2,500, and when you divide that by 30 you get $83.33 as the average daily balance.

A second billing procedure uses a simpler way of calculating the balance. It's called the adjusted-balance method (or the unpaid balance method). With adjusted balance, you pay interest on your balance as of the last day of the billing cycle. So, in the example given, you would pay interest only on the $50 you still owed as of day 30. Clearly, the adjusted-balance method is better for you in the example used here. But that's because, in this example, you were paying the merchant back. If, instead, you had made further purchases from him during the month, then the adjusted-balance method would prove worse for you. If, for example, you had bought a $50 coat on the twenty-ninth day of the billing cycle, you would be charged interest for the whole month on $150 (the cost of the coat plus the $100 you already owed).

The third basic billing method uses what's called the previous balance. With this method, you're billed for the month based on how much money you owed at the start of the month. So, in the example given, where you owe $100 but pay off $50 during the month, you would still be charged interest on the entire $100. Not until the following month would you have your balance reduced to $50. It's clear that this method is the least favorable to you. For that reason it's wise to avoid buying anything on credit from any store that uses the previous-balance method. Some state and local governments (Massachusetts, Maryland, and Washington, D.C., for example) have gone so far as to outlaw the use of the previous-balance method.

Well, now that you know all this, how's it going to save you money? Like this, in three easy lessons: (1) Pay your average-daily-balance accounts early in the billing cycle; (2) Pay your adjusted-balance accounts late in the billing cycle; (3) Avoid having any previous-balance accounts. That way, you'll always be paying on the lowest possible balance and you'll keep your interest charges down.

That kind of juggling will help if your credit pinch is of the normal, everyday variety. But what if you're really in over your head? Then more drastic steps may be called for. Some areas have nonprofit credit counseling agencies you can go to. They'll sit down with you (at no charge) and help you work out a plan for getting out of debt. If you can't find counseling, or if the advice you get still isn't enough to pull you out of the morass, you should consider a plan known as "Chapter 13." Under that plan, a court-appointed referee handles your debts. It costs you something, but it's a less drastic procedure than bankruptcy, and it's designed to ensure that eventually all your creditors will be paid. Your last resort is to declare yourself bankrupt. Bankruptcy is a subject worthy of a whole book in itself, and whole books have, indeed, been written about it. Rather than attempt a capsule explanation here, we suggest you read one of them.

Falling into debt is easy. In fact, if you do it with some flair and imagination, it can be downright fun. Pulling yourself *out* of debt, however, is a different story. The more you know about the wise use of credit, the less likely you are to need to learn about bankruptcy and its alternatives.

14

Sales Stratagems
You Should Know

As a consumer, you shop in a market place that is almost schizoid
in its functioning. The market place is designed on the one hand
to serve you, and on the other hand to take your money away.
That's fine as long as the two elements of the market place's personality stay in balance. But you don't have to be paranoid to suspect that the second element sometimes becomes dominant.

There are almost endless variations of sales tricks that you
should watch out for. We can't hope to discuss them all. But in
this chapter, we'd like to alert you to four areas where abuses are
common: (1) misleading advertising, (2) pyramid plans, (3)
high-pressure door-to-door sales tactics, and (4) deceptive mail-
order sales. The principles involved in these areas will help you
in other areas as well.

To start with, let's see how familiar you are with some of the
forces operating to affect you in the market place.

CSK Quiz

1. True or false: Manufacturers spend about $13 a year for every
   American consumer to determine his buying habits and bom-
   bard him with an average of at least 100 advertising messages
   a day.

2. True or false: Women are more susceptible to the pitches of door-to-door salesmen then men.
3. True or false: Pyramid sales meetings are well publicized to attract as many people as possible.
4. True or false: If you receive unsolicited merchandise through the mail, you may legally treat it as a gift—that is, you may keep it and not pay for it.

Here are the answers. Number 1 is false, because the figures given *understate* the impact advertising has in our daily lives. In 1970 manufacturers spent an average of $95 per person (not $13) to determine each consumer's buying habits. And that research is followed up by an advertising bombardment which subjects the average person to some 600 (not 100) advertising messages per day.

Number 2 is also false. You may be surprised by this, fellows, but research shows men, not women, to be the softer touch for door-to-door sales presentations. According to industry data, door-to-door salesmen also find that people under twenty-five, the elderly, and the poor make good sales prospects.

Number 3 is false as well. People who run pyramid schemes don't publicize their sales meetings very well. The number in attendance is purposely held down so those who work for the operation outnumbered newcomers three or four to one. Many of the workers will pose as ordinary visitors, planting themselves throughout the unsuspecting crowd. Then they get extremely enthusiastic about the sales pitch, inspiring the newcomers to join the bandwagon.

Number 4 is true. According to postal law, it is illegal to send unsolicited merchandise through the mail, except for free samples or merchandise mailed by charitable organizations soliciting contributions. In any case, you can treat the merchandise as a gift. Do with it whatever you like. Keep it, destroy it, or mark it refused and send it back; it's entirely up to you. It's illegal for anyone to bill you for it or to send you dunning letters. (If they do, you can reply by sending them a bill for storage charges. This isn't encouraged by the Post Office, so we're not really recommending it. But the thought is rather amusing.)

If you answered all four questions correctly, you're probably quite well equipped to protect your interests in the rough and tumble of the market place. But feel free to read on: You might find something to help you sharpen your skills still further.

You'll remember the first stratagem we wanted to warn you about is misleading advertising. Ads can mislead in a variety of ways. For one thing, they can lie outright (e.g., Super-Miracle Hair Tonic will make your bald head sprout hair again in just 20 seconds!). But plain lying is passé nowadays; it's done mainly by small, marginal firms. More common now is that an ad will use partial truths and emotional manipulation to distract you from a factual, rational analysis of the product's merits.

This kind of manipulation is accomplished through a variety of propaganda devices. For example, there's the testimonial. Sports heroes, movie starlets, and other famous people can always be found touting the merits of one product or another. Such people are paid well for their appearances on behalf of a product. But the viewer, or reader, is supposed to think, "Hey, if I use that product, I'll be as desirable as that person is." Then there's the opposite tack, the "plain folks" approach. Here, an ad uses people who don't look like models; they may even be homely or bumbling. You're supposed to buy the product because the people selling it are "just good old plain folks." The trouble with these ads is the same as with those using celebrities: They're based on your emotional reaction to the person using the product. Meanwhile, they don't tell you anything about the merits of the product.

Then there are the glittering generalities. A product is "wonderful," "beautiful," "dynamite," or whatever. And it's being sold at "fantastic savings." When someone speaks in generalities like this, an intelligent consumer would be justified in assuming that he hasn't any specifics to back the claims up. Otherwise, why wouldn't he cite the specifics?

The reverse side of the glittering-generalities coin is the selective use of "studies." These are often done by unnamed "authorities." For health-related products, you are told that "doctors" recommend the product. Or the product's merits have been proven by a "leading" or "major" consumer organization or testing center. Your basic rule should be to distrust all studies cited in ads, unless the people who conducted the study are named. Any company can finance a "study" to prove whatever it wants or find an "expert" to testify to the merits of its product. As for endorsements by consumer organizations, these should be taken with several grains of salt. Truly objective consumer organizations protect their reputation for impartiality by refusing to allow their names to be used for commercial purposes.

Another advertising technique that plays on your emotions rather than telling you about the product is the "transfer" tactic. With a transfer, an advertiser attempts to take your good feelings about something entirely unrelated to his product, and associate them (illogically) with the product. Thus, you'll see products wrapped in the theme of motherhood, America, the flag, and moral fiber.

A final propaganda device that's often used is the bandwagon effect. In substance, the ad says, "Everybody, or at least the majority, is doing it. If you want to be in, you have to get with the majority." The ad plays on the desire to be accepted, to be part of the crowd. The same technique is used, as we noted before, in pyramid sales.

None of the techniques we've been discussing is illegal. But all of them are methods you, as a discerning consumer, should suspect. There are times to let your emotions govern your actions. But not when someone is trying to sell you something. Then you should be interested in the cold, hard facts.

The same philosophy applies with double strength when it comes to pyramid plans. Advertising, after all, may steer you to a worthwhile product or service. But pyramid plans are always designed to line someone else's pockets at your expense.

A pyramid plan is a money-making enterprise in which the chief source of money is the recruitment of new members into the plan. There is a product involved to give the whole operation the appearance of legitimacy. The product may be cosmetics, fire alarms, motivation kits, or some other item. But peddling the product is not how you'll make your big money, according to the promises dangled before you. The big money, they say, comes when you, the distributor, recruit new members as sub-distributors.

When you sign up as a distributor, you have to pay a large sum of money, perhaps $6,000. In return for this money, you get a few crates full of the product, and, more important, the right to recruit new members as sub-distributors. Each of the sub-distributors you bring in must pay, say $2,000 to the enterprise. Of that sum, perhaps $700 would go to you. In this case, you would have to recruit nine people to make your original money back. What you're likely to find, as many pyramid-plan victims have found to their sorrow, is that recruiting nine sub-distributors is almost impossible. After all, why should anyone want to become a sub-distributor of your product . . . unless he's gullible enough to think he'll make his money back by signing up nine sub-sub-distributors? So what's likely to happen is that you'll end up having poured money down the drain. As a consolation prize, you'll have a few leftover crates of unsold goods.

Conversations with people who have lost money in pyramid schemes consistently reveal one fact: The emotion-charged pyramid sales meeting is the crux of the entire fleecing operation. As we've already noted (in the answer to quiz question 2), these meetings are packed with people who pose as new prospects. But they're really members of the pyramid scheme who try to whip enthusiasm to a frenzied pitch, making you feel alone and ashamed if you don't go along. The atmosphere of the pyramid sales meeting closely parallels that of the revival meeting. It's full of exhortation, repetition, litany. And a religion is indeed preached there—the religion of the fast buck. The emotion appealed to is greed, a very natural emotion that's present in almost all of us. When a person's interest is aroused, he's asked to put down $100 or so to show "good faith," and invited to another meeting. The second meeting, sometimes called a "golden opportunity weekend," is often a sort of a retreat lasting a couple of days and held out in the country. In this isolated setting, the pyramid propaganda machine goes into high gear, working on the prospective recruit until he plunks down his $6,000 (or whatever sum) to become a distributor.

The only people who actually make money in pyramid operations are the founders, people like Glenn Turner. Turner, running such pyramid operations as Koscot cosmetics and Dare to Be Great, accumulated immense wealth as he zoomed around the country. But let's put it this way: When you go to a pyramid sales meeting, you're already late. Those giving the speeches are the early birds. And those listening often end up as the worms.

Should someone try to recruit you for a pyramid plan, don't get involved. You might want to contact local law-enforcement authorities, since pyramids are beginning to be outlawed in some localities. Don't try to give the cold shoulder to the recruiter by telling him you don't have any money. That will only encourage him, since the operations tend to prey on have-nots. Pyramid personnel have been known to advise prospects on the best method of securing a loan. There's no record, though, of their ever having helped to pay one off. They may suggest the prospect go to several different banks, or even lie about the reason for borrowing (which is illegal conduct in itself).

In the interest of fairness, it's important to draw a distinction between pyramid schemes and legitimate multilevel operations. Legitimate multilevel operations do use distributors, many of whom are part-time recruits. But they charge no enormous initial investment fee. They do not use high-pressure tactics to recruit distributors. They let you back out and sell back your goods to the company (often at 90 per cent of what you paid for them) if you become disenchanted. And they *do not* promise you a get-rich-quick pot of gold at the end of the rainbow. Pyramid plans *do* use high-pressure tactics, emphasize recruiting rather than selling the product, and make you keep the product you've committed yourself to distribute. And they *do* promise you a pot of gold. But if you fall for it, you end up only chasing the rainbow.

Let's turn now to our third area of consideration, door-to-door sales. Some people think door-to-door salesmen are like pyramid operators, slick hucksters out to take away their victims' hard-earned money. That characterization is not really fair. There are at least 1,500 companies that market products door-to-door. These companies employ well over 2 million sales persons, most of whom are honest.

Nevertheless, authorities report many complaints about salesmen's using dishonest means to make a sale. Complaints include the use of deceptive means to get inside the door; high-pressure sales tactics; little untruths about the quality, price, or character of the product; overpricing; and the nuisance aspect of the salesman's knocking on the door in the first place. Then, of course, there's the whole separate question of sales resistance. Some people feel so charmed by (or sorry for) certain salesmen that they buy things they really didn't need. Even if the salesman's pitch was honest, that kind of spending can quickly blow a big hole in the family budget.

If you get talked into buying something from a door-to-door salesman that you don't really want, you have three days to cancel the deal. What you must do is notify the company, *in writing*, that you've changed your mind and you want to cancel the contract you've just signed. Just telephoning or talking to the salesman or the company won't do. You must send notice in writing. And it's best to go to the post office and send it by certified mail. (Sending something by certified mail isn't hard or expensive. If you've never done it before, a postal employee will be glad to show you how.) This way, you have proof that you sent the company written notice. You should also keep a copy of your letter for your own records, in case there's any dispute. And remember, the letter must be sent within three business days of the day you made your purchase.

This three-day "cooling-off period," as it's known, is provided for by Federal Trade Commission regulations passed in 1974. So it applies all over the country, to any purchases of goods or services costing $25 or more. (In addition, many states have similar three-day cooling-off-period laws.) The FTC rule protects you whether you make your purchase in your own home or someone else's home (as long as it doesn't take place in a store). Unlike many state laws, it protects you even if you *asked* the salesman to come (as long as you weren't in his store when you asked him). There are a few cases where the FTC rule doesn't apply. It won't help you if you're buying supplies for your business, insurance, real estate, or securities. But it covers just about everything else.

Under the FTC cooling-off rule, you can waive your three-day cooling-off period if there's an emergency. This happens most often when a consumer wants to contract for emergency home repairs. But to waive your rights, you must write out (in your own handwriting) a statement that the situation was an emergency and that you therefore have decided to waive your three-day-period rights. Companies are not allowed to give you a form for you to sign, waiving these rights. Thus, consumers are protected against the quickie home-repair operator who says, "Just sign here, buddy," and goes to work before the consumer can change his mind. Of course, the protection is of the most use to consumers who know what their rights are under the law. The FTC regulation supersedes all state cooling-off-period regulations, except where the state statutes are stronger in protecting the consumer.

Before you sign any contract with a door-to-door salesman, you should of course read it carefully. One thing that should be in the contract is a section explaining your right to cancel it (titled, "Buyer's Right to Cancel"). If it's not there, there's something wrong, and you shouldn't sign. While you're reading the contract, watch out for some of the dangerous clauses we described on pages 196-197. Remember that neither you nor the salesman is legally bound to any verbal agreement, only to the written contract. Be sure everything you've agreed to is in writing, including the exact amount of money involved. Be certain there are no blank spaces that could be filled in without your knowledge. And don't forget to get a copy of the contract.

In general, don't be rushed, whether the contract is for home repairs, an encyclopedia, a vacuum cleaner, or any other product or service. If you want to think it over, ask the salesman to leave the contract with you. Don't sign unless you're sure you want the product or service being offered. It's risky to rely on the three-day cooling off period. Something might go wrong, and you'd lose part or all of your money. Or you might change your mind after three days were already gone. You have all the time in the world *before* you sign the contract. If a salesman is really trustworthy, he won't insist on rushing you.

There are some other signs, besides the high-pressure rush, that should make you look suspiciously at a salesman. If he offers to loan you his own money for the first installment of a purchase, consider it a definite danger signal. The practice is unbusinesslike on the salesman's part. As likely as not, it's intended to shame you into a purchase you don't need or can't afford.

Beware, too, of salesmen who base their pitch on the educational welfare of your children. Especially pernicious are those who claim to have been sent by your child's school to offer a possible remedy for his poor performance. The remedy turns out to be an encyclopedia, teaching machine, or some other expensive item you have to buy. Parents, concerned about their children, sometimes don't stop to think that school systems don't operate this way. If someone tells you he was sent to you by your child's school, tell him you'll check with the school to verify that claim.

Other danger signs include extravagant bargain claims and razzle-dazzle bonuses. If a door-to-door salesman tells you an item normally costs $700 but he can offer it to you for $298, you have reason to question his honesty. Discounting is an accepted practice, but claims of 50 or 75 per cent discounts are likely to be exaggerated, at best. And if a salesman offers you all kinds of free "extras" when you buy his basic product, it's a good bet strings are attached somewhere. Perhaps the attractive-sounding bonuses are really cheap or shoddy. Or perhaps the basic product's cost is partly hidden, so you'll end up paying more than you anticipated.

A variant of the bonus pitch is the old "free-gift" gimmick. You're told, either by mail or by a salesman, that you have won a free gift. Some consumers are very excited by this prospect. What they find out, all too often, is that in order to collect the "free" gift, they have to buy something else first, or at least listen to a sales pitch. As often as not, that pitch is a high-pressure barrage designed to make you feel like a worm if you don't buy something to compensate the company for its generosity.

The free-gift gimmick is legal in most places, so long as the company spells out clearly what you have to do to earn the gift. But if they claim the gift is offered "with absolutely no obligation" on your part, and then it turns out there *are* strings attached, they are violating FTC regulations. You should report the violation to a regional office of the FTC.

A final tactic to watch out for when you deal with the door-to-door brigade is referral selling. The way it works is simple: The seller induces you to sign a contract by telling you he'll give you a commission, a discount, or some other financial consideration if you will give him the names of other people who might buy his product. His promises are often just a pitch to get you to sign the contract. If you run into this tactic, show the salesman the door. And you might contact your state consumer protection agency as well, since referral selling is illegal in some states.

Many of the same gimmicks that mar the door-to-door sales scene are present in mail order sales as well. Referral selling, for example, is often part of a mail-order pitch. According to the U.S. Postal Service, "Each year thousands of families end up paying exorbitant prices for . . . central vacuum cleaning systems, color TV, intercom systems, and burglar alarm units" bought through mail-order referral-selling schemes. These families, the Postal Service says, "were lulled into believing there was an unlimited market . . . and that 'with all our friends we won't have any trouble getting enough commissions to reimburse us for our purchase.'" But in fact, postal inspectors have found that "in almost every instance the victim is lucky to earn even one or two commissions, and the family is stuck with an appliance they couldn't afford at half the price."

The razzle-dazzle bonus, the free gift, the extravagant bargain claim—all of these are as much a part of the mail-order scene as the door-to-door scene. So many of the precautions already mentioned in this chapter will help you resist phony pitches in the mail-order area. As with door-to-door salesmen, most mail-order houses are honest. But there are plenty of exceptions. The very anonymity of mail-order transactions lends itself to chicanery. So does the fact that you don't see the merchandise until *after* you've paid for it. Too often, the mail-order game turns out to be (if you'll pardon the pun) a lick and a promise. Sometimes your purchase never arrives. Sometimes it does arrive, and you wish it hadn't. Too often, the glowing promises of the ad are broken and you discover too late that *you're* the one who's been licked.

Thousands of mail-order rackets are in operation today. There are business opportunities, land grabs, charity gifts, correspondence schools, dance studio offers, foreign employment, lonely hearts clubs, work-at-home proposals, unordered merchandise, chain letters, and so on. One high-ranking postal official estimates the public is taken for well over $500 million a year by mail fraud. You shouldn't, though, let that figure scare you into thinking all mail-order merchants are frauds. Shopping through the mail can be convenient, easy, and fun—*if* you know what you're doing.

First of all, you should know about a group called the Direct Mail Marketing Association (DMMA). It's a trade association representing some 1,600 businesses that either sell or advertise by mail. The DMMA will try to help you if you have a problem with a mail-order house. It will advise you to complain to the company if your merchandise is defective in some way or if it hasn't arrived thirty days after being ordered. If thirty more days go by and you haven't gotten satisfaction as a result of your complaint letter, then write to the DMMA. The address is: Mail Order Action Line, Direct Mail Marketing Association, Inc., 6 East 43d Street, New York, N.Y. 10017. The DMMA has more success in dealing with its own members than with firms that aren't members (some of the latter are fly-by-night outfits), but it will try to intercede on your behalf with both.

The DMMA has two more programs of possible interest to many consumers. One of them is for people who don't like getting third-class mail, or "junk" mail as it's often called. If you are among them, you can write the Mail Preference Service of the DMMA and ask to have your name taken off the mailing lists of the association's 1,600 members. This will result in a significant decrease in the amount of third-class mail you get. It won't end it completely, since some mailers don't belong to the association. (If you've been getting pornographic mail that you don't want, the DMMA can't help you, since none of its members are pornographers. But there is a way you can stop getting sexually oriented ads. Go to the main post office in your town and fill out Postal Service form 2201.)

Besides getting your name off of mailing lists, the DMMA can help you get *on* them, if you wish. The association has a list of some twenty-seven interest areas, such as books, stamps, stocks, gardening, and so on. You can write their Mail Preference Service and ask for a list of the interest areas. After checking off the ones that interest you most, you can send the form back and start getting *more* ads in the area of your choice. One caution: Once your name gets on any mailing list, it's bound to end up on other mailing lists as well. (That's because mailers swap or sell the lists to each other.) So if you want to get your name off any DMMA lists, you must have it taken off all of them.

Knowing about the DMMA is a good start for any mail-order consumer. There is more you should know, though, to protect yourself. Here are a few tips, culled from brochures put out by the DMMA, the Council of Better Business Bureaus, and the U.S. Postal Service:

• Don't rely solely on the picture of the item in the ad. Instead, note the size, weight, color, contents, or other aspects of the item, as described in the text of the ad. Note the facts on your order, next to the order number, if possible.

• Always keep a copy of the ad or brochure you order from.

• Beware of fake "contests" that you have "won." These are simply another version of the free-gift gimmick described earlier.

• See if the ad promises a guaranteed delivery date. And if you're ordering holiday gifts, do it well in advance.

• If you're in doubt about the reputation of a mail-order firm, check with the Better Business Bureau, the Chamber of Commerce, or your state or local consumer protection office. (State offices are listed in the Appendix to this book.)

• Be leery of mail-order "debt consolidation" offers. According to the Postal Service, your first few checks to a mail-order debt-consolidation service may well go to pay the consolidator's fee instead of being credited to merchants threatening to repossess your car or appliances. So you will have only deepened your financial troubles.

• Look for a company policy on returns. If the policy isn't stated, ask for it before sending any sizable order. It's sometimes wise to test out a mail-order firm you haven't used before by making your first order a small one.

• Place your order at least thirty days before you want the goods. See if there's a cut-off date for the placing of your order, after which delivery won't be guaranteed.

• Watch out for mail-order insurers who say they'll insure you no matter how many accidents you've had. If they don't care about your driving record, it may well be because they don't plan on your being able to find them when it comes time for them to pay a claim.

• If you won't accept a substitute for the item you're ordering, say so on your order.

• Pay by check or money order; otherwise you have no proof you've paid. Keep a record of your order also, including the name and address of the company.

• Don't buy real estate you haven't seen, no matter how good it sounds in the ad. Clever wording can disguise a lot's faults to a great degree. Some land sold through the mails turns out to be under water, miles from the nearest utility connections, or in the middle of a desert.

• When you receive your merchandise, check at once to see that it's intact and that it's what you ordered. If it's not, notify the company at once. Don't try to send the package back COD. Save a copy of your letter and wait for the company's instructions. After thirty days, contact the DMMA if you haven't gotten satisfaction.

• If you think you've been defrauded by a mail-order firm, notify the postal service. One reason mail fraud flourishes is that only one out of ten victims takes this step.

• If you receive unordered merchandise, remember that you can treat it as a gift. If you didn't order it, you don't have to pay for it.

• Don't give money to mail-order charities you haven't heard of; some are frauds. Be aware that some phony charities use names designed to sound like genuine and well-known charities.

• Be skeptical of any mail-order offers to help you find an inheritance from a long-lost relative. These offers are always contingent on your paying a fee. In one such recent scheme, thousands of families named Kelly received such offers.

• Be wary of work-at-home plans. Usually you have to pay a fee to join such plans or you have to order raw materials from the company. Yet often, when you've performed your part of the bargain, the company finds a loophole to avoid doing anything to help you sell the items you've made. Usually, it's that your work doesn't measure up to the company's (unspecified) "high standards."

• Plants and trees are another commodity you should be cautious about ordering through the mails. Some firms specialize in marketing weeds under imaginative names, such as Golden Crowns (dandelions), Pink Magic (burrs), and the Incredible Snowstorm Plant (milkweed).

One area that deserves special attention is that of mail-order study courses or vocational training. More than half a million people a year enroll in private home-study schools. No one knows for sure how many private correspondence schools there are, but estimates range into the thousands. They offer courses in everything from auto mechanics to wildlife training. Some of them advertise, on matchbook covers and in magazines, that they'll dramatically increase your earning potential.

You should be quite skeptical about home-study ads. No reputable correspondence school will imply that you are guaranteed a job of any kind upon completion of its course. And no correspondence school can qualify you to practice as a doctor, nurse, or lawyer. Claims of the salaries earned by graduates are often greatly exaggerated or based on the school's handful of most-successful graduates.

One of the most successful come-ons used by phony schools is fake accreditation by some agency. It often turns out that the "agencies" are composed of none other than the officials of the school. The U.S. Office of Education does not have any ratings for correspondence schools. But one private body, the National Home Study Council, does issue accreditation to some schools, and its seal of approval is meaningful. It evaluates not only a school's curriculum and faculty but also its financial status and advertising practices. You can get a directory of accredited schools for home study by writing the National Home Study Council, 1601 18th Street N.W., Washington, D.C. 20009.

Accreditation is a good sign. But the mere fact a course is accredited doesn't mean it will necessarily meet your needs. Before you sign any contracts, check with businesses in your area to make sure they do hire correspondence graduates from the school you're interested in. It's also a good idea to contact your state department of education (or related state agency). They can tell you if the course you're considering meets their guidelines. What you learn *about* correspondence schools is free. And in the long run that education may be more helpful than the course you were planning to pay for.

15

Defogging the World
of Insurance

Quick, now, how much health insurance do you carry? How much life insurance? How much auto insurance? If you don't know, you're not unusual. Most people have some insurance, but many of us do not know how much protection it really provides. Often we don't even know the limits on what the insurance will pay, let alone the conditions for payment spelled out in the fine print. It needn't be that way. In fact, you can probably learn a tremendous amount about insurance in less than a week. How? Take one evening to read this chapter. Then take another three or four evenings to sit down and read your insurance policies. It won't be the most exciting week you've ever spent in your life, but it might be one of the most informative.

Let's face it: Insurance policies are boring to read. They're meant to be, for two reasons. First, the complex legal jargon is intended to stand up technically in a court of law. Second, that same jargon keeps you, the consumer, from knowing what's really in your policy. And often the companies would just as soon you didn't know.

Recently, a welcome trend was started by Herbert Denenberg, often described as a maverick in the world of insurance regulation. Denenberg was (until he resigned in 1974 for an unsuccessful run for the U.S. Senate) Insurance Commissioner of Pennsylvania. In that office, he did things for consumers that insurance commissioners had never done before. One thing he did was apply a "readability" test to some insurance policies. Using a statistical measure of readability developed by Rudloph Flesch, Denenberg said, in effect, "If an insurance company's policy is too difficult to read, then it can't be sold in Pennsylvania." The procedure provoked an uproar, and Denenberg wasn't in office long enough to apply it to all policies. (Nor, probably, did the commissioner's office have sufficient staff to do that.) But the concept attracted a wave of favorable publicity and got across to the public. As a result, some companies are now stressing the readability of their policies. Some of them even make it an advertising point. And well they should, since a policy he can read is worth much more to a consumer than one he can't.

You, however, would be unusually lucky if your policy is easily readable. We can hope that this chapter will help you unfog some of the language you encounter in your policies and understand better what policies you own, and what policies you may need.

Let's take life insurance first. We might begin by testing what you already know in the life insurance field.

CSK Quiz

1. True or false: Cash-value insurance provides a lifetime of protection.
2. True or false: The cash value in an insurance policy is the same as in a savings account.
3. True or false: The best place to keep your policy is in a safe deposit box, in your name only.

Now let's look at the answers. Number 1 is true. There are two major types of life insurance, term and cash value. A term policy, as its name implies, insures you only for a specific term of years, though it may be renewable after that, up to age 65 or so. A cash-value policy (often called a whole-life, or straight-life policy) will provide insurance protection as long as you live and pay the annual fee (called the "premium") to the company. This difference is important, but it does not mean that you should necessarily buy a cash value policy, as we'll see.

Number 2 is false. The cash value in an insurance policy resembles a savings account in many ways, but there are some key differences. If you put money in a savings account, you can get at it any time, at no cost to you. Not so with the cash value in an insurance policy. To get the cash value, you either have to give up the policy (ending your insurance protection) or borrow from the insurance company, using the cash value as your collateral. If you borrow, you must pay the company interest, ranging from 4 to 6 per cent a year. So the cash value in an insurance policy is less accessible than money in an ordinary savings account. But there's also another angle (significant mainly to people in high tax brackets). While interest paid to you from a savings account is taxable every year, the buildup of cash in an insurance policy is not taxed until you surrender the policy. (And even then, it's taxed rather lightly.)

Number 3 is also false. If you want to keep your policy in a safe deposit box, the box should be in the name of your spouse, not in your name. Once you die, it takes a court order to open a deposit box with your own name on it. So your policy would be unavailable to your spouse just when it was needed. Actually, there's no need to keep the policy in a safe deposit box at all. Companies can replace a policy if it's lost (you might keep a record of the policy *number* in your safe deposit box, as a precaution). The policy should be kept someplace easily accessible, and you should be sure that your beneficiaries know where it is.

With those questions and answers in mind, let's examine the basic mechanisms of life insurance. The concept, at its root, is simple enough. You pay the life insurance company a certain number of dollars a year, called the premium. In return, they agree to pay your beneficiary (your spouse, for example, or anyone else you name) a specified sum of money when you die. This specified sum is called the face value of the policy, or the death benefit. If the policy you buy has cash value in it, your beneficiary still gets the same death benefit, *not* the death benefit plus the cash value. Another way of putting it is that the cash value goes to pay part of the death benefit, and the company makes up the rest from its own funds.

The last point may be clearer if we use an example. Take a cash-value policy with a death benefit of $10,000. Its premium would stay the same every year. If you were thirty-five years old when you bought the policy, the premium might be about $180 a year. The cash value would gradually go up as shown in this table:

	$10,000 Cash-Value Policy		
Age	Premium	Cash Value	Death Benefit
35	$180	0	$10,000
45	$180	$1,600	$10,000
55	$180	$4,000	$10,000

If you surrendered the policy at age fifty-five, you would get $4,000 back. If you died at age fifty-five while the policy was still in force, your beneficiaries would get $10,000 (not $10,000 plus $4,000).

The same kind of chart for a term policy would look quite different. Let's take what is probably the most common type of term policy, five-year level renewable term:

	$10,000 Level Term Policy		
Age	Premium	Cash Value	Death Benefit
35	$66	0	$10,000
40	$82	0	$10,000
45	$107	0	$10,000
50	$152	0	$10,000
55	$210	0	$10,000

These tables tell you a lot about the differences between term and cash-value policies. You'll note that the term policy has a cash value of zero throughout its life. That's typical. Term policies normally have no cash value; occasionally they have a token amount. You'll note also that the premium for this type of term policy gets higher as you get older. It goes up at the end of each term if you elect to renew your coverage. What you *also* will note is that the premium for the term policy, until you reach age fifty-five, is cheaper than the premium for the cash-value policy. That's also typical. And that's the appeal of term insurance. It is in many ways cheaper than cash-value life insurance. We'll elaborate on that point shortly.

You noticed that the policy illustrated was called "level" term. That means that the death benefit stays level (in this case at $10,000). There's also a type of policy called *decreasing* term. With it, the premium stays the same every year, but the amount of protection (the death benefit) drops at each renewal period. A decreasing term policy might be tabulated something like this:

	$10,000 Decreasing Term Policy		
Age	*Premium*	*Cash Value*	*Death Benefit*
35	$71	0	$10,000
45	$71	0	$6,670
55	$71	0	$3,340
65	0	0	0

Decreasing term policies are often used to cover the declining balance on a home mortgage. That way, if the breadwinner dies, the family is assured of keeping its house. Decreasing term is very well suited for this purpose. As general life insurance, though, it has its drawbacks. The smaller death benefit in the later years may just not be enough, and if the breadwinner goes out to buy more insurance, he'll find his increased age makes his rates much higher. Or he may have developed medical problems and have difficulty finding insurance at all.

For your basic life insurance protection, you'll probably want to choose a cash-value policy, a level term policy, or a combination of the two. The big advantage of term is that it's cheap in the early years. A man in his twenties or thirties can easily buy three or four times as much protection in the form of term as he could buy for the same money in the form of a cash-value policy. Often, that is the period in a breadwinner's life when young children at home make the need for life insurance protection the greatest.

If you buy a term policy, you should get the kind that's renewable at the end of each term (every five years, ten years, or whatever). However, even renewable term policies end at age sixty-five or so. Cash-value policies don't, which is a possible advantage for them. On the other hand, most people with cash-value policies would normally surrender them at retirement age anyway to augment their retirement income.

This money tucked away may seem like a big advantage in the cash-value policy. But of course the consumer has paid a price for it all along, in the form of higher premiums. Which type of policy, then, is really more economical? Actuarial tests performed by Consumers Union lead to these conclusions:

- If you die while the policy's in force, term is always more economical.
- If you buy term and invest your savings (from the lower premiums) at about 5 per cent return after taxes, then a good term policy and a good cash-value policy are about equally economical.
- If you have great difficulty saving, or if your investments earn 4 per cent or less (after taxes), then a good cash-value policy is more economical for you than a term policy, *assuming* you live to cash it in.

These considerations aside, the most important thing is for you to protect your family adequately. For some people, buying term insurance is the only way they can afford to do that. As for figuring out how much insurance you do need, there are no simple rules. A good insurance agent will be a help to you in this regard. Another valuable resource is a book called *The Consumer's Union Report on Life Insurance*. It contains worksheets to help you figure out how much coverage you need. One thing to guard against is the assumption that your family will need the full amount of your present salary year after year after you're gone. They won't need that much. And besides, to insure yourself for that much would simply be prohibitive. Remember, too, that your family is probably entitled to survivor's benefits under Social Security. A good agent will help you find out how much these benefits will amount to and deduct that from the amount of other life insurance you'll need.

And how do you find a good agent? Again, there's no magic formula. A starting point might be to talk to your friends and business associates. The agent you're looking for will answer your questions fully and clearly. And he'll be willing to leave his proposals in writing for you to examine at your leisure. Nor will he object if you do some comparison shopping with other agents or companies. Such shopping may save you a lot of money, since surveys have shown the cost of similar policies can vary 100 per cent or more.

Adding to the general confusion prevailing about life insurance is the plethora of so-called "riders" available with most policies. Riders are simply options. When you consider them, you should find out from your agent exactly how much they add to the cost of the policy each year. Then weigh that cost against the rider's value to you.

One rider is called "waiver of premium in the case of disability." Under this clause the company will pay your premiums if you become disabled for six months or more, and some will reimburse you for the premiums you paid during the first six months of your illness. It's a way of keeping your insurance in force in time of financial hardship. If you're considering this rider, be sure to read the policy's exact definition of "disability." Some companies don't believe you're disabled unless you've lost a couple of limbs. Others use a more lenient, more reasonable standard.

Another option is called double (or triple) indemnity. It often works like this: The company will agree to pay your beneficiary twice the stated death benefit of the policy if you die in an accident, and three times the stated death benefit if you die as a fare-paying passenger on a common carrier. So, if you held a $10,000 policy with double and triple indemnity and you died in a car crash, your beneficiary would receive $20,000. If you died in a plane crash (or a train or bus accident), your beneficiary would get $30,000. This option typically costs a thirty-five-year-old man with a $10,000 policy about $9 a year. (The price goes up as the size of the policy goes up.) If you select this option, you're actually gambling on how you're going to die. And the companies will take your bet because they know how slim are the chances of an accidental death.

Another option is the guaranteed insurability rider, offered in connection with cash-value policies. It's the company's promise that you will be able to buy at least a certain amount of additional insurance from them in the future at standard rates. Thus, if you find you have a serious disease, you can still buy insurance for the same price as someone who is healthy. For our hypothetical thirty-five-year-old, this option will cost roughly an extra $15 a year on a $10,000 policy (more on a bigger policy). Some people feel that the guaranteed insurability rider is just an effort to tie up your future insurance purchases with the same company. Others feel it's a small price to pay for the security of knowing you can always get insurance. You'll have to decide whether it's valuable enough to add to *your* policy.

Let's turn next to the realm of health insurance. Unlike life insurance, health insurance is commonly provided as a fringe benefit to a job. That's nice for your pocketbook. But if you're not paying directly for your health insurance coverage, you may not be too familiar with its provisions. That would be unfortunate, because you're more likely to need your medical insurance than you might think. Every year about one out of every seven Americans is hospitalized. Of those, 60 per cent require surgery. More than 8,000 workers become disabled every *day*. When these misfortunes occur, tens of thousands of Americans find themselves paying medical bills they *assumed* were covered by their insurance. Let's get a feeling for how much you already know about this vital area with a quick quiz.

CSK Quiz

1. True or false: Mail order is the best way to buy health insurance.

2. True or false: The best way to protect yourself is to buy many health insurance contracts.
3. True or false: If you are under thirty, you are more likely to need disability insurance than life insurance.

Now let's see the answers. Number 1 is false. Far from being the best way of buying medical insurance, mail order is often the worst. In fact, mail order deception in the health insurance field is so widespread, the federal government has deemed it necessary to issue the following warnings: "Most insurance sold by mail requires no medical examination. However, the application form requires you to state whether or not you have received medical attention in the past five years, and to list any disease or other physical difficulties you may have had during this period. Unless you complete this form carefully and accurately, you may find that when you purchase the policy and make a claim, the company will refuse to pay, contending that you have a pre-existing condition which you failed to mention on the application form." In short, the risk involved in purchasing mail-order health insurance may not be worth the possible reward.

Number 2 is also false. Purchasing many different insurance policies is not your best course. It often results in duplicate coverage, hiking your bill unnecessarily. And many group policies contain a provision limiting benefit payments from *all* plans to no more than 100 per cent of the cost of treatment. Profiting from illness is contrary to the purpose of medical insurance, so the companies protect themselves against it. If they didn't, insurance costs would have increased even more dramatically than they have in recent years.

Number 3 is true. For most people the statistical risk of being disabled is substantially greater than the statistical risk of dying. It's seven times as great for a person under thirty, and twice as great for a person sixty-two years old. So you should give serious thought to buying disability insurance, if you don't already have it.

Now it's time to get out the old magnifying glasses again, as we take a tour through some of the fine print of your health insurance policy. Policies vary, of course, but we'd like to point out some features that affect the benefits offered by most of them.

- If you want a private room, you'll have to pay extra for it (if you can get one at all). Most policies pay only for a semi-private room, which normally means you share with one other patient.
- The average cost of a day in the hospital was $92 in 1973. That means a five-day stay would cost, on the average $460. A twenty-day stay would cost an average of $1,840. You can see why it's important to see how much your policy will pay per day and how many days it will pay for.
- Policies vary in how they pay for surgery. Some pay a flat rate for each type of operation. That's fine, if the benefit paid is big enough to cover what the surgeon charges. The other type of policy pays a fixed *percentage* of the surgery cost. If you have such a policy, you'd better check what that percentage is.
- Many policies have deductibles. That means you pay the first $100 (or some other fixed amount) before the insurance company starts paying anything. You should know exactly what the deductible is in your policy. It shouldn't be more than you can afford to pay yourself. On the other hand, if you can afford to carry a larger deductible, you may be able to save some money on your premium. Some deductibles apply just once a year, others apply each time you make a claim. The first type is better, of course.
- Even after you've paid the deductible amount to the hospital or doctor, most policies don't cover you completely. They often pay only 70 or 80 per cent of expenses above the deductible. You must pay the rest. (This is called a "co-insurance" provision.)
- There's also a maximum, or a lid, on what your policy will pay. This maximum may be expressed as a fixed dollar amount ($25,000, for example), or as a number of days of care.
- Some policies are cancelable; some are noncancelable. With a cancelable policy, either you or the company can cancel the contract any time. The premiums are cheaper, but *don't* buy a

cancelable policy. If you do, the company could just drop you when you start costing money.

• Besides being noncancelable, your policy should be guaranteed renewable. Otherwise, the company can decline to renew your policy when it expires. If you buy a noncancelable, guaranteed renewable policy, you'll be pretty well assured of coverage. And the company can't raise your rates unless they raise the rates for all their policyholders.

• If you read your policy carefully, you'll find the exclusions. These are the items the policy won't pay for at all. Typical exclusions are self-inflicted injuries, war injuries, and care you receive in a government hospital. Some policies exclude occupational injuries and diseases. In this connection, you should accept only a policy that reads, "Excluded are accidents at work or occupational diseases *if actually covered by workmen's compensation benefits.*" Reject any policy that says, "Excluded are injuries at work or conditions *arising* from work." Many conditions *arise* from work that aren't covered by workmen's compensation. On the whole, if you find too many exclusions, exclude that insurance company.

To be adequate, your health insurance coverage should include five areas. The first is *hospital expense*. That's the $92 a day we mentioned earlier. However, the cost of hospital care (room, meals, routine nursing care, medical supplies, diagnostic tests and x rays) has been rising steadily, with no end in sight. By the time you read this, even the $92 figure will probably be a substantial underestimate.

The second area is *doctor bills*. Some policies cover these regardless of where the doctor treats you; others only if the doctor treats you in a hospital. Coverage for doctor's charges is also known as physician's expense insurance.

The third is *surgical expenses*. Just as you might have guessed, this applies to the cost of surgery. As mentioned, some policies pay a flat rate, others a percentage of the cost.

The fourth area is *major medical insurance*. This applies to those expensive, serious illnesses, such as strokes, cancer, and heart disease, for which the normal hospital coverage may have been exhausted. (But a major medical policy shouldn't be limited to these or any other specific diseases. You might come down with a rare ailment that keeps you hospitalized for months, exhausting the money in your standard hospital expenses coverage. Major medical should cover that situation.)

The fifth area is *disability income coverage*, which we've already mentioned in regard to quiz question 3. If you can't work, this type of insurance provides income to replace your lost wages until you get back on your feet.

If you're very lucky, you may buy all five types of coverage in one policy. More typically, you'll need two or three (major medical and disability policies are often sold separately, for example). Of course, you should try to avoid costly duplication of the kind we mentioned in discussing quiz question 2. Let's look now at some of the key considerations in each of the five areas.

When you investigate hospital expense insurance, you should ask how many days in the hospital it covers. Coverage usually ranges from 70 to 365 days. The longer the better. Check to see if benefits are paid starting the first day you're hospitalized. With some policies, you must pay for the first three days (or more) of a hospital stay out of your own pocket. Find out if the policy pays the full hospital bill, a percentage, or a fixed allowance per day. If it's a fixed allowance, check how that allowance compares with actual hospital costs in your area. Check out the deductible and the exclusions in the way we described on pages 230 and 231.

When you buy physician's expense insurance, you should be clear on whether it covers treatment only in a hospital or in the doctor's office as well. (This is particularly important for families expecting to have babies, since maternity-care costs are substantial.) Find out how much the policy pays for each visit and what limits there are on the number of visits covered.

With surgical insurance, the deductible and the exclusions are again important considerations. As we mentioned, you should also determine whether benefits are based on a flat rate schedule ($225 for an appendectomy, $200 for a tonsillectomy, and so on), or on a percentage of the actual cost. If a flat rate schedule is used, you'd be wise to compare the benefit amounts to what surgeons are actually charging in your area.

With major medical insurance, the single most important factor is the maximum lid on benefits the company will pay you. Sometimes the lifetime maximum is no more than $25,000, no matter how many times you're ill. That may not be enough. A young man in Nassau County, New York, totally paralyzed from a football injury, runs up medical expenses of $6,500 a *month*; they may stay that high the rest of his life. A middle-aged New York City man with kidney disease requires dialysis to purify his blood; it costs $10,000 a year. He, too, will probably be paying the rest of his life. So, when buying major medical coverage, find out what the maximum benefit is. Ascertain whether that's the maximum that can be paid out over your entire lifetime, or whether the maximum coverage can be restored again after your recovery from a given sickness. Check the deductible, the exclusions, and the co-insurance feature (the percentage *you* have to pay). And, as with other kinds of health insurance coverage, be sure the policy is noncancelable and guaranteed renewable.

With disability income insurance, a key element is the waiting period (also known as the elimination period). That's the time between the first day of disability and the time the benefits start. Common waiting periods are thirty days, sixty days, and ninety days. The longer the waiting period, the lower the premium, but the more money you'll lose if you *do* become disabled. Even more important is the definition of disability. Some policies define it as "inability to perform duties pertaining to *any* occupation." In other words, in order to collect, you must be a total cripple. That's not what you want. You want a policy that defines disability along these lines: "inability to perform duties pertaining to *his or a similar* occupation." A technicality you say? That technicality could save you from selling pencils on the street corner. Other questions to ask about a disability income policy are whether you must be confined at home to receive payments, what the amount of the benefits is, and how long the benefits continue. And, as always, check the exclusions.

No matter what type of health insurance you're buying, you're likely to be better off if you can purchase it through a group plan. Such a plan may be available where you work or through some association to which you belong. Of course, if any group plan for which you're eligible proves inadequate, you'll end up having to buy individual coverage. But the reasons for joining a group plan are compelling. First, group policies are usually one-third to two-thirds cheaper than individual policies. Second, you don't have to prove that you're healthy to join a group plan, or demonstrate that you have no pre-existing medical conditions. Third, although group plans *can* sometimes be canceled, individual members can't be singled out and canceled because they're sick. And when you leave a group plan (by changing jobs, for example), you're often given the right to take out a guaranteed renewable individual policy to replace the group policy you're losing. So look over any group health plans available to you, and if one looks pretty good, by all means sign up for it.

Before leaving the subject of health insurance, we'd better say a word about national health insurance. Congress has been considering various national health insurance plans for more than twenty years. As of 1974, none had passed. Many experts in the mid-1970s, however, felt that national health insurance in *some* form was bound to come soon, perhaps even by the time you read this book. If that happens, your tax dollars will pay the premiums for much of your health coverage, leaving you with less need for private insurance. But it's unlikely that any national plan will give you comprehensive coverage in all five areas that we've discussed. So, if national health insurance is enacted, get a detailed list of the benefits you have coming to you and compare them against the benefits you need for full-fledged protection. This will give you an agenda for shopping in the private insurance market.

Let's move on now to the field of auto insurance. While no one forces you to buy life insurance or health insurance, many states do require you to carry auto insurance if you want to drive. Like the other two forms of insurance we've discussed, auto insurance can be expensive. But, again like the other two forms, it has costs that can be minimized by alert comparison shopping.

If you have any doubts about the benefits of shopping around, consider a sample case. Let's say we take a secretary, twenty-three years old. She's been driving since she was eighteen; her car is a 1973 Ford Pinto; she lives alone in her own apartment in Baltimore; and she drives to work each day, four miles one way. Two years ago she got a ticket for speeding; she has no other blemishes on her driving record. Here are some of the premiums that would be quoted to her by major insurers in her area:

Annual Premiums for Hypothetical Applicant
(Secretary, 23, one speeding ticket on record)

Company	Premium
Hartford	$212
Traveler's	$308
Nationwide	$169
GEICO	$136
Allstate	$180
State Farm	won't insure single people under 25 living away from home.
Aetna	won't insure applicant because of speeding ticket.
Maryland State Fund	$542

(Information for the chart above was gathered by phone by the staff of Consumer Survival Kit in 1973. Agents have been known to quote incorrect rates on the telephone, so be sure to ask for written quotes to follow up your phone conversations.)

You can see that there's a tremendous spread in premiums, from $136 to $542. The table also shows that you shouldn't get too discouraged if you're turned down for a policy by one company. You may still get a good rate with another company. By the way, don't assume that this table will tell you anything abut what kind of premiums the companies named would charge *you*. Each company has a different weight that it puts on such factors as age, location, and driving record. So it's best to shop around and ask the agents for the companies to send you their price quotes in writing.

In understanding your auto insurance policy, a vital piece of information comes in the form of three little numbers separated by slashes, like this: 15/30/5. These three numbers stand for three elements in your auto insurance policy: bodily injury liability *per person*, bodily injury liability *per accident*, and property damage liability. Each figure is a multiple of $1,000. So, in the example given, the policyholder is insured for up to $15,000 for injuries he causes to any one person, up to $30,000 for injuries he causes to *all* persons involved in the accident, and up to $5,000 for any fences he smashed, lawns he plowed up, and so on. These three elements together make up your *liability coverage*, which is probably the single most important part of your auto insurance package. In view of the large awards juries give nowadays to people who are injured in auto accidents, the figures given above (which happen to be the minimum required in Maryland) are lower than the amount you probably should carry. If you can possibly afford it, *Consumer Survival Kit* would recommend minimum liability limits of 50/100/10 ($50,000 per person, $100,000 per accident, and $10,000 property damage). If you can afford more than that, so much the better.

In many states, all motorists are required to pay for something called *uninsured motorist coverage*. The money you pay for this feature goes into a pool, which is used to compensate the victims of hit-and-run drivers or drivers who carry no insurance. Even if your state doesn't require you to buy this coverage, it's worth it in case you should ever be injured by a hit-and-run driver. The cost is modest and is sometimes lumped in with the charge for liability coverage.

A third feature in the auto-insurance package is *collision coverage*. It's optional; no one requires you to buy it. It covers the cost of repairing your car if you're involved in an accident that's your own fault. (If it's the other fellow's fault, you'll collect from *his* insurance company.) Collision coverage is purchased with a deductible. As in the case of health insurance, the deductible is the amount you must pay toward the repairs before the company pays anything. Typical deductible amounts are $50, $100, and $250. The larger the deductible, the smaller the premium (but the greater the chance that you'll be stuck with a sizable portion of a repair bill). Collision insurance can be a worthwhile purchase, especially if you're protecting your investment in a new car. But if your car is old, you should consider doing without collision coverage and shouldering any necessary repair bills yourself.

Another element you may want in your policy is *comprehensive coverage*, which, like collision coverage, is optional. It pays for your loss if your car is stolen or damaged by fire, hail, hurricane, vandalism, and most other noncollision causes. This coverage, too, might be skipped on an older car.

Then there's *medical payments coverage*, another option. It pays for your medical and hospital costs if you're injured in an accident, regardless of whose fault the accident was. Typically, it covers anyone riding in your car; it also covers you and your family, even if you were riding in another car. There's a limit on how much the policy will pay (often from $500 to $5,000). Be sure to check the limit, and also check carefully to see whether you need medical payments coverage at all. It sometimes is a needless duplication of protection you have under a state no-fault auto insurance system or under your own health insurance policy.

In jurisdictions that have no-fault laws (they include Connecticut, Delaware, Florida, Maryland, Massachusetts, Michigan, New Jersey, New York, Oregon, and Puerto Rico), there will be another type of coverage in your policy, often called *personal injury protection*. This covers not only medical payments but also a major portion of lost wages. Sometimes it also provides money to cover "loss of services." If, for example, a family has to hire a housekeeper because the family member who usually does the housework was injured in an accident, some portion of the housekeeper's wages will be paid for by this feature in the auto insurance policy. The exact nature of benefits paid under no-fault laws varies from state to state. So find out what coverage *you* have if your state has the no-fault plan. Don't hesitate to keep asking your insurance agent questions until you're sure you understand your own coverage.

And don't hesitate to shop around for auto insurance the same way you would shop for a refrigerator. As we've seen, prices vary tremendously. And the price a company will charge you depends on a large number of variables: the type of car you drive, your age, where you live, how much you drive the car each year, whether you drive to work, whether you're single or married, how many accidents you've had, how many tickets you've gotten, whether you've had driver training, whether your car has safety bumpers, and even (in some cases) what the company thinks of your personal habits. Now, it's important to remember that different companies put different amounts of emphasis on each of these factors. So you might be a bad risk in one company's eyes, a good risk in another's. If you already have auto insurance, you may be able to find a lower price for next year's coverage by shopping around. But here's an important caution: Never drop your current policy unless the new one is paid for, signed, sealed, and delivered.

Up to now we've been considering life insurance, auto insurance, and health insurance as separate items. Obviously, though, they have certain things in common. From your point of view as a consumer, perhaps the most important thing they have in common is that they're all regulated by the same state insurance department. If you have a problem with an insurance company, your state insurance department is usually the best source to turn to for help. This is true whether the problem is a life insurance payment that's late in arriving, an auto insurer declining to renew your policy, or a health insurance payment that's smaller than you think it should be. Personnel at state insurance departments are also often helpful when all you want is information. If this chapter has inspired you to read your own policies, and you find some features you don't understand, you may be able to get an interpretation from the folks at the insurance department. You can get the address from a state government directory, from a telephone book, or from your state consumer protection agency listed in the Appendix of this book.

Checklist for Insurance Buyers

(Note: For any insurance purchase, get price information from several companies.)

Life Insurance
1. Do I want a term policy or a cash-value policy?
2. Do I want a rider waiving the premium if I'm disabled?
3. Do I want a double or triple indemnity rider?
4. Do I want a guaranteed insurability rider?

Health Insurance
1. Is my hospitalization coverage adequate?
2. Is my physicians' expense coverage adequate?
3. Is my surgical coverage adequate?
4. Is my major medical coverage adequate?
5. Is my disability income coverage adequate.

Auto Insurance
1. Do I have enough liability coverage?
2. Do I have uninsured motorist coverage?
3. Do I want collision coverage?
4. Do I want comprehensive coverage?
5. Do I want medical payments coverage?
6. Do I have personal injury protection coverage?

SUNDRIES

16

Prescription
for Drug Buyers

Laxatives and sleeping potions,
Cold remedies, pimple lotions,
Analgesics, stimulants,
Handy antiperspirants,
Anti-infectives, antitussives:
Heaven knows what all that stuff is.

Do *you* know what all that stuff is? If not, it might benefit you to
find out. Americans spend at least $8 billion a year on drugs.
About half that total goes to pay for presecription drugs (an average of five prescriptions a year for each man, woman, and child
in the country). The other half goes to pay for so-called over-
the-counter (OTC) medications, that is, drugs available without
a prescription. It would be a full-time job for anyone to keep up
with the names and properties of all the drugs on the market. But
every consumer ought to know at least some fundamentals about
drugs, about how to use drugs and how to shop for them.

To test the state of your knowledge about some very important
consumer products, try our little quiz.

CSK Quiz

1. True or false: You get what you pay for in medications. For

example, the more expensive brands of aspirin work faster and more effectively than the cheap brands.

2. True or false: The government screens all drug commercials prior to broadcast.

3. True or false: The price of a prescription drug can vary up to 1200 per cent in the same area.

Now let's consider the answers. Number 1 is false, as illustrated by the example used. Some television commercials to the contrary, all aspirin *is* alike. It *has* to be. All aspirin must meet the same standards of quality set by the U.S. Pharmacopeia. (That's what the initials USP on the bottle stand for.) Aspirin is a standardized drug; it must be made according to a set formula. Any departure from the USP standards would be a violation of the law. Later in this chapter we'll see other illustrations of the fact that the most expensive medication is not necessarily the best.

Number 2 is also false. A survey done by the Food and Drug Administration (FDA) found that three out of eight Americans believe that ads for health products must be true or the government wouldn't let the manufacturers make the claims. It's just not so. When and if the government takes action against misleading or deceptive advertising, it is *after* the fact. So let a doctor, not the ads you see, be your guide to medicines.

Number 3 is true. The price of a prescription drug can vary tremendously, up to 1200 per cent according to some surveys. Cost for non-prescription drugs vary widely too. Unless you need a drug within minutes, you would do well to shop around for the best price. You might save a lot of money.

There are, as we've noted, two kinds of drugs: over-the-counter and prescription. Let's focus on OTC drugs first. Those most commonly used are aspirin (and other pain relievers), antacids, cough drops, and some antihistamines. In return for the privilege of selling these drugs without a prescription, drug companies are required by the government to provide quite a bit of information on the label. It's there for a reason, and any consumer who doesn't read every word on the label of any drug he buys is asking for trouble.

Each OTC drug label must provide the following eight pieces of information: (1) The name of the product; (2) the name and address of the manufacturer, packer, or distributor; (3) adequate directions for the safe use of the drug for each of the purposes the drug is intended to serve; (4) any cautions of warnings needed to protect the user; (5) the names of all active ingredients; (6) the quantities of some ingredients; (7) the name, quantity, and a specific warning about the properties of any habit-forming drug contained in the product; and (8) the net contents of the package (usually expressed in grains, milligrams, and/or number of capsules).

Of these pieces of information, the most important of all is number 4: cautions or warnings needed to protect the user. OTC drugs are safe only if you follow the directions and pay attention to the warnings. For instance, a label might read, "Do not apply to broken skin," or "Do not drive or operate machinery while taking this medication," or "Do not exceed recommended dosage." They mean what they say. The warning section may also tell you to stop using the drug ("discontinue use") if certain things occur. Some OTC drug labels tell you to stop using the drug if you develop a skin irritation. Others warn you to "discontinue use if rapid pulse, dizziness, or blurring of vision occurs."

You may wonder why the authorities let drugs be marketed over the counter if they're strong enough to cause blurring of the vision in some people. It's a good question, and it has an important answer. All drugs have side effects. But, as the FDA says, "if the drug is necessary, a calculated risk is justified." When the side effects are strong enough, the drug is made a prescription item, so that a physician must make the decision about that risk. But, as you can see from reading the labels, even OTC drugs are often strong. So avoid unnecessary self-dosage and *do* read labels carefully.

OTC drugs shouldn't be used over an extended period of time. The FDA warns in its booklet *First Facts About Drugs*: "An OTC drug may relieve your symptoms, but that's all it does. You may think you are getting better while the disease is getting worse. Do not use an OTC drug steadily except at your doctor's order."

Another worthwhile warning from the FDA is this: Don't take

several OTC drugs at the same time without consulting a doctor. The ingredients in the various preparations may react chemically with each other to produce some undesirable effect on your body.

Of all the money spent by consumers on OTC drugs, more than half goes for painkillers. We've already seen (in the answer to quiz question 1) that aspirin is a standardized product, and that you may as well buy the cheapest brand you can find. But perhaps you don't take plain aspirin for pain relief. Perhaps you take one of those super-duper extra-ingredient tablets. If so, you're not alone. Americans spend three or four times as much for combination ingredient tablets as they do for plain aspirin. But whether they really feel better as a result is open to question.

Let's have a look at the labels of pain relievers. There are at least sixty-three OTC pain relievers containing aspirin or an aspirin substitute as their major ingredient. As for the added ingredients, there are several possible combinations. Caffeine is one substance added to aspirin in several products. One grain of caffeine is about as much as you get in half a cup of coffee. According to the American Medical Association (AMA), such small doses of caffeine have no analgesic (pain relieving) effect. Nor does caffeine affect the activity of the ingredients that *do* fight pain. So the caffeine's effect, if any, is to pep you up, which would be achieved equally well by drinking coffee.

Next comes salicylamide, which is itself an analgesic. Unfortunately, AMA drug evaluations classify salicylamide as "not recommended" because it is much less effective than aspirin for pain or fever—indeed, "too weak and unreliable to be useful."

Acetaminophen is found in several so-called extra-strength pain relievers. Now, acetaminophen is a useful drug. It acts on most symptoms in a manner very similar to aspirin, although it lacks aspirin's direct effect on inflammation. It is very useful for people who are allergic to aspirin or who get heartburn or a stomach ache from aspirin. You *can* purchase acetaminophen by itself without a prescription. But when it's combined *with* aspirin in the same tablet, as it often is, all of its virtues are basically wasted.

In some OTC drugs, aspirin is combined with an antacid.

Alka-Seltzer, the most widely advertised combination product, combines aspirin and sodium bicarbonate (baking soda). The FDA tells us that sodium bicarbonate is one of the best antacids there is. It should, however, be avoided by anyone on a low-salt diet because of its high sodium content. Such combination products may be all right for occasional use as pain relievers. But their regular use should be avoided, according to Consumers Union, which warns that too much sodium bicarbonate can cause kidney and bladder problems. And these products should never be used as antacids, since the aspirin in them is counterproductive.

A number of other products contain small amounts of other antacids mixed with aspirin, the intention being to "buffer" the aspirin so it's gentle on the stomach. One best-selling buffered aspirin product has .75 grains of aluminum glycinate and 1.5 grains of magnesium carbonate per tablet. The maker says these ingredients "help prevent the stomach upset often caused by aspirin." But in 1971 the National Academy of Science's National Research Council seemed to disagree. Its Panel on Drugs for Relief of Pain reported that most studies it evaluated showed "little difference in the incidence or intensity of gastro-intestinal side effects after ingestion of (the buffered product) or plain aspirin."

A final ingredient often found in combination with aspirin is methapyrilene fumarate. It's an antihistamine. The chief use of antihistamines is to dry up secretions in your nose and throat. They also have a side effect: They make you drowsy, which is why you're warned not to drive or operate machinery while taking them. Sometimes antihistamines and aspirin (perhaps along with a decongestant) are marketed for the relief of cold symptoms. Here's what *Consumer Reports* said about that (in a January 1974 article titled "Cold Remedies: What Helps and What Doesn't"): "While antihistamines are useful in treating some allergic conditions, such as hay fever, they are worthless against the common cold. Extensive clinical studies over more than 20 years show that antihistamines do no more for a cold than a placebo—a dummy medication such as milk sugar."

It's interesting to note that, even though the main ingredient of numerous pain relievers is aspirin, the cost varies quite a bit. Though the extra ingredients in combination tablets don't do much to help the user, they go a long way to jack up the price of various OTC pain-relief products. Here's a table based on some shopping done by *Consumer Survival Kit* in 1973:

Cost of Pain-Relief Aids

(Arranged in ascending order of cost;
price shown is for 100 tablets)

Product	Price	Comment
Aspirin	20¢–70¢	depending on brand
Excedrin	$1.20	
Anacin	$1.30	aspirin, but with six grains per tablet instead of five.
Bufferin	$1.50	
Vanquish	$1.80	
Alka-Seltzer	$2.10	
Excedrin P.M.	$2.20	
Cope	$2.70	

Some consumers will still figure, "What's a few bucks when I can have a taste of magnesium hydroxide or methapyrilene fumarate?" But maybe you'll count yourself out of their number. To put it as plainly as we can, no independent study of the combination ingredient tablets has ever proved them more effective than plain, ordinary, inexpensive aspirin.

From the government's point of view, regulating OTC drugs is something like doing battle with a Hydra, that mythical sea monster with multitudinous heads. For every head the government chops off, two more grow in its place. No one even knows precisely how many OTC drugs there are. Estimates range from 100,000 to half a million.

The agencies charged with making the OTC hydra behave itself are the Food and Drug Administration (FDA) and the Federal Trade Commission (FTC). Basically, the FDA takes charge of drug content and labeling, while the FTC handles advertising. Long ago, the courts decided that the adage "Let the buyer beware" could not apply to drugs. Agencies and laws to protect the public were set up, starting with the Pure Food and Drug Act of 1906. Unfortunately, the philosophy at the turn of the century was, "If it can't be proved bad for you, then it must be okay." The result of that approach is that today thousands of nonprescription drugs are sold with little knowledge of their effectiveness or long-term safety.

To remedy the situation, new standards are being established requiring a manufacturer to prove the safety and effectiveness of a new product before it is sold. But subjecting all the drugs already on the market to the new standards is a lengthy task. The FDA has set up review panels to evaluate nonprescription drugs according to class (all the antacids in one group, cold remedies in another, and so on.) The review of OTC drugs should be completed sometime in the mid-1970s.

Let's turn now to the even more potent world of prescription drugs. Many of them deserve the name once bestowed on the antibiotics: "miracle drugs." They can work wonders in restoring the health of sick people. Unfortunately, they can also do harm if overprescribed or taken without prescription. And, because of the system under which they are marketed, they can do considerable damage to the pocketbook.

The prescription drug marketing system is conditioned by the patent laws. When a new drug is developed, a company normally patents it. That means no other company can sell that particular drug (as defined by its chemical formula) for the term of the patent. The term is normally seventeen years.

Every drug has at least two names, its *generic name* and its *brand name.* The generic name is the drug's official name and usually gives some hint of the drug's chemical composition. The brand name is the name under which a company markets a drug. Generic names are often long and difficult to pronounce. Brand names, in contrast, are generally short and easier to pronounce and remember. For instance, the sedative drug known generically

250 / CONSUMER SURVIVAL KIT

as pentobarbital sodium is sold by a drug company as Nembutal, a brand name.

Once a patent expires, other companies can duplicate a competitor's brand name formula and sell the same drug under its generic name. Drugs sold under generic names are exact chemical equivalents of the brand name drugs they replace. They contain the same amount of the same active ingredient in the identical dosage form. Generic drugs cost *much less* than their brand-name equivalents.

Drug companies sometimes say that brand-name drugs work better on patients than their hard-to-pronounce chemical twins. If this is true, it would presumably be because of a placebo effect, that is, a psychological reaction on the part of a patient who has greater confidence in a drug whose name is familiar to him. However, the Task Force on Prescription Drugs of the U.S. Department of Health, Education, and Welfare didn't put much stock in that theory. It reported that "instances of clinical inequivalency among chemical equivalents" have been rare. And even when they did occur, only a few had significant therapeutic consequences.

So you as a consumer should feel free to buy your prescription under generic names rather than brand names whenever possible. Doing so will save you considerable money. All set to go? Well, hold on a minute. Unfortunately, it's not as easy as it ought to be.

You see, in almost all areas of the country, if you walk into a drug store carrying a prescription for, say Nembutal, the pharmacist is *required by law* to give you Nembutal, and not the generic equivalent pentobarbital sodium. The same goes for all other prescription drugs. If a brand name is on the prescription, a brand-name is what you'll get. Discussing the situation with your pharmacist won't change the law. You've got to get your doctor to prescribe for you by generic name rather than brand name.

There are several reasons why this might be difficult. Some people are just plain intimidated by their doctors; others are embarrassed at having to discuss finances with them. Try not to feel that way; if your doctor knows you're concerned about the financial aspects of your health care, he may be able to make some valuable suggestions for cutting the cost.

Just as important, doctors themselves may be unaware of the existence of a generic equivalent for the brand-name drug he's prescribing. Or he may not know what the cost differential involved is. For a long time, doctors had no more information about the retail costs of drugs than their patients. Some have been surprised to find out that one drug used interchangeably with another might cost more than twice as much. Doctors, after all, get much of their information about drugs from the drug companies. The companies spend about $4,500 a year per physician to promote their products. Since the doctor isn't going to pay for the prescription, the advertising doesn't usually go into much detail about price.

It certainly can't hurt, though, to *ask* your doctor whenever he writes a prescription for you whether he's prescribing a drug by its generic name, and if not, whether he can. Once you've breached the white-coat-mystique barrier, you can ask him to help you save in other ways too. If he has you on a maintenance medication for a long-term illness, ask him to prescribe in quantity. Pills and capsules in lots of 100 or 500 are often more economical than a bottle of 25. But be prepared to take "no" for an answer; some kinds of medication become chemically unstable quickly and *should* be bought in small containers.

Another thing you might request of your doctor is two copies of prescriptions for drugs you'll be reordering. You can leave one with a drugstore that delivers and the other with a discount store. If the discount outlet is cheaper for your particular prescription, you can buy the drug there and use the other pharmacy in an emergency.

While you're talking with the doctor, be sure to tell him if you're taking more than one drug. Perhaps you have an OTC drug that you plan to take along with his prescription. Or perhaps you have another prescription for some other problem from another doctor. What we said about the hazards of mixing OTC drugs goes double for prescription drugs. Mixing medications can be dangerous, even fatal.

After you leave the doctor's office, you can minimize the cost of your prescriptions with just a little investigation. If you're past retirement age, ask your pharmacist about a possible discount for those over sixty-five. Or check into discount programs of groups like the American Association of Retired Persons. If you're younger, there are other plans for reducing drug costs sponsored by unions, group health cooperatives, local government agencies, and retail pharmacists themselves. Ask your union representative, your pharmacist, or your local health clinic for information.

The biggest step you can take to lower the cost of your prescription is to *shop around*. Ask the pharmacist what your prescription will cost *before* he fills it. If the price seems too high, try another store. If he won't give you the price in advance, try another store!

In Baltimore, the Junior League of Baltimore, Inc., visited sixty-nine pharmacies to fill prescriptions for three commonly prescribed drugs. The three drugs chosen—tetracycline, an antibiotic; Darvon, a pain killer; and Valium, a tranquilizer—are among the four most often prescribed drugs in the country. The Junior League researchers found price spreads of 250 to 500 per cent, as shown in the table below.

Prescription Drug Price Differentials

Drug	Price	Pharmacy	Neighborhood
Tetra-cycline	Highest, $5.00	independent	black working class
	Lowest, $1.00	chain	white working class
Darvon	Highest, $6.00	independent	white middle class
	Lowest, $2.40	chain	white middle class
Valium	Highest, $9.50	independent	white upper-middle class
	Lowest, $3.77	chain	white middle class

The Junior League concluded that chain stores generally had lower prices, though in at least one case prices varied from store to store within the same chain. The independent drug stores had slightly higher prices, on the average, than chain stores. But they often had delivery service and kept patient profiles on their customers, both of which are valuable services.

The League's survey results dramatize what we've said about the value of comparison shopping. By all means shop around and save money. But when you get home don't think the battle's over. You still need to have your wits about you to make proper use of drugs, whether prescription or OTC. The word "survival" in *Consumer Survival Kit* can be taken literally in regard to many of the following precautions:

- Don't take any drug unless you have to.
- Don't ask your pharmacist to refill a prescription without checking with your doctor (unless the original prescription says that refills are okay). No drug should be used for a long time without the supervision of a doctor.
- Know what you're taking.
- Follow the directions on the label to the letter.
- If you have an allergy or chronic illness, check with a doctor before taking any OTC drug.
- If a circular comes with the drug, that's part of the label, so don't throw it away, read it too.
- If you think you're experiencing a side effect from a drug, stop using it and call your doctor.
- Date all drugs when you buy them, including OTC drugs, and clean out your medicine cabinet regularly. Old drugs may deteriorate and become ineffective or even dangerous.
- Avoid alcohol when you're taking any drug, unless your doctor has given you specific permission to drink. Alcohol is especially dangerous if taken in conjunction with sleeping pills or tranquilizers.
- Flush discarded drugs down the toilet, rinse the containers, and throw them away.
- Buy medicines in realistic quantities, only enough for your immediate needs.
- Store all drugs out of reach of children, under lock and key if necessary.

- Never give or take medicine from an unlabeled bottle, and never give or take medicine in the dark.
- As mentioned earlier, don't take several drugs at one time without consulting a doctor.
- Avoid buying flavored children's drugs; kids can mistake them for candy, with disastrous results. By the same token, never cajole a child to take medicine by telling him it's candy.

If you follow the suggestions in this list and on the preceding pages, there's a very good chance that you will gain the therapeutic benefits of drugs without suffering damage to either your health or your pocketbook.

17

Looking Cosmetics in the Eye

When my social life's a drag
And my espirit's begun to sag,
Help is never very far:
I find it in a magic jar.
I dab some on my pasty face,
And, presto! I've got instant grace.

The business of cosmetics is an old one, dating back as far as 3500 B.C. In fact, there's evidence that during the reign of King Ramses III of Egypt workers went out on strike because they weren't given sufficient ointment. Nobody, they seemed to think, should have to work under such terrible conditions.

You can be sure the ancient Egyptians would raise their penciled eyebrows at the scope of the cosmetics industry today. It's a $6 billion a year business. Chances are your money provides part of the figure, since everything from baby powder to suntan lotions and deodorant comes under the heading of cosmetics. You can get an idea of how wisely you're spending your cosmetics dollars by trying our brief quiz.

CSK Quiz

1. True or false: Regardless of their cost, most cosmetics are made from the same basic ingredients.

2. True or false: The federal government pretests cosmetics for safety and effectiveness before the products reach the market.
3. True or false: About 60,000 people every year are disabled for at least a day, or seek medical help, as a result of an injury caused by a cosmetic.

Now let's take a look at the answers. Number 1 is true. There really isn't much of a difference between expensive and cheaper cosmetics. Differences between brands are usually determined by which of the standard ingredients are used, and in what proportion. One component that *may* vary considerably is the kind of perfume used in a cosmetic. (The fragrance, by the way, is usually the most expensive ingredient in a cosmetic.) Tests have shown that consumers link a product's fragrance with its "perceived quality." One product was tested twice in a controlled experiment. In the second test, the only change in the product was an improvement in its perfume. Consumers testified to all kinds of dramatic improvements in the *effectiveness* of the product the second time.

Quiz item 2 is false. The government does not pretest cosmetics for safety or effectiveness. The Food and Drug Administration (FDA) does act to take a product from the market if it receives too many reports of allergic reactions to that product. According to Dr. Richard Sykes, a cosmetics specialist associated with Ralph Nader, the FDA generally takes steps if it believes a product is causing reactions among one out of a thousand users. But such steps are taken only *after* the product has been in the market place. The government relies on the manufacturers for pretesting.

Number 3 is true, unfortunately. Some 60,000 people *are* injured by cosmetics every year, according to the Department of Health, Education, and Welfare. The typical allergic reaction is a rash, ranging from a mild skin irritation to a reaction about as severe as a case of poison ivy. But there have been more serious injuries, including blindness, baldness, and disfigurement. Severe allergic reactions have been reported from the use of hair dyes, vaginal sprays, and nail polish, among other products.

Historically, the use of cosmetics was originally bound up with religion, medicine, and magic. Gradually, those meanings gave way to the purely practical one of enhancing the appearance. But somehow the magical aspect persists, especially in cosmetic advertising. At moments, it's hard not to be swayed by the mysterious allure of a promising potion. After all, it offers to turn you into a Venus or an Adonis, to make you look and feel desirable, to help you ensnare the love-mate of your choice. And, besides, it's available only at "better stores," so it must be a quality product.

In truth, cosmetics ads often masterfully project an image (an "aura," as they would probably say in the trade) while saying nothing specific about the product. Supposing you are disappointed in a product's results, there would probably be little you could say in a letter of protest to the company. After all, if a product's promise was to "awaken the goddess within you," what are you going to write? Perhaps: "I bought a jar of your miracle cream for $18, and as far as I can tell, the goddess within me is still asleep." You probably wouldn't get very far with that complaint. In the meantime, you've spent $18 for, say, a jar of cold cream.

If the ingredients in an $18 jar and a $2.50 jar are basically the same, what does the extra money buy? In part, it goes to pay for the prestigious aura we were talking about. In order to present and sell his product at "better stores everywhere," a manufacturer must pay and train a salesperson, provide for displays and demonstrators, and spend heavily for time and space on TV or in fashion magazines. The former vice president of one major cosmetics firm figures that a dollar you spend on a big-name cosmetic gets distributed something like this: First, 40 cents goes to the retailer. Then, 5 or 10 cents goes to the demonstrator; 1 to 10 cents goes for advertising; 10 to 15 cents goes for sales and distribution costs; 1 or 2 cents goes for payment discounts; about 10 cents goes for general overhead; and 5 to 20 cents goes for the manufacturer's profit. Only 20 to 30 cents goes to pay for the manufacturing process, including ingredients, salaries, packaging, and so on.

It's apparent that the ingredients are only a small fraction of the ultimate cost of a cosmetic product. What this means to you is that you can save if you make your cosmetics yourself. It's possible, and no more difficult than making, say, a hollandaise sauce.

Let's start with basic cold cream. To make it, you need some mineral oil, beeswax, borax, and distilled water. You'll also need a candy thermometer. All are available at your drug store or supermarket. If you want your cream to be fragrant, you'll also need some perfume oil. That may be slightly harder to come by, but with a little effort you can find it at a drug store or chemical supply house.

Now, it's just like following a recipe. You take half a cup of mineral oil and a one-ounce block of beeswax. Measure carefully! Place them in the top of a double-boiler. (You can make a double-boiler out of two ordinary pots if you don't have one. A deep, narrow container is best, because the candy thermometer's bulb should be completely covered, and it should not be touching the sides of the container.) Heat the mineral oil and the beeswax over boiling water until the wax is completely melted.

In the meantime, start some water boiling, distilled water this time. Use ¼ cup of distilled water, plus one teaspoon more. To this you add the borax—just two-thirds of a quarter-teaspoon. To get this amount, take a quarter-teaspoon, put it on a clean piece of paper, and divide it with a knife into thirds. Discard one third and—Voilà!—there's two thirds of a quarter-teaspoon.

Pour the boiling-water-and-borax solution into the mineral-oil-and-melted-wax mixture in a steady stream. As you do, stir steadily and vigorously. Stir either clockwise or counterclockwise, but in one direction only. When all the borax-and-water is added, turn off the heat but continue stirring. Watch the temperature on the candy thermometer. When it drops to 140 degrees, you can add a teaspoon of perfume oil if you want. Keep stirring. When the temperature drops all the way down to 120 degrees, the cold cream is ready to be poured into jars. This procedure makes cold cream of perfect quality, and for only pennies a jar.

Cold cream is only one of the concoctions you can make at home. There's also vanishing cream, hand lotion, astringents, suntan lotion, and after-shave lotion, to name a few. Your local library probably has books telling how to make cosmetics from scratch. One good one is *Cosmetics from the Kitchen* by Marcia Donnan, the source of our recipe for cold cream. It contains numerous recipes and detailed instructions for the home cosmetics cook, as well as an appendix listing chemical supply houses.

If you're not ambitious enough to set up a mini-chemistry lab in your kitchen, there are even easier ways to make simple cosmetics. Honey, corn meal, mayonnaise, egg whites, and avocados can all be put to work. Plain old corn meal is a great skin cleanser and refresher. Lather up your hands with mild soap, sprinkle some corn meal into the suds, and scrub your face. Be gentle, but get the job done. Because it's ever-so-slightly abrasive, the corn meal will remove the dead outer tissue of your skin, open the pores, and leave your face feeling dewy and new.

If you have a sensitive complexion, or if yours has become that way through overexposure to sun, cold, or wind, try cleaning your face with mayonnaise. Yes, mayonnaise. Its light vegetable oil penetrates the skin more easily than the heavier petroleum oils contained in store-bought creams. The egg yolk in it is a good source of Vitamin A, and the vinegar in it helps the surface of your skin keep what is called the proper "pit balance."

How about a mask? A slightly beaten egg white, applied with a generous hand and then permitted to dry, makes a fine toner and tightener. After the first coat dries, give yourself a second one. Then grab a couple of used teabags (or slices of raw potato or cucumber, or cotton pads soaked in witch hazel) and find yourself a quiet place to lie down. Put your feet up and toss the pillow aside. Take your tea bags (or whatever) and place them over your closed eyes. Lie quietly, thinking pleasant thoughts, for twenty or thirty minutes. Then rinse off the mask and rub on a little almond oil, avocado oil, or fresh cream. Any of these will counter the drying effect of the egg white.

Another good skin mask is honey. You can apply it by itself at room temperature, after you moisten your face with water. It will be even more effective if you warm it slightly and mix it with a little dry skim milk, cream, or egg white.

Then there's the avocado, a truly amazing fruit. Its oil contains eleven vitamins and seventeen minerals. For a gooey but effective avocado treatment, do the following: Cut one fruit in half, remove the seed, and scoop out the pulp into a bowl. Mash the pulp until it's no longer lumpy, adding a little water if necessary to make a cream. Smooth it over your face and your just-shampooed hair, massaging it into the scalp. Then use the inside of the peel to rub your elbows, hands, feet, and other dry spots. Wait a half-hour and get under the shower. The avocado won't stick or cling, and it will give your hair lots of body. (You might also want to plant the seed; it grows into a beautiful plant.)

An excellent skin lubricator is fresh cream. It is absorbed quickly, feeds the skin, and leaves it nice and soft.

Hippocrates, the ancient Greek, had some words of advice for the women of Athens concerning rough, red, dry skin. The father of medicine advised them to moisten their legs and hands in the morning, rub them lightly with honey, and a bit later on rinse the honey off with clear water. It worked then, and it works now.

How about an egg shampoo? Mix one yolk in a pint of warm water, add just a pinch of borax, and rinse first with hot water, then with cold. Our sources tell us thorough rinsing is the secret of shampoo success. They also recommend rainwater for rinsing whenever possible. It will make your hair shine, they say, no matter what sort of shampoo you use.

Until very recently, making your own cosmetics was the only way you could be sure what was in them. The idea of labeling cosmetics with the ingredients they contained was scorned by the industry. To consumers' requests for ingredient labeling, industry spokesmen had a variety of answers. Such labels, they protested, would reveal trade secrets. They would not fit on small items, such as lipsticks (some lipsticks have dozens of ingredients). They would be too costly to produce, since every time a slight change was made in a cosmetic's formula, a new batch of labels would be needed. And they wouldn't help consumers much anyway, the industry spokesmen concluded, since those few people who have allergic reactions usually don't know what they're allergic to.

Pressure from consumers succeeded in overriding each of these objections. In 1973 the Food and Drug Administration issued an order with an effective date of March 31, 1975. All cosmetics packaged after that date must be labeled with a complete list of the ingredients (in descending order of weight). If the list is too long to be printed on a normal product label, a tag must be attached to the product bearing the list. There is a procedure under which companies can petition to have some ingredients left unlisted on the grounds that they're trade secrets. But the FDA intends to be quite strict about granting such exceptions: As of late 1974, none had been granted. An FDA spokesman said that any ingredient with a known potential for causing allergic reactions would not be allowed to slip through the trade-secret loophole. (According to Dr. Sykes, the Nader cosmetics specialist, the trade secret argument was silly anyway. Analytical chemists working for one company can always figure out what went into a product prepared by another company, he says.)

In stores where the turnover of merchandise is slow, cosmetics without ingredient labels will continue to be sold for months (perhaps even years) after the new requirements have taken effect. But for the consumer the task is now easy. Cosmetics with listed ingredients are available; one has only to choose them. And if you *do* suffer an allergic reaction, by all means telephone the nearest office of the FDA to describe your experience. Much of the point of the new labeling law will be lost if consumers don't act to share information with the government and, indirectly, with each other.

You can lessen your own chances of suffering an allergic reaction to a cosmetic by knowing something about cosmetics and how to use them. One thing you should know is that certain hair dyes are exempt from the safety requirements the FDA applies to most cosmetics. Here's an excerpt from an FDA fact sheet: "It is known that coal-tar hair dyes can cause allergic reactions in some persons. The law requires the label of this kind of hair dye to bear a conspicuous warning that it contains ingredients which may irritate the skin, and to give adequate directions for the user to make a preliminary sensitivity test, called a patch test. This is to enable a person to tell whether she will be sensitive to the dye, and to avoid its use if she is. In addition, the label warns against use of the dye on eyelashes or eyebrows because of the possibility of serious eye injury or blindness." Dr. Sykes says, "We're very concerned now that certain of the ingredients (in some hair dyes) may possibly be cancer-causing. There's a certain amount of research being done on a few of the ingredients. We feel that a lot of the other ingredients need public-oversight research."

The kind of patch test that's mandatory for coal-tar hair dyes is also a smart idea if you're trying any new cosmetic. It's especially necessary with any hair-dyeing or hair-tinting formula, suntan lotion, skin treatment, or hormone cream. Follow directions *exactly* when using these products. It's a good idea to repeat the patch test each time you use the product, since most allergies show up only after repeated use.

Be especially careful with hormone skin creams, limiting applications to small amounts, and never more than the label calls for. Hormones absorbed through the skin can disrupt your normal hormone balance. Physicians warn that sex hormones, even in small amounts, are a potentially powerful drug. Rather like a fissioned atom, they can start a chain reaction out of all proportion to their size. That's why the FDA limits the amounts of hormones used in cosmetics to 10,000 microscopic units per ounce. The maximum recommended limit per person is 20,000 units monthly. A little arithmetic will tell you that means you normally shouldn't use more than two ounces a month. Labels are supposed to instruct you on a safe dosage—probably no more than half a teaspoon a day. But the instructions are sometimes pretty casual, and often the maximum monthly limit is nowhere to be seen. Don't forget it.

If you have several hormone products, you'd be most safe to use only one of them on any given day. By the way, there's a good deal of debate about the effectiveness of hormone treatments in the battle against wrinkles. The consensus among scientists seems to be that they are probably not much help. Where, then, you may wonder, do the companies find the basis for the fantastic ad claims? Well, here's an example. In one case, tests were done that permitted the ads to claim "dramatic changes in just two weeks." The tests showed that dry, wrinkly skin looked younger and smoother. But the ad didn't mention that the skin appeared that way only under a microscope, not to the naked eye, only on women over fifty, and mostly on women over seventy; nor did it mention that the "dramatic changes" reached their zenith in about four weeks. Following that, there was a "slow decline to the original atrophic state."

Real skin problems, including warts, dandruff, wrinkles, and pimples, should probably be treated by a dermatologist. A doctor who specializes in skin treatments may not promise to work miracles on your skin. But you'll probably end up getting better results from the doctor (and spending less money, at that) than you would trying to treat persistent skin problems with a sequence of store-bought cosmetics.

Another area that deserves some special attention, and some caution, is eye makeup. The FDA says that "each year many women suffer eye infections from cosmetics." It blames these infections not on the cosmetics themselves but on consumer misuse. To help keep you from making one of the mistakes many women *do* make, the FDA offers the following eye-makeup tips:

- Wash your hands before applying cosmetics to your eyes. Your hands contain bacteria that, if placed in the eye, could cause infections.
- Make sure any instrument you place in the eye area is clean.
- Discontinue immediately the use of any eye product that causes irritation. If the irritation persists after that, see a doctor.
- Don't let your cosmetics get covered with dust or contaminated with dirt or soil. If the outside of a cosmetics container get dusty or dirty, wipe it off before the inside is contaminated (use a damp cloth).
- Date your eye cosmetics when you buy them and use them up within three months. If a product is older than that, it's best to discard it.
- Don't spit into an eye cosmetic to ease application. The bac-

teria in your mouth may grow in the cosmetic and cause irritation when you use the cosmetic later. If you need to thin an eye cosmetic, use boiled water.

- Be stingy. Don't share your eye cosmetics. Another person's bacteria in your cosmetic can be hazardous to you, and vice versa.
- Don't keep cosmetics in the glove compartment of your car or in any place where the temperature is likely to rise above 85 degrees. Cosmetics that are heated for very long are susceptible to deterioration of their preservatives.
- If you have an eye infection, or if the skin around the eye is inflamed, don't use eye makeup. Wait until the area is healed.
- Be careful in removing eye cosmetics. Instances of scratched eyeballs and other eye irritations sometimes stem from a slip during removal.

A final product that deserves special, and unfavorable, mention is the so-called feminine hygiene spray. A number of medical authorities have commented that any useful purpose served by these sprays can be better performed by soap and water. And, to the extent that an unusually strong odor might be a sign of disease, deodorant sprays' masking effect could run counter to a person's welfare by preventing her from discovering a disease at a time when it's most susceptible to treatment. Here's what Dr. Sykes says about the feminine hygiene sprays: "There have been a lot of problems, a lot of complaints. A number of women have suffered infections or serious irritations. My own feeling, my own judgment, is that they're quite unnecessary, that they're a form of product that really shouldn't be called a cosmetic, and that they've come to be used as widely as they have because of very heavy advertising."

Heavy advertising is, of course, the name of the game in the cosmetics business. One major company, for example, had a sales income of $170 million in a recent year and spent $55 million, or almost a third, on ads. Well, we have a free enterprise system, and companies are free to spend as much on ads as they want.

Keep those figures in mind, though, next time you see a cosmetics ad or step up to the counter to buy a high-priced beauty aid. If you make some of your own cosmetics at home from simple ingredients, you may avoid irritation to your body and simultaneously to your pocketbook.

18

Your Child's Toys

Though I am just an infant
I deserve the very best,
So when you go to buy a toy
It better pass the test.
It better be safe,
It better be good,
It better be able to take it.
If it's not right,
Don't mess around,
Send it back to the people who make it!

If your infant could talk (in spontaneous rhyme), the poem above probably comes pretty close to what he or she would say about toys. But let's face it, what babies can do as dissatisfied consumers is limited: They have to take whatever *you*, the all-knowing parents, give them.

Playing the role of omnipotent protector for your child may not be easy. But if you don't play that role, nobody else will. Not even, we're sorry to say, the toy manufacturers. Judging by some of the products on the market, some toy makers are more interested in raking in money than in contributing to the physical, mental, or moral welfare of children.

Let's begin our consideration of toys with a few questions

designed to see how much you already know about the toys your children use.

CSK Quiz

1. True or false: A toy labeled "safe" or "educational" generally can be expected to be hazard-free.
2. True or false: Toy-related injuries number some 700,000 a year.
3. True or false: The federal government tests toys before they go on the market to make sure they're safe.

Now let's look at the answers. Number 1 is false. Toy makers are free to use words like "safe" and "educational" whenever they please; there are no regulations concerning the use of the words. Any toy, indeed any object in the world, can be considered "educational" by a stretch of somebody's imagination. As for "safe," it's a standard practice to put the word on the package to reassure parents (or even, perhaps, to forestall their making their own inquiries into how safe a toy is). Although some toy manufacturers use these and other words more intelligently than others, there is no way you can accurately rely on them to tell you anything about the product.

Number 2, sadly, is true. In 1970 the National Product Safety Commission estimated that some 700,000 injuries a year are toy-related. And those are only the injuries that require medical treatment; thousands of other injuries go unreported. The overwhelming majority of these injuries could be avoided.

Number 3 is false. The federal government does *not* test all toys before they go on the market to ensure their safety. As with cosmetics (see Chapter 17), the government does have the power to ban toys that it decides are hazardous; and since acquiring this power in 1969 the government has banned more than 1,500 toys. Here are some examples:

- baby rattles that can break open and allow an infant to swallow the rattles inside
- squeak toys with squeakers that can fall out in the course of

rough play, creating a danger of an infant's swallowing the squeaker

• dolls with wire frames inside, constructed so that a wire can conceivably come loose and scratch a child, or even poke out an eye

• toxic chemical toys. (So-called vampire blood was being sold at Halloween time. The label said, "A few drops on your skin or in the corner of your mouth looks like the real thing! Harmless. Nontoxic!" Well, the first part of the label was true. Children with the fake blood on did look as if they'd been mortally wounded. The trouble was, some of them really were hurt. Vampire blood was toxic and caused a severe skin rash.)

These toys, as we said, have been banned by the Food and Drug Administration (FDA). But don't be lulled into a false feeling of security. The system does have its shortcomings. If the government decides a toy is dangerous, it can initiate proceedings to ban it, in which case the manufacturer is expected to remove it from sale voluntarily. But the manufacturer has sixty days to protest the ruling. If the manufacturer does protest, the government must then prove in court that the toy is unsafe. Court action can drag on for months, even years. And while due process is running its course, the toy can still be sold. And, of course, a dangerous toy could injure a child before the toy's hazards ever came to the attention of the government.

There are other problems, too. The government can *ban* toys, but it cannot *recall* them. Once a toy is sold, it stays in a child's home. There would be no way a parent would normally know about an FDA ban on the toy unless parent happened to read about it in the newspapers or hear about it on TV or radio. And the simple fact is, most toy bans attract very little press attention.

A further problem occurs with toys that aren't physically dangerous but that might be mentally or emotionally bad for a child. A case in point was a kit sold under the enchanting name of "How To Kill A Cop." The kit consisted of a toy gun, a blackjack, and a knife. It hardly seemed the type of toy to build the character of tomorrow's citizens. Yet the FDA couldn't legally ban the toy. To do so, the government would have had to prove in court that the toy actually led someone to assault a policeman. That's a very difficult legal task. This particular toy is now off the market, but only because of voluntary action by the distributor.

One expert who feels many toys *still* on the market are dangerous is Edward Swartz, a Boston attorney. Swartz, the author of the book *Toys That Don't Care*, has testified before the National Commission on Product Safety concerning the hazards of toys. His work as a lawyer and author has earned him the informal title "the Ralph Nader of toy safety."

Swartz itemized for *Consumer Survival Kit* some of the types of toys that concern him, all of which are still being sold. They include:

• fuzzy toys with the fuzz loosely attached, sold without an indicated age restriction. Young children can (and will) pull off the fuzz and eat it.

• some goggles sold for children's use, made of glass that can shatter and cause serious eye injury

• boomerangs. The authentic boomerang is a hunting weapon, not a toy. Real boomerangs and their imitations made of heavy materials are dangerous and don't belong in the category of playthings.

• balloons that can explode in a child's face. One danger is that a flying particle may shoot into a child's open mouth and be inhaled into the lungs. Since there's no way a parent can readily distinguish a potentially dangerous balloon from a safe one, Swartz uses this hazard as an example of the need for the pre-market testing of toys. (In the meantime, *Consumer Survival Kit* advises parents to keep balloons away from children who are still young enough so that they normally put playthings in their mouths.)

• ornamental bells and other doodads attached to shoes or clothing. The adult knows these are intended for decoration. But to the child, the doodad looks like an interesting toy. This can lead to swallowing or choking, if the ornament is loosely attached.

• caps. Some caps are sold with a caution on the container that they should not be exploded too close to the ears or eyes. Such a written caution is unrealistic in a product intended for children. The container will be thrown away, in all likelihood, before the caps are used. And the very nature of children's play is rapt and spontaneous; a youngster is unlikely in the enthusiasm of the moment to remember a warning read or heard some time before.

If you want to get information on toy safety, there are a number of sources you can turn to. You can write to the American Toy Institute, 200 Fifth Ave., New York, N.Y. 10010, and to the U.S. Consumer Product Safety Commission, Washington, D.C. 20207. They'll send you literature on choosing, caring for, and using toys.

The nature of your thinking about a toy has to be conditioned to a large degree by your child's age. One cardinal rule is to keep the toys of your older children separate from those of little ones. Otherwise the small ones are exposed to items they simply aren't prepared to handle. Likewise, think twice before you disregard the age range printed on the box of many toys. Many times the manufacturer has a good reason for the age range indicated.

The largest single cause of play-related injuries to children from age two to seven, according to the Department of Health, Education, and Welfare (HEW), is playground equipment. The obvious implication for parents: Supervise your children when they're around jungle gyms, swings, merry-go-rounds and the like. There's a tendency for parents to think that a child is getting pretty self-sufficient once the toddler stage is left behind. Yet, according to the HEW figures, age five is the most vulnerable time for toy-and play-related injuries.

If you're choosing toys for an infant, you need to be especially vigilant. Watch like a hawk to make sure your child's playthings don't have small parts that can lodge in the windpipe, ears or nostrils. Dolls and teddy bears must be checked for eyes that can be pulled off. Be sure the eyes are sewed or glued securely in place, not held in by the friction of a jagged piece of metal.

Some toys are safe enough to begin with but dangerous when broken. Pretest playthings to be sure they're reasonably rugged. Examine a child's play area from time to time to make sure nothing has shattered or splintered, leaving sharp points or edges exposed. In this connection, glass toys are out. Plastic toys are often good, provided the plastic is strong and not brittle.

Paint is another important factor in toy safety, especially with very young children. Make sure there's no lead paint anywhere around the house, since children do eat paint chips, and ingested lead paint can cause brain damage. Try to avoid painted toys altogether for infants who put playthings in their mouth. As the next best thing, use only paints that are labeled "lead-free" or "nontoxic." Nontoxic paints do not contain antimony, arsenic, cadmium, mercury, selenium, or soluble barium, any of which could be harmful to your child. Another marking to look for on a paint label is one saying, "Conforms to American standard Z66.1-9: For use on surfaces that might be chewed by children."

Yet another consideration you, the omniscient parent, should have in mind is the length of the cord on a pull toy. For very young children, the cord or string shouldn't be longer than 12 inches. When you decide your child can have toys with longer cords, you should continue to exercise close supervision over play with such toys until the danger of accidental strangulation is passed.

Older children shouldn't be rushed into toys until they're ready for them. This injunction applies with particular force to bikes, electrical toys, and chemistry sets. More than one set of parents has bought their budding genius a chemistry set, only to have the little Einstein surprise them by eating the chemicals. Electrical toys should be used only under close supervision. Tricycles, bicycles, wagons, and roller skates must be accompanied by safety training that includes the habit of avoiding the street.

If all of the safety advice we've been parceling out so far sounds like a lot to remember, that's partly because it is. But, we repeat, if you don't protect your child nobody else will. One way of summarizing much of what we've been saying is that you should always buy toys keeping in mind Murphy's law (if anything can go wrong, it will). Realize that your child may misuse, abuse, or (at the very least) use a toy in a manner that was not intended. Ask yourself what would happen to the toy, and the child, under those circumstances.

Despite your best efforts, you may some day buy a toy that turns out to be hazardous for one reason or another. If that happens, your first obligation is of course to keep it away from your children. But your responsibility doesn't end there. You should inform the proper authorities of the problem. Your action may prevent injuries to other children.

The agency to contact is the Consumer Product Safety Commission (CPSC). It has the legal power to take a hazardous toy off the market (having inherited this power from the FDA, which supervised toys before the CPSC came into existence.) Write to a local CPSC office, if you can find one in your area. If not, write to the Consumer Product Safety Commission, Washington, D.C. 20207. With some 1,200 U.S. companies turning out some 150,000 different varieties of toys (not to mention the 83,000 imported toys hitting the market every year), the CPSC has its hands full. It can't possibly keep surveillance over every toy. Your complaint could lead to an investigation and eventually to the banning of a toy. You should also report the hazard you've found to the manufacturer of the toy.

If your child was injured before you could discover the hazard, you may want to consider a lawsuit against a toy maker. A lawsuit, of course, requires a lawyer, and that in turn means paying legal fees. But you can often get inexpensive legal advice from a local lawyer referral service. (If you don't find "lawyer referral" listed in your phone book, ask your local bar association if there's such a plan in your area.) For a few dollars, you can often sit down with a lawyer to discuss your situation for half an hour. That's usually enough time to find out whether you have a strong enough case to sue.

No doubt the biggest toy-buying time of the year is Christmas. That also means Christmas can be a dangerous time. In the hustle, bustle, and excitement, parents and children alike may forget about safety. Make sure your Christmas stays as happy as it starts, and don't forget to observe the safety tips in this chapter.

If you have a Christmas tree, remember that those beautiful decorations are often highly flammable, and in many cases so is the tree. So keep the tree far away from any fireplace or stove. Avoid smoking near near the tree or decorations. Be especially careful to keep candles, matches, and lighters out of the reach of children.

Remember that a fresh tree will stay green longer and present less of a fire hazard than a dry tree will. You can tell that it's fresh if the needles are hard to pull off the branches and don't break easily. In addition, the trunk butt of a fresh tree is likely to be sticky with resin. After you've chosen a tree that's fresh, you should keep it fresh at home by treating it much the same as you would a cut flower. Keep it in a water-holding stand, and be sure you refill the stand with water when needed. The dry air inside a house often tends to dry out a tree quickly.

Take care, likewise, with decorations. Leaded icicles or baubles with lead paint are out. If your children are young, avoid decorations that are sharp, could break easily, or have small removable parts. And avoid trimmings that look like candy or food. A child could eat them. Think twice about dusting a tree with artificial snow. If often contains ingredients that can irritate the lungs if inhaled. If you must use it, be sure to follow the directions carefully.

So called "fire salts" can produce colored flames when they're thrown on wood fires. This display may be a treat for your kids, but it's a treat you should be careful with. Fire salts contain heavy metals and can cause gastrointestinal irritation or vomiting if they're eaten. So be sure to keep them out of children's reach.

Last, but not least, let's consider those attractive Christmas lights. The Department of Health, Education, and Welfare offers these suggestions:

• Use only lights that have the Underwriters' Laboratories (UL) label.

- Check every set of lights for broken or cracked sockets, frayed or bare wires, and loose connections. Repair or discard any sets with any of these defects.
- Lights are labeled for indoor or outdoor use. Don't use indoor lights outside, or vice versa.
- Three set of lights is the limit for a single extension cord.
- When you go to bed or leave the house, turn off all your electrical decorations. A short circuit could start a fire while you're away or asleep.
- If you have a metal tree, don't string electric lights on it. (You can use colored spotlights instead, with an equally attractive effect.) It's true metallic trees *can* be safely strung with lights. But the risk if something goes wrong is too great to take. If a metal tree gets charged with electricity from faulty lights, a person touching a branch could be electrocuted.
- Keep "bubbling" lights away from children. Their bright colors and bubbling movement can tempt a curious child to break the glass, which can cut, and attempt to drink the liquid inside, which contains a hazardous chemical.

In making these suggestions, HEW isn't trying to pour cold oatmeal over anyone's Christmas fun. Nor is *Consumer Survival Kit* trying to take all the fun out of toy-buying. But, at the risk of offending some manufacturers in the $4-billion-a-year toy business, we do have one other suggestion: You can make many of your child's toys yourself. In the words of Edward Swartz, "Toys are overbought, overpromoted, oversold. For virtually no cost at all, from things we discard at home, we can make adequate playthings for our children—toys they can interact with, toys they don't feel guilty about if one should break, because they know we can make another tomorrow morning. You can take discarded milk cartons, for example, and make the most glorious boats. We've done it at home. So I say to parents, one solution to the problem of commercial toys being unsafe and overpriced is to make your own." You can probably find books at your library giving you suggestions for homemade toys. If you don't find any by looking under "toys" in the catalog, try "crafts" or "arts and crafts." Many of these books will include some toys among the other articles they tell you how to make on your own. Who knows? You may find that toys are as much fun for you to make as they are for your child to play with.

Whether you're buying toys or making them, we hope you have better luck than the Consumer Product Safety Commission had at Christmas time in 1974. The Commission had ordered some 80,-000 buttons bearing a picture of a teddy bear and the legend, "Think Toy Safety." Unfortunately, the CPSC apparently failed to give the manufacturer sufficiently detailed specifications. The buttons that arrived at CPSC offices for distribution had sharp edges, parts that a child could pull off and swallow, and paint with a dangerously high lead content.

19

Your Family's Pet

I bought a little doggy in the window,
He looked so appealing and frail.
His price was two-hundred and fifty—
I'm lucky that he was on sale.

I spent a lot of money on vet bills,
I fed him the best I could buy;
Now he's very happy and healthy,
But I live on chicken pot pie.

They said he was a miniature schnauzer.
Now, I'm not the sort to complain,
But two years have passed and he's still growing;
He sure does look like a Great Dane.

There seems to be a need in many of us for the company of animals, a need that urban civilization only accentuates. In response to that need, an entire industry has grown up and flourished. First there are pet suppliers themselves; sales of cats and dogs were estimated at $310 million in 1974. Then there's the even bigger business of feeding the pets. Pet food is outselling baby food four to one in the supermarkets, bringing in a hefty $2 billion in annual sales for the pet food makers. And all of that is only the beginning. There are gourmet restaurants for pets, featuring dishes like kidney ragout and chicken supreme. Last summer Saks Fifth Avenue's Dog Toggery quickly sold out a lightweight tennis coat—for dogs—with red, white, and blue stripes and a racquet emblem. The cost? Twenty dollars. Luxury hotels for dogs and cats are springing up, with fully carpeted rooms, raised beds, and piped-in music. And then of course there are grooming salons where dog owners spend about $200 million a year. At the end of the line are pet cemeteries, where bereaved owners can hold memorial services and purchase plots, caskets, vaults, and gravestones.

Thus, economics plays a major role in pet ownership. It's far from the whole story, though. There are emotional factors in the person-pet relationship. And there's knowledge needed for owners to take good care of their pets. Let's check the state of *your* readiness for pet ownership with a quick quiz.

CSK Quiz

1. True or false: The best diet for a cat or dog is any nutritional canned food.
2. True or false: The temperature of a dog's nose is a good indication of his general health.
3. True or false: Neutering an animal changes its disposition.

Now to look at the answers. Number 1 is false. A steady diet of canned food is probably not the best diet for your pet. Many people are under the impression that canned pet food is meat, while dry food—the kind sold in sacks or boxes—is cereal. It's not true. Both contain meat, and the dry food usually has much more protein. Most dry pet food, if it's well balanced, has about 23 per cent protein and about 10 per cent water. Canned pet food is usually only about 10 per cent protein and up to 75 per cent water. Thus you get more protein for your dollar when you buy dry food. Dry food is also better for your pet's teeth and gums. Because it contains little moisture, however, it's important to serve it with plenty of fresh water or moisten it with water before serving. Generally, veterinarians agree that a good dry food (one with at least 23 per cent protein) is sufficient for a maintenance diet. If you plan to follow this course, check with your vet to see if it will meet your particular pet's needs. As a bonus, dry food is cheap, especially if you buy it in large sacks. The only problem with it seems to be that people don't like it. A consumer research project done for Ralston Purina found that dogs are commonly looked on as "one of us" or "members of the family." Consequently, "the more meaningful the dog food can be made to seem in terms of the dynamics of family feeding and care, the more likely it is to interest and motivate the homemaker." In the first nine months of 1973, the pet food industry spent $54 million advertising "meaningful" (and expensive) canned pet food.

Number 2 is also false. The temperature of a dog's nose in no way indicates his health. There are ways, however, to tell if your dog is sick. Symptoms like discharge from the nose or eyes, loss of appetite, hiding in dark places, or a lifeless, dull coat of hair are all signals for you to visit the vet with your dog. Don't try to treat him yourself.

Number 3 is true. Neutering often *does* change a pet's disposition—for the better. Cats, for instance, become less nervous, less noisy, and more relaxed and playful. All neutered pets tend to be more gentle and affectionate. They are less interested in other animals, spend more time with the family, and are easier to get along with. There are other benefits, too: Surgical removal of the reproductive organs eliminates a female's chances of uterine infections and reduces the possibility of mammary cancer. Males usually becomes less aggressive and spend more time at home, thus decreasing their chances of being injured in fights or automobile accidents. However, neutering does alter a pet's metabolism, and this may cause him to gain weight if he is permitted to overeat. It's up to you to watch your pet's diet. In the long run, neutering a pet is beneficial to you, the animal, and the community.

Whether or not to have your pet neutered is one of the first decisions you'll face as a pet owner (unless you buy a pet that's already been neutered). If you're having trouble making the decision, consider the following scenario. Just how far away do you think this news broadcast is?

ANCHORMAN: Good evening, earth brothers and sisters. Tonight I have a special report on the critical proportions of the animal population explosion. Between 2,000 and 10,000 dogs and cats are now being born every hour in the United States alone, compared to only 415 human beings.

Desperate attempts are being made to find homes for these animals, yet only one or two out of every ten are being placed with families. The rest, about 13 million dogs and cats a year at the current rate, must be destroyed.

The cost to taxpayers and humane societies has reached a staggering $100 million a year. But for every litter located, three more may remain undetected.

In cities across the country, reports are coming in of packs of stray dogs running wild, terrorizing children, particularly in slum areas. The dogs are also roaming streets and alleys, overturning trash cans, scattering garbage which attracts swarms of rats. Children are contracting diseases from contact with animal wastes. The incidence of dog bites is rising alarmingly. City residents report being kept awake at night by loud, incessant barking.

Experts say one cause of the crisis is that dogs are about fifteen times as prolific as humans, and cats are thirty-five to forty-five times as prolific. The experts warn that sterilization of animals kept as pets will not entirely solve the problem. But they say that such sterilization is absolutely essential if the crisis is to be brought under control.

Well, how far away did you guess that scenario to be? Did you guess the year 2020? The year 2000? Perhaps 1984? In any of these cases, you would have been wrong. The events and situations described are already happening. If you have any doubts about the wisdom of neutering your pet, perhaps that information will eliminate them. Many pet owners think neutering is a good idea—for somebody else's pet. Don't fall into this kind of fuzzy thinking.

You'll have many responsibilities as a pet owner, and having your pet neutered is just one of them. You'll need to be home at regular hours. If you have a dog, he'll need to be walked. And arrangements must be made for your pet's care if you're going to be away. Large dogs require room for exercise. Then there's money for food and the vet. Dogs and cats should see their doctor once a year, and that means bills. There's no Medicaid for pets, unfortunately. What it adds up to is that you shouldn't buy a pet unless you're sure you can care for him properly. Too many animals are abandoned by their owners already. Contrary to popular opinion, cats and dogs cannot fend for themselves. The life expectancy of a stray is about one year.

Let's suppose you've decided that you're ready to take on the responsibility of a pet. Your first impulse might be to rush right out to a pet store and buy one. But you'll have a better chance of a happy experience with your pet if you don't do that. First of all, a pet store isn't always the best place to find a pet. (We'll go into that in more detail later.) Second, you should take some time to consider exactly what kind of pet you want. A pet should fit your personality almost as well as a mate does. In fact, you can almost imagine a sort of computer-dating firm set up to match pets with people. It might work something like this:

WOMAN: Well, hello, Mr. Bates. Welcome to the Psychological Pet Placement Center. According to your computerized personality analysis and pet preference test, you want a dog. Is that right?

MAN: Yes, but it's absolutely imperative that he won't shed, smell, or require toilet training. And I'd prefer a dog that will walk himself.

WOMAN: I see. Well, I'm afraid what you really want is a cat. Cats are a great deal less trouble than dogs, you know. They're very clean, and they don't need any (lowers her voice) toilet training. And you wouldn't need to walk your cat, unless, of course, you wanted to train him to a leash.

MAN: No, I definitely don't want a cat. They're too—uh— cat-like. Besides, I have small children. I'm afraid a cat wouldn't like having his ears pulled. You know how little kids are around animals.

WOMAN: Well, Mr. Bates, children have to be taught how to treat their pets, regardless of what kind of animal it is. Generally, we recommend one of the larger breeds of dogs for households with small children. The smaller, more excitable breeds may tend to feel threatened, and that makes them more prone to nip or bite. We've found the dogs bred originally to herd sheep or cattle or to hunt game are especially adaptable to life with children.

MAN: Don't they eat a lot?

WOMAN: Well, naturally they eat more than the very small dogs. But not as much as a Great Dane or Irish Wolfhound, for instance. *They* can consume from three to five pounds of food a day. Now, you mentioned you were concerned about toilet training. You can avoid house-breaking your pet if you buy an older dog rather than a puppy.

MAN: Yes, I know that. But the kids want a puppy.

WOMAN: Puppies do attach themselves to a family more easily than older dogs do. But I'm afraid there's just no way to get around house-breaking a puppy. We do advise our clients to purchase puppies when they are from four to six months old. By that time they will have survived most of the illnesses that afflict puppies. The puppy should also have had its first shots and been wormed. Have you decided on a male or female?

MAN: I hadn't given it much thought.

WOMAN: Females are generally supposed to be gentler. They don't roam as much, and they are a little more responsive to the family, as a rule. But, of course, a male dog won't present you with an unwanted litter.

MAN: Unwanted litter? Good grief, I hadn't bargained for that. House-breaking, shots, worms! It sounds to me like a puppy is a lot of trouble. They must have developed a breed without all those defects.

WOMAN: Hmmmm. I think I know exactly what you want. There's a particular type we recommend in cases like yours.

MAN: Really?

WOMAN: Yes. (Reaches in a drawer and pulls out a stuffed toy puppy.) Isn't this what you really had in mind, Mr. Bates?

MAN: Why, er, I mean, um . . .

You probably won't need the aid of a computer in choosing your pet. Nevertheless, it's a choice requiring a lot of serious thought. If you buy a kitten or puppy, you may be living with him for as long as ten or fifteen years. So choose carefully. Go to the library and read about the different kinds of animals that make good pets. If you've decided on a dog, check the characteristics of the various breeds. Don't buy a particular type of dog simply because the breed is in vogue.

You'll remember we said a pet shop isn't necessarily the best place to find a pet. Most licensed pet dealerships are reputable in their practices, hygienically safe, and a good place to buy *most* pets. But if you've decided on a puppy, a pet shop is not the best place to go. United States Humane Society Investigators have found numerous cases of seriously diseased puppies available for sale in franchised pet shops. The problem does not stem with the shops themselves, but rather the puppy mills—dog farms designed for the wholesale markets. The bulk of the puppy mills in the United States are located in the Midwest. When the pups are anywhere from four to eight weeks old, they're crated and shipped to various parts of the country. Before shipment across state lines can take place, a veterinarian is supposed to inspect each puppy, state the types of inoculation given, and make a general statement of health. Due to the volume of pups, it's not uncommon for only a few in a crate to be thoroughly inspected.

Even if a puppy is in good health before shipment, he will probably be traveling in areas of planes and trucks not designed for animals. That means lack of oxygen, food, water, and sanitation. The farther a puppy travels, the greater his chance of illness. So it's always a good idea to ask a pet dealer where he gets his animals.

If you're not going to buy a dog from a pet shop, where can you buy one? The answer depends in part on what kind of dog you want. Some people prefer a purebred dog, that is, one whose parents were both of the same breed. Others will happily settle for a puppy of mixed parentage, technically called a mongrel. If it's a purebred you want, a good place to look is at a local kennel. The puppy you find is likely to have traveled less, and seen less abuse, than one you'd find in a pet shop. With less travel and fewer middlemen involved, a kennel puppy is also likely to cost less. One federal investigation, for example, found a doberman puppy selling for $250 at a Maryland pet shop. At a local kennel, the same breed of puppy was available for $125.

Local kennels offer other advantages too. As a prospective buyer, you can see how the pups have been raised. Usually the dam and sire are there. A close look at them offers a good clue to how their puppies will look when full grown. Local breeders rely on word-of-mouth advertising, so they want their customers to be pleased. Like pet shops, they usually offer guarantees and will honor them.

An organization called the American Kennel Club (AKC) operates a registration program designed to make sure that buyers who want purebred dogs are getting genuine purebreds. If you are told a dog is eligible for registration with the AKC, you are entitled to receive from the seller an application form that will enable you to register your dog. This form should be complete and accurate, so read it carefully. If the seller can't give you the application, you should demand and receive full identification of your dog in writing, signed by the seller. This should include the breed, the registered names of your dog's sire and dam, you dog's date of birth, the name of its breeder, and, if available, its AKC litter number. Don't be misled by promises of papers later. Demand a registration application form or proper identification. If neither is supplied, don't buy the dog.

One thing you should know about this registration business (and the AKC is very emphatic about it) is this: Registration in no way indicates the quality of a dog. Surprised? Many people are. Some people seem to think that just because a dog is registered with the AKC it should take first place in every dog show for miles around. But all a registration certificate means is that the puppy is the product of a registered purebred sire and dam of the same breed. He may not win any prizes at shows, but on the other hand he could very well make a great pet.

Cats can be registered too, if they are purebred. (There are thirty-six recognized breeds of cats.) Be sure to get your kitty's registration papers before you take him home, if breeding concerns you. One last note of caution: Avoid so-called good deals when buying a purebred dog or cat, especially if registration papers aren't available. Something may be seriously wrong with the animal's health or disposition. Check around with breeders to find out the going price of the breed you're interested in, and be very careful if somebody offers you an animal at a substantially lower price.

Now let's suppose that you really don't care about pure blood lines in your pet, that "just a nice puppy" or "any cute little kitten" will do fine. In this case, you might try the local animal shelter. The only requirement is a small fee to cover the cost of shots. You might happen to get a purebred pet this way, by happenstance. But more likely it will be of "interesting mixed heritage," as they say in the trade.

No matter where a dog or cat is purchased, there are a few buying tips you should always follow. Check out the environment where your prospective pet is being kept. Does it look and smell clean? Are the cages excessively crowded with animals? Is there ample food and water in the cages? Ask if the dealer offers written guarantees as to the state of the animal's health. And make sure there's a compensation clause if the pet doesn't get a clean bill of health from a veterinarian. Get a certificate of inoculation showing what shots the pet has had. In the case of a dog, shots for distemper, hepatitis, and a disease called leptospirosis are usually given in combination. Rabies shots aren't ordinarily given until a puppy is about six months old. You should also find out if a dog has been wormed. Cats also require worming and should have shots for feline distemper, rabies, and pneumonitis. Check with a veterinarian on the timing of the shots. Incidentally, for tips on where you can get shots for your pet economically, try asking your local animal shelter or a local chapter of the American Society for Prevention of Cruelty to Animals (ASPCA).

Up to now, we've been talking exclusively about cats and dogs —and for a pretty good reason. The large majority of people who own pets have either a cat or a dog, or both. The range of other animals with some potential for pethood is almost endless. If you're going to be part of the 14 per cent of the population owning an unorthodox pet, here are a few tidbits of information you should know.

- Many animals carry salmonella bacteria, which can cause severe intestinal distress in humans. Turtles are especially prone to carry the disease. According to an estimate by the Department of Health, Education, and Welfare (made in 1973), some 280,000 cases of human salmonellosis per year are caused by turtles. Since then, due partly to pressure from Consumers Union, regulations have been tightened for the inspection and shipment of pet turtles. But if you do bring a turtle into your home, you should follow certain precautions. Never kiss a turtle, and don't put one near your mouth. Don't let a child drink the water from a turtle bowl or put pebbles from the bowl in his mouth. And *always* wash your hands after playing with a turtle.
- Don't paint your turtle's shell. Paint can restrict its growth, or even kill it.
- If you have a rabbit, don't feed him too many carrots. If you feed a bunny carrots more than twice a week, he may refuse to eat other foods.
- If you're buying a canary, be aware that only the male canary can sing. For a beginner, it's almost impossible to tell a male canary from a female. So, if you want a singing canary, go to a reliable shop and get a guarantee that the bird you're buying is a male.
- Snakes are not slimy. Many of them are harmless and make fine pets. But don't be a do-it-yourself snake collector unless you really know what you're doing. Either buy a snake at a pet shop or read extensively about snakes and study the pictures carefully before finding one in the woods. If you don't know what variety a snake is, leave it alone. Never touch any snake you cannot identify as harmless.

Whether you finally choose a hamster or a hippopotamus, a pet is bound to have a noticeable impact on your life. So choose carefully and take the time to read extensively about your pet. The more you know, the more fun you'll have, and the better you'll be able to meet the responsibilities that go with the fun.

20

It's Your Funeral

Although death is a private, personal subject, the funeral business isn't and shouldn't be. Like thousands of other businesses, it involves the exchange of the consumer's money for goods and services.

Most of us don't like to face unpleasant subjects like death and funerals. Statistics show that the average American will be involved in the planning of two funerals during his lifetime, and that planning must often be done at a time of emotional trauma. Some advance knowledge can help keep the experience from becoming financially traumatic as well.

Man has always disposed of his dead in symbolic fashion. The Egyptians, for example, had a strong belief in an afterlife and acted accordingly. When a man of prominence died, his survivors buried with him what they thought he would need in the afterlife: tools, gold, jewelry, clothing, and food, among other things. Even the man's servants were executed and buried with him the better to serve their master in the hereafter. (That may explain why it was hard to get good help even in those days.)

American funeral practices were carried over from those in seventeenth- and eighteenth-century Europe. In Colonial times, when someone died the body was laid out, usually by the women, in the home. Mourners would gather there for a two-day wake, during which someone was awake at all times looking for any slight movement of the body that would indicate life. After two days without a twitch, the body was put in a hearse and taken to the church cemetery for graveside service and burial.

By 1900, the undertaker was on the scene. He would dress and embalm the body, place it in a plain pine box built by a local carpenter, and transport it to the cemetery. Most of this work was done in the home of the deceased, where, as before, the wake was held.

By the 1920s and '30s, undertakers (like men in many other professions) began to become conscious of their public image. Their profession was viewed with some disdain by the general public, so they began an effort to improve their image. The fruits of those labors can best be seen in a curious change in language. Undertakers became funeral directors or morticians. As the wake moved from the home to the funeral home, it became a "viewing." Dead bodies (the phrase, that is) disappeared. The deceased became known by his name in life, "Mr. Jones."

As the American standard of living soared, so did our standard of dying. The plain old pine coffin has been replaced by hermetically sealed metal caskets with fifty-year warranties. Last year, we spent over $2.6 billion to bury, burn, or otherwise dispose of our dead, which is just about as much as we spent on primary and secondary education.

Today, some Americans are looking for new ways to handle the rites and rituals associated with death. Some are looking for economy in the face of spiraling funeral prices. Others questions the traditional rites because they are looking for something more meaningful in terms of today's values. On the other hand, some Americans strongly believe in the religious or psychological value of the traditional funeral. The important thing is that the choice of the kind of funeral be made consciously and with full knowledge of the alternatives. Let's begin our discussion of funerals, then, by seeing how much you already know about some of the issues involved.

CSK Quiz

1. True or false: The law says that all dead bodies must be embalmed before burials.
2. True or false: A casket is required before a cremation can be performed.
3. True or false: Most cemeteries require a vault before a casket can be buried.

Now for a look at the answers. Number 1 is false, except in a very few states. In the vast majority of states, embalming is *not* required by law, although some funeral directors have been known to imply that it is. Embalming merely postpones immediate decomposition and supposedly gives the body a lifelike appearance. If cremation is going to take place within a day or two of death, there is usually no need to pay for embalming. Likewise, if there is to be no viewing and burial takes place within a day or two, there's usually no need for embalming. Unfortunately, some funeral directors charge a flat fee, so the customer pays for it whether he has it done or not.

Number 2 is also false. A casket is *not* required for a cremation in most states. In some cases, people are led to believe that they must purchase an expensive casket in order to have a cremation. Such is not the case. Of course, if there is to be a viewing of the body before cremation, a casket may be used as a practical matter. But in cases where the relatives want the body cremated very soon after death, with no viewing, a casket is not needed.

Number 3 is true. Most cemeteries do require a vault. A vault is simply a large box, usually cement, in the ground, into which the casket is placed. Its purpose, cemeteries usually say, is to prevent the earth from settling in around the casket, causing the ground to sink in, and requiring the cemetery to spend money to fill in the hole. Vaults can be an expensive item. But then, so can many of the features that go to make up the standard funeral and burial.

The American funeral industry exists, after all, for two reasons.

One is to fill a basic need. The other is to make a profit. The profit, of course, comes out of our pockets, so let's take a look at what we get for our money. The costs of a funeral and burial can be realistically broken down into six areas, which we'll examine one by one:

1. services of the funeral home and funeral director
2. embalming
3. casket
4. vault
5. cemetery plot
6. marker, gravestone, or monument

The first item covers the costs of transporting the body and arranging for death certificates, newspaper notices, clergy, and burial. The price you pay for this service, of course, also goes to pay the salaries of the funeral home staff and the rent or mortgage on the building.

The second item, embalming, involves the preparation of the body for viewing, including the services of a cosmetologist. Taken together, charges for funeral home services and embalming (frequently offered as a package) are likely to run between $700 and $900. For purposes of illustration, we'll call it $800.

The next major item to consider is the casket. For that, you go to a selection room to examine caskets of wood or metal in a variety of styles. You'll probably find caskets to fit a variety of budgets and tastes. A typical "inexpensive" casket is made of pine. It has square ends and a flat top and is covered with pink embossed doeskin. The interior is an inexpensive twill material with a wool bedding. Such a basic casket would take you off to your final reward for about $300.

If you think your final hurrah deserves a little more style, you can have your heirs buy you a "medium-priced" casket. Typically, it would be made of 20-gauge steel in a half-couch design. It has what's known in the business as stationary hardware, which means it's all one piece. The interior is crepe. This popular model costs about $800 (at 1974 price levels.).

If you really want to pull out all the stops, you can choose a veritable Cadillac of caskets. If you ask the funeral director for one of his very best caskets, he'll probably show you one made of solid copper, with a bronze, hand-rubbed finish of baked enamel. The lining material will be velvet. The casket will have two mattresses, to assure maximum comfort to the deceased. In all likelihood, it will be a casket with a gasket. That is, a rubber gasket will allow the container to be hermetically sealed, like a can of tennis balls. This will keep you firm and bouncy for the journey to the great hereafter. To go in such luxury will run you about $2,900. There are many variations, of course. Although metal caskets now dominate the market, you can still get wood. For example, you can buy a mahogany casket with a hand-rubbed finish and velvet interior for around $2,500.

At this point you may be wondering what happened to the old-fashioned pine box. *Consumer Survival Kit* wondered too. And we found one maker who still turns out old-fashioned pine caskets, with a slight twist. The twist is that you can use it as a wine rack until it's ready for its ultimate purpose. This pine box casket is completely handmade by two skilled carpenters at the Rocky Mountain Casket Company in White Fish, Montana. When last we checked, it was selling for only $180.

Let's say you select a medium-priced casket from a funeral director's selection room. We'll add its cost (about $800) to the $800 you've already paid out for basic services. That brings the cost of the funeral so far to $1,600.

Now we move on to the fourth element, the vault. As we said, it's required by most cemeteries. And it's usually bought from the cemetery. Prices for vaults can range from $215 to $945. One very widely sold model costs $240. It's made of concrete reinforced with steel and has an inner lining covered with asphalt. We'll assume that's the vault you select. So, adding $240 to the previous total of $1,600 makes $1,840. And that covers the funeral. But burial expenses have to be considered too.

A single cemetery plot usually costs around $150, though that figure can vary widely. The opening and closing of the grave will add on about $180. All of this means that the entire funeral and burial will cost something like $2,170. Unless, of course, you want a marker or monument of some kind over your grave. Bronze or stone, they start at $75 and run into the thousands of dollars. Selecting the most reasonable marker will boost our cost to a grand total of $2,245.

It happens that the average cost of childbirth in the United States is now about $1,000. For the consumer, there isn't much consolation in the fact that it costs twice as much to leave this world as it does to enter it.

The trend in American funerals has been toward more and more elaborate and expensive services. One man who has seen this change firsthand is W.W. Chambers, Jr., a funeral director in Washington, D.C. His three funeral homes handle up to 1,400 funerals a year. Says Chambers: "I think it's a fair criticism to say that people in our business do take advantage of those in distress. Naturally, they're in a very vulnerable position at that time. And people do try to suggest to them a more elaborate funeral than is necessary, one that's over and above their means. I believe in telling people the exact cost of a service, and exactly what they're getting. And I find today a trend for people to call various funeral homes and inquire what is the price. What is the cost of this particular service? There is a trend toward cremation, toward closing the casket, toward having a memorial service instead of a funeral. But people following these trends are in a minority. If anything, the majority of people today want to be quite elaborate on funerals. They want to have something nice. I don't know whether it's to impress their friends or to impress themselves. But everything has modernized—cars, buildings, everything. So funerals have improved."

Perhaps the minority Chambers describes as wanting economical funeral arrangements would be a larger number if the wishes of the deceased were governing. A great many people say something like, "When I go, I want it to be simple, quick, and cheap." But not many people want to spend the time to see that it will indeed turn out that way. Since the survivors, not the deceased, usually plan the funeral, that often-expressed desire for simplicity is rarely carried out.

One way you can spare your survivors a great deal of expense and help all of humanity at the same time, is to donate your body to science. There is a great need for cadavers in medical schools. In some states, there are organizations that will pick up a body anywhere in the state, free of charge. After it has been used for instruction, it is cremated. Survivors can claim the ashes. This procedure eliminates the funeral altogether, reducing expenses to zero. To get information about bequeathals in your state, call or write a medical school in your vicinity.

There are other ways the dead can help the living without doing away with the traditional funeral service. For one, you can donate various organs of your body. Your eyes could give sight to someone who is blind. Your kidneys could save the life of someone with kidney disease. Your pituitary gland could save a child from growing up as a dwarf. There's also a need for tissues for therapy and skin for grafting. Organs and tissues are only suitable for transplant for a short time after death. For that reason, it's important that your wishes to donate organs should be clear immediately upon your death. To make your wishes clear, carry a Uniform Donor Card. The card is a wallet-sized document that is legally binding. All you have to do is fill it out and have it witnessed by two people. Then, at the time of your death, the organs you specify are put to constructive use. You can get a Uniform Donor Card from a number of organizations. One is the National Kidney Foundation, 116 East 27th Street, New York, N.Y. 10016. If you ever change your mind about the donation, all you have to do is tear the card up.

Donation of some of your organs doesn't preclude a conventional funeral, if your survivors want to give you one. They can give you a closed-casket funeral or have a cosmetician disguise any traces of your posthumous operation.

Use of the donor card does require a bit of planning. Some people have enough trouble planning their vacations, never mind planning for their funerals. But there's a movement afoot that's trying to convince people that planning is the way to go. The spearheads of the movement are called memorial societies. Contrary to what you might suppose, memorial societies do not have any connection with funeral homes or with cemeteries. They are independent, educational organizations. Their purpose is to help their members make rational plans for after death. The societies are not for or against the traditional funeral and burial arrangement *per se*. But they are against choosing that traditional arrangement without knowledge of the alternatives. So they disseminate information not only on traditional funerals but also on cremation, organ donation, and memorial services.

A memorial service is an alternative to a funeral. The chief difference between the two is that the body isn't present at a memorial service. Proponents of a memorial service say this allows the emphasis of the service to be on life and not on death. Memorial services are often much more economical than conventional funerals—an added advantage, in the view of their proponents.

Opponents of memorial services argue that the viewing of the body is a necessary part of "the grief experience." Without a viewing, they say, survivors may tend to deny (in the inner depths of their psyche) that the death has really occurred. Until that denial is broken down, some say, it will be impossible for the bereaved to make a satisfactory adjustment. The presence of the body, it is argued, breaks down this psychological denial and helps tears to flow in an honest and therapeutic expression of grief. Yet another argument for having the body present is that the deceased may have died in a distant city or in the seclusion of a hospital. With the aid of a cosmetician, the viewing supposedly enables those who were fond of the deceased to see him one last time as he was.

Whether or not to have a viewing is, in the last analysis, a very personal decision. The important thing to realize is that it is an option, not a necessity. It should be included in the final arrangements only if you believe that it will be of real benefit to the survivors, psychologically or spiritually.

A memorial service often follows a cremation. The body is taken away and cremated soon after death. Then, a few days later, a service fondly recalling the deceased is held. This, however, is not the only possible pattern involving cremation. You can have a service with the body present (and the casket either

open or closed) followed by cremation. Cremation saves cemetery costs. There's no expense for a plot, none for opening and
closing the grave, and none for a vault. Many people think that
land should be used by the living, not the dead. Cremation (or
donation of the body for medical purposes) is likely to appeal to
them.

Of course, after cremation, you have remains, commonly
though inaccurately referred to as ashes. You can have them scat-
tered by your heirs in a place of your choice. Or they can be put
in an urn. The urn can be kept in the home of one of your survivors. Or they can buy a columbarium niche for it. That's a place in
a cemetery for an urn. The cost of a columbarium niche runs anywhere from about $35 to $750. Of course, the purchase of a niche
tends to negate the "land-is-for-the-living" assertion. But in terms
of economy, cremation plus a niche certainly beats funeral plus
burial. In California, yet another alternative has recently become
available: cremation, with scattering of the remains at sea. That
type of final arrangement has proved quite popular, with people
apparently finding it both uplifting and economical.

You can learn more about the various alternatives to conventional funeral arrangements by joining a memorial society. The
cost of joining will usually be from $3.50 to $15. And that fee is
paid only once. In addition to providing information, memorial
societies often have standing negotiated arrangements with local
funeral homes for discounts. Each society will operate in a
slightly different way, since each one is run by its own membership. All reputable memorial societies are nonprofit organizations.
You can be sure that a memorial society is legitimate by seeing if
it is a member of the Continental Association of Funeral and
Memorial Societies. Write to the association's headquarters at 59
East Van Buren Street, Chicago, Illinois 60605, to get more information or to find the name of a memorial society near you.

In spite of all your precautions and foresight, it's possible that
you might become involved in a disagreement with a funeral
home, just as you might with any other vendor of consumer services. In some states, funeral directors must be licensed. Where
they are, there's usually a State Board of Funeral Directors, or

some similar organization. Get in contact with it if you find the total bill for a funeral far exceeds the estimate given before the service. If there's no such organization in your state (or if you can't locate it), call or write the consumer protection agency listed in the Appendix to this book.

All of this talk about funerals may save you (or your heirs) a lot of money. But perhaps it has you feeling depressed. If so, here's a bright note to consider. You may be able to write your own obituary. At newspapers, obituaries are typically considered drudge-work and are generally assigned to relatively inexperienced hands. They also must often be written under heavy time pressure. So if you prepare your own and have a relative send it in after your death, there's some chance it might be printed verbatim. Just think: "John J. Consumer, noted bon vivant and renaissance man, took his final bow yesterday at the age of —. Friends and professional associates regarded him as at the peak of his chosen profession, and as an unusually wise and kindhearted individual. Consumer, who was often seen by friends reading a book called *Consumer Survival Kit*, used the money he had saved to build a magnificent . . .

Appendix

A Listing of State Consumer Agencies

The consumer protection agencies listed below are state agencies. If you have a consumer problem and are in doubt as to where you should turn, they are often the best place to start. You may well find, though, that the state agency will refer you to a city, county, federal, or private organization to deal with your problem. A directory of *State, County & City Government Consumer Offices* has been compiled by the federal Office of Consumer Affairs. You can order it from the Superintendent of Documents, U.S. Government Printing Office, Washington, D.C. 20402. As of 1974, the price was $1.10.

The phone numbers and addresses of state consumer protection offices, listed below, may change from time to time. For that reason, we have left enough room so that you can pencil in any corrections. Phone numbers beginning with 800- are toll-free.

ALABAMA
Consumer Protection Officer
Office of the Governor
138 Adams Avenue
Montgomery, Alabama 36104
205-269-7477 or 800-392-5658

ALASKA
Office of the Attorney General
Pouch "K", State Capitol
Juneau, Alaska 99801
907-586-5391

ARIZONA
Director, Consumer Protection and
   Antitrust Division
Office of the Attorney General
159 State Capitol Building
Phoenix, Arizona 85007
602-271-5510

ARKANSAS
Consumer Counsel
Consumer Protection Division
Office of the Attorney General

Justice Building
Little Rock, Arkansas 72201
501-371-2341 or 800-482-8982

CALIFORNIA
Director, Department of Consumer Affairs
1020 N Street
Sacramento, California 95814
916-445-4465

COLORADO
Office of Consumer Affairs
Office of the Attorney General
112 East 14th Avenue
Denver, Colorado 80203
303-892-3501

CONNECTICUT
Commissioner, Department of Consumer Protection
State Office Building
Hartford, Connecticut 06115
203-566-4999 or 800-842-2649 or 800-842-2220

DELAWARE
Director, Consumer Affairs Division
Department of Community Affairs and Economic Development
201 W. 14th Street
Wilmington, Delaware 19801
302-571-3250

DISTRICT OF COLUMBIA
Director, Office of Consumer Affairs
1407 L Street, N.W.
Washington, D.C. 20005
202-629-2617

FLORIDA
Consumer Counsel, FTP Office
Department of Legal Affairs
The Capitol
Tallahassee, Florida 32304
904-488-2719

GEORGIA
Assistant Attorney General for Deceptive Practices
Office of the Attorney General
132 State Judicial Building
Atlanta, Georgia 30334
404-656-3346

HAWAII
Director of Consumer Protection
Office of the Governor
250 S. King Street, 602
Kamamalu Building, P.O. Box 3767
Honolulu, Hawaii 96811
808-548-2540

IDAHO
Deputy Attorney General for Consumer Protection
Office of the Attorney General
State Capitol
Boise, Idaho 83720
208-384-2400

ILLINOIS
Chief, Consumer Fraud Section
Office of the Attorney General
134 N. LaSalle Street, Room 204
Chicago, Illinois 60202
312-641-1988

INDIANA
Director, Consumer Protection Division

Office of the Attorney General
215 State House
Indianapolis, Indiana 46204
317-633-6496 or 317-633-6276 or
    800-382-5516

IOWA
Assistant Attorney General in
    Charge
Consumer Protection Division
Iowa Department of Justice
220 East 13th Court
Des Moines, Iowa 50319
515-281-5926

KANSAS
Chief, Consumer Protection Divi-
    sion
Office of the Attorney General
State Capitol
Topeka, Kansas 66612
913-296-3751

KENTUCKY
Consumer Protection Division
Office of the Attorney General
Room 34, The Capitol
Frankfort, Kentucky 40601
502-564-6607 or 800-372-2960

LOUISIANA
Director, Governor's Office of Con-
    sumer Protection
Capitol Station
P.O. Box 44091
Baton Rouge, Louisiana 70804
504-389-7483 or 800-272-9868

MAINE
Consumer Protection Division
Office of the Attorney General
State House
Augusta, Maine 04330
207-289-3716

MARYLAND
Chief, Consumer Protection Divi-
    sion
Office of the Attorney General
One South Calvert Street
Baltimore, Maryland 21202
301-383-3713

MASSACHUSETTS
Consumer Complaint Division
Executive Office of Consumer Af-
    fairs
State Office Building
100 Cambridge Street
Boston, Massachusetts 02202
617-727-7755

MICHIGAN
Consumer Protection and Anti-
    trust Division
Office of the Attorney General
Law Building
Lansing, Michigan 48902
517-373-1152

MINNESOTA
Director, Office of Consumer Ser-
    vices
Department of Commerce
Metro Square Building, 5th Floor
7th and Robert Streets
St. Paul, Minnesota 55101
612-296-2331

MISSISSIPPI
Consumer Protection Division
Office of the Attorney General
Gartin Justice Building
P.O. Box 220
Jackson, Mississippi 39205
601-354-7130

MISSOURI
Consumer Protection Division
Office of the Attorney General
Supreme Court Building
Jefferson City, Missouri 65101
314-751-3555

MONTANA
Administrator
Department of Business Regulation
805 North Main Street
Helena, Montana 59601
406-449-3163

NEBRASKA
Assistant Attorney General for Consumer Protection and Antitrust
Office of the Attorney General
State Capitol
Lincoln, Nebraska 68509
402-471-2211

NEVADA
Deputy Attorney General for Consumer Affairs
Office of the Attorney General
Supreme Court Building
Carson City, Nevada 89701
702-882-7401

NEW HAMPSHIRE
Chief, Consumer Protection Division
Office of the Attorney General
State House Annex
Concord, New Hampshire 03301
603-271-3641

NEW JERSEY
Director, Division of Consumer Affairs

Division of Law and Public Safety
State Office Building
1100 Raymond Boulevard
Newark, New Jersey 07102
201-648-2012

NEW MEXICO
Director, Consumer Protection Division
Office of the Attorney General
Supreme Court Building
Box 2246
Santa Fe, New Mexico 87501
505-827-5237

NEW YORK
Chairman, State Consumer Protection Board
Executive Department
Twin Towers Office Building
99 Washington Ave.
Albany, New York 12210
518-474-3514

NORTH CAROLINA
Consumer Protection Division
Office of the Attorney General
Box 629, Justice Building
Raleigh, North Carolina 27602

NORTH DAKOTA
Assistant Attorney General and Counsel
Consumer Fraud Division
State Capitol
Bismarck, North Dakota 58501
701-224-2217

OHIO
Chief, Consumer Frauds & Crimes Section
Office of the Attorney General

State House Annex
Columbus, Ohio 43215
614-466-8831

OKLAHOMA
Governor's Adviser on Consumer
Affairs
3033 N. Walnut Avenue
Oklahoma City, Oklahoma 73105
405-521-3653

OREGON
Consumer Protection Division
Department of Justice
1133 S.W. Market
Portland, Oregon 97201
503-229-5522

PENNSYLVANIA
Director
Bureau of Consumer Protection
Department of Justice
23A South Third Street
Harrisburg, Pennsylvania 17101
717-787-9714

RHODE ISLAND
Consumer Affairs
Department of the Attorney General
250 Benefit Street
Providence, Rhode Island 02903
401-831-6850

SOUTH CAROLINA
Coordinator
Office of Citizens Service
Governor's Office
State House
P.O. Box 11450
Columbia, South Carolina 29211
803-758-3261

SOUTH DAKOTA
Commissioner of Consumer Affairs
Office of the Attorney General
State Capitol
Pierre, South Dakota 57501
605-224-3215

TENNESSEE
Assistant Attorney General for
Consumer Protection
Office of the Attorney General
Supreme Court Building
Nashville, Tennessee 37219
615-741-2041

TEXAS
Chief, Antitrust and Consumer
Protection Division
Office of the Attorney General
P.O. Box 12548, Capitol Station
Austin, Texas 78711
512-475-3288

UTAH
Assistant Attorney General for
Consumer Protection
Office of the Attorney General
State Capitol
Salt Lake City, Utah 84114
801-328-5261 Ext. 71

VERMONT
Assistant Attorney in Charge
Consumer Fraud Division
200 Main Street
P.O. Box 981
Burlington, Vermont 05401
802-864-0111

VIRGINIA
Assistant Attorney General (Consumer Affairs)

Room 401, 203 North Governor Street
Richmond, Virginia 23219
804-770-3518

WASHINGTON
Chief, Consumer Protection and Antitrust Division
Office of the Attorney General
1266 Dexter Horton Building
Seattle, Washington 98104
206-464-7744 or 800-552-0700

WEST VIRGINIA
Assistant Attorney General (Consumer Affairs)
Office of the Attorney General
State Capitol
Charleston, West Virginia 25305
304-348-3377

WISCONSIN
Consumer Affairs Coordinator
Department of Justice
State Capitol
Madison, Wisconsin 53702
608-266-7340

WYOMING
Consumer Affairs Division
Office of the Attorney General
Capitol Building
Cheyenne, Wyoming 82002
307-777-7775